D1500385

Protecting Children Online?

The Information Society Series

Laura DeNardis and Michael Zimmer, Series Editors

Protecting Children Online?

Cyberbullying Policies of Social Media Companies

Tijana Milosevic

foreword by Sonia Livingstone

The MIT Press
Cambridge, Massachusetts
London, England

This book was set in Stone Serif by Westchester Book Composition. Printed and bound in the United States of America.

Library of Congress Cataloging-in-Publication Data

Names: Milosevic, Tijana, author.
Title: Protecting children online? : cyberbullying policies of social media
    companies / Tijana Milosevic.
Description: Cambridge, MA : MIT Press, [2017] | Series: The information
    society series | Includes bibliographical references and index.
Identifiers: LCCN 2017017866 | ISBN 9780262037099 (hardcover : alk. paper)
Subjects: LCSH: Online social networks--Moral and ethical aspects. | Internet
    industry--Moral and ethical aspects. | Cyberbullying--Prevention.
Classification: LCC HM742 .M58 2017 | DDC 302.30285--dc23 LC record
    available at https://lccn.loc.gov/2017017866

10   9   8   7   6   5   4   3   2   1

To my aunt, Vesna, for stepping in when it was tough

Contents

Foreword

In this age of social media, society finds itself paying extraordinarily close attention to phenomena that have, through past decades or even centuries, lurked well under the radar of public attention. The bullying and hostilities that occur among children at school and elsewhere have long been dismissed as banal—just what kids do, hardly deserving of public scrutiny or effortful intervention. The ambiguities of children's play, including the dubious pleasures of testing personal boundaries, transgressing adult norms, and, on occasion, experimenting with hurting others, have until recently been firmly relegated—if noticed at all—to the private realm, a matter for parents, perhaps teachers.

But today, many of children's interactions—what they like or say, who they know or hate, when they behave well or badly, and whether they are happy, bored or desperate—all of this is recorded, tracked, monitored, and monetized on proprietary networks. Thus, children's troubles are newly accessible to intervention and regulation, in principle at least, and not just by the parents, teachers, or community actors who know them as individuals, nor even by the government that, after all, bears the ultimate responsibility for their welfare. Also implicated are the biggest multinational corporations the world has ever seen: technology companies headquartered elsewhere, driven by financial and political interests to innovate fast in the global competition to dominate society's collective attention. Their corporate concerns are so distant from the realities of their users' lives that many of these companies even refuse to recognize that children use their services, let alone take responsibility for them. Why should these corporations care that their services have become so meaningful to children that they couldn't live without them, checking for updates every few minutes, pinning their hopes on the next notification and, sometimes, tragically, dreading the next message so intensely that they may take their own life.

The loudest chronicles of this transformation are the news stories that proclaim with indecent relish the suffering among young social media users. Often cavalier in their reporting of prevalence statistics and simplistic in inferring technological causes for psychological effects, the news media are proving effective in banging the drum for society to "do something." But what exactly should be done, who should do it, and will it work? Tijana Milosevic's insightful book shows how complex and difficult it is to find effective solutions to cyberbullying, among other online problems. And there are a host of reasons why this is true. As Milosevic clearly explains for the benefit of those new to this field, there are some genuine organizational, technical, and regulatory challenges, which dispel any hope of a quick-fix technical solution. But there are also some political challenges arising from shifting power struggles between states and corporate entities, being played out in the esoteric but crucial domain of internet governance.

While the media, NGOs, children's rights activists, and parenting groups call for action to prevent cyberbullying, the numerous small companies they try to target keep changing, thus continuing to be blind to the needs of children on their networks. Meanwhile, the public relations and corporate social responsibility teams at the big companies have become proficient at claiming the operation of proprietary solutions, albeit with little transparency or accountability to the public, thereby adeptly evading regulatory responsibility for children's welfare. Further complicating matters, it is also the case that society does not want multinational corporates acting *in loco parentis* (or, as one of Milosevic's informants puts it, as "judge and jury" when relations among children become fraught). And, for reasons of free speech, expression, and rights to privacy, society does not want social network companies surveilling and intervening in the everyday interactions of either adults or children.

In trying to unravel the pressing conundrum of incidence, causation, responsibility, and practicalities regarding cyberbullying, Milosevic urges us to look more deeply at the ethical infrastructure of the society that has both produced and failed to address this problematic behavior. As she argues, it is incumbent on society now to debate the critical consequences of the privatization of the digital public sphere, and to address the challenges this poses to human dignity—for children in particular, but also for those who live among them. In this sense, cyberbullying is a highly visible manifestation of a much larger set of problems facing all of us. If society would commit to taking forward Milosevic's recommendations to reduce cyberbullying, children and the wider public would benefit. I hope you. To Gligor Cvetkovski for an extraordinary friendship, for *always* being there for me, and especially for helping me find the fastest way around London tube, making sure I was on time for the interviews. To Douglas LaBier, who believed in me when I did not, and selflessly invested in me throughout the years. To two remarkable women, Nita Gojani and Lynsea Garrison, for being there when I needed them during my MA and PhD journeys. To Vera Korab and her family and to Studenka Ivkovic, for all the wonderful support. To the memory of Ljudmila Kattan-Tomasevic, a rare individual and beautiful person who is very much missed. To my dear friends who cheered me up when writing, editing, and research became slightly overwhelming—Zorana Jovanovic, Aleksandra Stojanovic-Milic, Tatjana Kojic-Cehic, Tamara Djordjevic, Maja Medovic, Ksenija Bogetic, Lazar Milic, Ana Vuckovic, and Marija Vucinic—and their significant others. To an outstanding group of people gathered around Urban Artistry, who helped me feel at home in Washington, DC. To Gordana, Ratko and Sofija Musicki for all their support. And the very last but most certainly not least: to Vladimir, who took care of me and helped me become more of who I am.

I Cyberbullying, Dignity, and Children's Rights

1   When Cyberbullying Ends in Suicide

"do us all a favour n kill ur self"

This was one of the comments that 14-year-old Hannah Smith from the UK received on the social media platform Ask.fm, prior to hanging herself in her bedroom (Henley, 2013; Smith-Spark, 2013). The teen had allegedly been exposed to a series of online taunts on the site, which allows users to pose questions to each other anonymously. The powerful influence of the site at one point, particularly among youth, is best exemplified by a recorded "13 billion page views from 180 million unique visitors" in 150 countries in April 2013, approximately half of whom were under 18 (Henley, 2013). In response to her suicide, some 15,000 people signed an online petition requesting the UK government to act against Ask.fm (Dunn, 2013). The UK prime minister, David Cameron, called the website "vile" and asked its advertisers to boycott it. Ask.fm issued a statement of condolence and promised to improve its safety measures and cyberbullying policies.

This case joins a long list of incidents involving social media platforms that attract public attention because of their connection to self-harm (Bazelon, 2013b). Almost without an exception, every cyberbullying incident with such a tragic outcome kindles a blame-gaming rally that can result in arrests of individuals—often the children who posted the offensive material[1]—and calls for tougher cyberbullying laws. But there is little research-based evidence to support the effectiveness of such laws aimed at children (Bulger, Burton, O'Neill, & Staksrud, 2017). Bullying is a complex behavioral issue and, as I reveal in this book, a *cultural* issue. It can hardly be solved by punishing, and especially not by stigmatizing, individuals.

Public reaction to high-profile cyberbullying incidents can spark "media panics" of a kind not uncommon around children's use of technology (Drotner, 1999; Buckingham, 2011; Staksrud & Kirksæther, 2013). Exaggerated anxieties about the negative effects of children's use of social media and internet have surfaced historically in reference to the advent of TV, video games, and every previous "new" technology. This does not mean that the concerns expressed are necessarily invalid, but they can be misdirected to blame the technology itself for broader social problems (Livingstone, 2009a).

As I note above, the children themselves can become the focus of concern and punishment. Take the case of 12-year-old Rebecca Ann Sedwick of Florida, who died by falling from a tower in an abandoned factory after allegedly being bullied on Ask.fm, Kik, and Voxer; the local sheriff arrested two girls, asserting that he feared for the safety of other children ("Rebecca Ann Sedwick suicide," 2013). After 17-year old Rehtaeh Parsons hanged herself in Canada, the local authorities in Nova Scotia voted in a new cyberbullying law that allowed victims to seek help in identifying anonymous perpetrators, as well as to sue individuals or even parents if the offender was a minor (CBC News, 2013).[2] The law was finally struck down in court as "colossal failure" for violating personal freedoms (Ruskin, 2015). Moreover, members of the hacking vigilante group Anonymous threatened to find Parsons's offenders on their own and publish their names, potentially exposing them to acts of revenge ("Rehtaeh Parsons suicide," 2013).

Projecting an Image of Safety

Cyberbullying cases exist on a spectrum of social media sites, and the case of Ask.fm and Hannah Smith illustrates particularly well how a company with a reputation as a breeding ground for bullying can suffer from far-reaching negative effects. Ironically, though, a year after Hannah Smith's suicide, the coroner's report concluded that the girl had been sending "vile" messages to herself on Ask.fm, and a police investigation could not find any evidence of digital bullying (Davies, 2014). Ask.fm had already been hurt by the publicity this high-profile case attracted, however, so the revelation appeared to do little to repair its reputation. The advertisers pulled out, causing the company to lose revenue, while educators and e-safety experts were warning parents against allowing their children to use Ask.fm.

By mentioning the ironic effect on the reputation of Ask.fm, I do not mean to gloss over the fact that this company and others like it have been riddled with many actual cyberbullying cases, or to suggest that companies should not take responsibility.

Rather, I mean to stress a key point that I will come back to throughout this book: social media companies are currently not obliged to provide information to the public (either the general public or international policy makers) about the prevalence of bullying on their platforms. This is equally true for Ask.fm and for much more successful companies with better reputations, such as Facebook, YouTube, Twitter, Snapchat, or Instagram. Therefore, very little evidence exists to show if children find the measures these companies take against bullying to be effective. Nonetheless, the actual prevalence rates and effectiveness of measures appear to matter less for companies' successful business operations than the good reputations they are able to maintain, especially when faced with real or alleged high-profile incidents.

What matters to them, in terms of their business success, is also the performative act of demonstrating to the public that a given company cares about fighting bullying—and is actively taking measures against cyberbullying. Typically the more experienced and older companies with more resources—those referred to as "more established companies" such as Facebook, Twitter, or YouTube—understand this point and take such measures on an ongoing basis, not just in response to a high-profile case. This is best illustrated when comparing the reaction of Ask.fm in the aftermath of the Hannah Smith case to actions that Facebook continuously undertakes to show to the public that it fights bullying.

Reputation Matters

In an interview with *Time* magazine titled "Meet the Brothers Behind the Web's Most Controversial Social Network," the two Latvian men who headed Ask.fm when the incident took place failed to show penitence or take adequate responsibility for demonstrating ways to ensure that their company would become bully-free (Dickey, 2014). Rather, they said, bullying would always take place, as it was a wider cultural and social problem: "We [society] teach people to bully. Look at the media. Do you have muscles? You're a cool guy. Are you fat? You're a loser." Short of providing tools with which to report cyberbullying and "punish[ing] whoever sent the bad comment or question," they said there was little that their company could do to prevent it. The brothers concluded that Ask.fm had itself been bullied by the negative media coverage (Dickey, 2014). Their observations about bullying being a wider social problem actually reflect some of the key tenets of dignity theory, which I adopt as the framework for this book. None of the brothers' defenses mattered, however, whether self-justifying or on point. Although the company had acquired a reputation in the UK tabloid press for being run by two obscure "playboy brothers" (Evans, 2013), it had been publicly expected to take responsibility and would have been well served by demonstrating decisive resolve for improvement.

Companies with more experience, such as Facebook, tend to handle the policy, the discourse and their reputations much better than Ask.fm did. Consider, as an illustration, an event called the Anti-bullying Ambassadors Program Showcase (Facebook London Showcase, 2014; see also Anti-bullying showcase 2013). The program itself, which is run by a UK charity or non-governmental organization (NGO), trains young people from schools in the UK and Ireland to fight against bullying, supports their progress, and bestows the title Anti-bullying Ambassadors on those who participate in the program (Antibullyingpro.com, n.d.).[3] Facebook organized the London showcase event for the program in cooperation with the NGO (I give attention to collaboration of various NGOs with companies in chapter 7). The company opened the doors of its London headquarters and invited numerous children, excited and honored to be there, to participate with MPs, celebrities, Facebook's Team, schools and parents, in demonstrating collaborative ways to fight bullying (see Anti-bullying Ambassador . . ., 2016, para 1).

By soliciting the help of, among others, the child hip-hop celebrity duo Bars and Melody—who are known for their participation in *Britain's Got Talent*, and who, for this occasion rapped against bullying—the event sought to send a powerful message designed to resonate with young people that bullying was *not* okay. It recognized as well that Facebook was not only willing, but had already been taking the responsibility, to fight against it.

Regulators seemed to agree. It was not uncommon for e-safety experts or policy makers I talked to—for instance Robert Madelin, former Director General for Communications, Networks, Content and Technology (CNECT) at the European Commission, who had extensive experience with alternative regulatory mechanisms—to cite Facebook as an example of a positive self-regulatory trajectory. It was widely recognized as a company that started with few options for users in the beginning and gradually developed a robust e-safety effort that served as a model for new companies in the industry, Ask.fm being one.

An Overall Lack of Transparency

While the more established companies appear to succeed in projecting an image of decisive and effective handling of bullying, they nonetheless provide extremely limited information about their operational policies. A widespread use of non-disclosure agreements (NDAs) in the industry prevents much insight into concrete evidence for the effectiveness of anti-bullying enforcement mechanisms, in both the less established and the more established companies alike. As a common industry practice, having an NDA in place prevents any use of these materials without explicit permission from the company; such measures tend to apply to NGOs and e-safety experts that collaborate with the companies as well (Carr, 2013b).

Social Media Companies among Other Stakeholders

In this book I trace a trajectory: from start-up companies developing their cyberbullying policies to more experienced companies that face continued challenges implementing them, all the while critically evaluating available data on the effectiveness of the self-regulatory systems in place. Cyberbullying has gained significant traction in the public agenda. When cyberbullying incidents are linked with suicides, social media companies find themselves in the spotlight, pressured to respond. Most scholarly research on cyberbullying, however, focuses primarily on the role of educators, families, and peers in handling cyberbullying. Legal studies discuss whether there is a need for introducing new laws specific to cyberbullying.

Accordingly, I address a gap in academic research concerning the role of social media companies in intervening with and preventing cyberbullying cases. It is first important to identify both the parameters and policies of social media. Social media platforms, as I define them in this book, are those that meet the first three of the four conditions proposed by the scholars Laura DeNardis and Andrea Hackl (2015): (1) "enable the intermediation of user generated content," (2) "allow for interactivity among users," and (3) "direct engagement with the content." Because some of the anonymous apps I analyze in this book may not allow users to know the identity of those they connect with, these platforms may not meet the fourth condition: "the ability of an individual to articulate connections with other users" (DeNardis & Hackl, 2015, p. 762).

Other, broader, definitions of social media include: "those that facilitate online communication, networking and/or collaboration" (Russo, Watkins, Kelly, & Chan, 2008, p. 22), or "a group of internet-based applications that build on the ideological and technological foundations of Web 2.0 and that allow the creation and exchange of user generated content" (Kaplan & Haenlein, 2010, p. 61). All these definitions would also include digital messengers, such as WhatsApp, Kik, and Voxer. Digital messengers enable private communication between two or more people, similar to short message service (SMS) or group chat, which is transmitted online. However, as the subsequent chapters detail, there are different interpretations within the industry as to what constitutes social media, and these companies nonetheless may not consider themselves as such.

By "cyberbullying policies" I refer to provisions against bullying, harassment, or abuse that companies stipulate in their corporate documents—such as Terms of Service (TOS) and Community Guidelines or Principles—and to subsequent enforcement mechanisms that social media companies have in place to intervene in existing cyberbullying and prevent future incidents on their platforms. These mechanisms include, but are not limited to: reporting tools; blocking and filtering; geofencing, which leverages global positioning system (GPS) to ban certain geographic locations from accessing a social media platform; any forms of human or automated moderation systems, such as supervised machine learning, various forms of artificial intelligence (AI) or algorithmic learning; as well as anti-bullying educational materials.

Some of these policies are aimed at intervention, in some cases by allowing users to block or report someone who they think is bullying them on the platform, or in others by flagging abusive content. The company can then decide if it wants to block such a user, remove the abusive content, or take some other action. Cyberbullying policies such as geofencing, supervised machine learning, and developing educational materials are oriented toward prevention. For instance, geofencing allows companies to prevent certain geographic areas, such as high schools, from accessing the service; educational materials that some companies develop in cooperation with e-safety NGOs are aimed at teaching children about positive online relationships in an effort to prevent bullying. Supervised machine learning would involve monitoring social media platforms for the content that can result in bullying incidents in order to prevent them before they escalate.

In the US, state laws and proposed federal laws contain anti-bullying or anti-cyberbullying provisions that stipulate the role of schools in working with parents and sometimes law enforcement to address cyberbullying. However, these laws do not contain provisions regarding the responsibility of social media companies on whose platforms these incidents tend to take place. Furthermore in the US, Section 230 of the Communications Decency Act (CDA) shields these services from liability in such cases. It stipulates that "where an entity has provided a forum for online speech, that entity shall not be held liable for tortuous speech of others who may use the forum for harmful purposes" (Lipton, 2011, p. 1132).[4] The European eCommerce Directive also provides safe harbor provisions (see chapter 5).

Although the companies regulate bullying on their platforms via private regulation in the EU as well, the situation there differs from that in the US in a number of important ways (Newman & Bach, 2004; O'Neill & Staksrud,

2012; see also McLaughlin, 2013; O'Neill 2014a, 2014b), as I elaborate later, particularly in chapter 5.

Such creation and enforcement of rules by the industry "with minimal or no intervention by the state" (Lievens, 2016, p.77, cf. Lievens, 2010) can be characterized as "self-regulation." But for the system to be classified as "self-regulatory," some conditions need to be met, other than an individual company's private regulation or the self-organization illustrated in their policies. Throughout the book, when referring only to a company's private policies—those that define the contractual relationship between the company and the user—the terms "private regulation" or "self-organization" will be used.

Liability exemptions can leave companies with little incentive to monitor posts on their platforms and the victim with few legal remedies when it is not clear who the anonymous perpetrator is, as is sometimes the case with cyberbullying incidents (Lipton, 2011; Citron, 2014a). Yet when an incident with severe consequences unfolds, such as the ones described in the beginning of this chapter, the ensuing controversy creates incentives for a company to assume corporate social responsibility and regulate cyberbullying behavior. Furthermore, a company's behavior is subject to regulation by the local laws in the countries where it operates, which can provide further incentive.

There is still a paucity of academic studies about the role of these technological platforms in intervening with and preventing cyberbullying incidents. Media reports have emerged in the recent past which discuss the slow response of some companies to bullying complaints (Franks, 2014); such reports raise concerns about the levels of transparency with which companies moderated the reports they would receive about abuse (Barnett & Hollingshead, 2012). And yet a systematic analysis of these tools across the industry has rarely been a subject of academic study. With this book I aim to contribute to this effort, which also includes the work of Bazelon (2013b), Schneider, Smith, and O'Donnell (2013b), Citron, (2014a), Matias et al. (2015), Crawford and Gillespie (2016), and Van Royen, Poels, and Vandebosch (2016).[5]

"Information intermediary" (or "online intermediary") is an umbrella term that applies to online service providers such as social media and digital messenger services. "Internet intermediaries are third-party platforms that mediate between digital content and the humans who contribute and access this content" (DeNardis, 2014, p. 154). I use this term as well to refer to the relevant social media companies.

While these online companies play an important role in addressing bullying, their operational or internal policies and enforcement practices are not
well understood. Although their official policies tend to be—to a degree at
least—spelled out on their websites, these written policies do not always
reflect the more complex operations that take place within these corporations. Thus, I set out in this book to explain what the policies mean, and
especially to determine how company representatives position their companies' roles in addressing cyberbullying on their platforms.

Moreover, non-governmental organizations play an important international role in how companies deal with online bullying by participating in
the design and execution of what is often described in the US and the EU
as a multi-stakeholder self-regulatory process.[6] Yet, except for news articles,
and a limited number of reports, little is understood about the role of NGOs
in helping companies address cyberbullying. Subsequently, in chapters 6
and 7, I examine what can be known about the effectiveness and implications of this process.

Social media companies' involvement with the content on their platforms
can be controversial as well, as it allows these companies, which are private
entities, to regulate free speech (DeNardis, 2014). By asking social media
companies to decide if a case constitutes cyberbullying, and consequently
make decisions about which content to take down, any law that would propose such a feature would delegate to private companies a regulation of free
speech that is forbidden to the US government by the First Amendment
and to many other governments by their constitutions. Social media companies already take content down if they decide that a case constitutes bullying and thus violates their TOS, a procedure that I analyze later in detail.

A much-discussed legal remedy is to institutionalize a procedure similar
to the US Digital Millennium Copyright Act (DMCA), which provides for a
"notice and takedown system" whereby a copyright owner can file a notice
to the platform whose user posted the material that infringed on copyright
material of the owner. The platform then avoids liability for the infringing
content as long as it removes such content upon notice from the copyright
holder. The legal scholar Daniel Solove (2007) proposed that a similar system should be instituted for reputational harm and privacy issues. Some
legal and communication scholars have pointed out that such a system
could be applied to cyberbullying cases (Chang, 2010; Poole, 2013). Nonetheless, this procedure could be prone to abuse. For instance, false bullying
reports could become a common occurrence; platforms would have to find
a way to penalize those who abuse the system, which would again mandate
a degree of involvement from private companies with content on their

platforms. Yet DMCA is prone to abuse as well and a broader normative question at issue here is why intellectual property seems to hold a higher value in the US culture than e-safety, dignity, privacy, and reputation—all of which can be at stake when cyberbullying is concerned. I will critically examine the application of such solutions in the context of bullying cases concerning children.

All intermediaries require that their users agree to the TOS, the contracts designed by companies that typically contain anti-cyberbullying provisions. In this book I incorporate a qualitative analysis of TOS, Community Guidelines/Standards/Principles, corporate statements and blogs, media coverage of cyberbullying, congressional hearings, and other relevant meetings and documents (in the US and EU) to explain the scope of anti-bullying policies and tools of enforcement employed by these companies.

When analyzing these policies, particular attention must be paid to how the texts used in these documents may emphasize certain facts over others and what implications such use of the text may have for users, companies, and policy in general. Of particular note for companies is the inherent profitability factor that underlies their policies and practices. In her seminal book, *The Culture of Connectivity*, scholar José van Dijck provided a framework for analyzing how social media companies engineer human connectedness as algorithmic expression. By actively steering and curating user connections in ways that are not always transparent, companies use data created thereby to "monetize engineered streams of information" (van Dijck, 2013, p. 12). For users, "connectivity" may mean accumulating friends and social capital, but for platform owners it refers to "amassing economic capital" (van Dijck, 2013, p. 16). Similarly, the word "platform" is discursively employed by social media companies to minimize the perception of any conflict of interest in companies' services to various constituencies, from advertisers to users and policy makers (Gillespie, 2010, 2015).

In this book I present an overview of five cases that were characterized as "cyberbullying incidents" and that were also said to have contributed to suicides of young people; these case studies provide a context for examining the interplay of factors that influence social media companies in such crises. Analysis of corporate documents and relevant media coverage, as well as the interviews with representatives of selected companies, NGOs, and e-safety consultants who participate in the design of these policies, or have an expert understanding of the issue inform the subsequent discussions.[7] I also draw from experience at international conferences, summits, or events organized by various stakeholders in the area of e-safety. I thus propose to shed light on the following overarching and pivotal questions:

• In what ways are online intermediaries addressing cyberbullying? How have their efforts evolved?

• What issues might these companies be encountering and what can be known about effectiveness of their policies? How do the companies understand and describe the relative effectiveness of their tools of enforcement?

• How do the companies measure this effectiveness and what evidence of effectiveness do they provide?

• What roles do e-safety NGOs play in the process of self-regulatory and self-organizational effort?

In addition to these empirical questions, I address several larger, normative issues:

• Whose responsibility should it be to handle cyberbullying cases on these platforms?

• Should laws require companies to intervene, and which interventions are supported by research?

• What implications would companies' actions have for freedom of speech?

• Should the burden of policing the platforms, and making decisions in terms of which speech is allowed, be left to private corporations?

• What should be done about the characteristics of platforms that are considered as particularly conducive to cyberbullying?

Addressing each of these questions involves a complexity of considerations. As an example of peripheral factors, anonymity is perceived as especially favorable to cyberbullying.[8] As I discuss in more detail in the subsequent chapters, some research shows that anonymity can disinhibit people in ways that can, under certain conditions, facilitate meanness. But anonymity also allows for a freedom of expression that people may be reluctant to adopt when they are bound by their real identities, and in that sense anonymity can be a valuable asset as well.

Overview of Cyberbullying (Digital or Online Bullying)

Bullying is often characterized as aggressive, typically repetitive behavior among school-aged children that also tends to involve a form of real or perceived power imbalance (Mishna, 2012). Likewise, cyberbullying is bullying that takes place using electronic and particularly digital technology—smart phones, computers, and social media (Kowalski, Giumetti, Schroeder, & Lattanner, 2014; Vandebosch & Van Cleemput, 2009). Research suggests that while bullying and cyberbullying tend to occur together, cyberbullying can be more difficult to escape by providing bullies with more access to the victim online, a wider audience to witness the humiliation, and a digital record that does not easily go away (Hinduja & Patchin, 2009; Katz, 2012; Patchin & Hinduja, 2012; Görzig & Macháčková, 2015). Specific qualities of online environments can create a false sense of privacy, escalate negative emotions, and increase impulsivity, all of which can alter the nature of bullying online or intensify its consequences (Englander, 2015). Cyberbullying can have negative impact on children's performance at school as well as on their self-esteem, and was sometimes found to be related to other psychological problems, substance abuse or maladaptive behavior (Hinduja & Patchin, 2010; Subrahmanyam & Šmahel, 2011; Kowalski, Limber, & Agatston, 2012; Patchin & Hinduja, 2012).

Rates of prevalence of cyberbullying differ significantly from study to study, depending on how cyberbullying studies are conducted and measured—ranging from as few as 6.5% to as many as 72% (Tokunaga, 2010; Kowalski, Giumetti, Schroeder, & Lattanner, 2014). The Cyberbullying Research Center in the US reveals that on average about 27 percent of students who participated in their ten most recent representative studies (from 2007 to 2016) reported being victims of cyberbullying at some point in their lives (Cyberbullying Research Center, n.d.). Relying on a robust, representative sample collected in 25 European countries, the EU Kids Online project reports that Internet-using children between the age of 11 and 16 were 7–12% more likely to be exposed to cyberbullying in 2014 than in 2010. EU Kids Online places these numbers in context: "being cyberbullied is reported by a small minority of 11- to 16-year-olds. However, this risk is the most likely to result in harm—half of these youngsters report being fairly or very upset by receiving nasty or hurtful messages online" (EU Kids Online, 2014, p. 16). Similarly, scholars Sameer Hinduja and Justin Patchin, who lead the Cyberbullying Research Center in the US, conclude that cyberbullying is "neither an epidemic nor a rarity" and that judging by media reports, a reader would think that cyberbullying is acquiring epidemic dimensions, which research does not support (Cyberbullying Research Center, 2013, title).

Bullying and cyberbullying disproportionately affect lesbian, gay, bisexual, transgender, and questioning (LGBTQ) youth. Research shows that LGBT youth are more likely to experience harassment than non-LGBT peers (Centers for Disease Control and Prevention, 2014). A national study in US schools revealed that more than 80% of LGBT youth reported being verbally harassed because of their sexual orientation and over 38% were physically harassed (Kosciw, Greytak, Bartkiewitz, Boesen, Palmer, 2012, p. xiv).

Research also suggests that bias-based harassment is more strongly related with psychological problems than general forms of harassment (Ybarra, Mitchell, Kosciw, & Korchmaros, 2015).

The online intermediaries' corporate documents such as TOS stipulate the range of acceptable behavior that users need to agree to in order to be able to use the platform, and provisions against abuse, harassment, or cyberbullying tend to be included in those. Cyberbullying policies can also fall under the companies' corporate social responsibility (CSR); this form of self-organization, incorporated into the business model, is designed to guide the company's ethical behavior in a way that ensures the company's engagement in actions that further social good (Haigh, Brubaker, & Whiteside, 2013).

I selected the companies I analyze in this book based on several criteria: the high number of users they had at the time of research and writing (see table A.1 in appendix A), their reported popularity among teen and preteen users, and/or their appearance in media reports in relationship to online bullying, especially in reference to self-harm or suicide. Some companies do not reveal the exact numbers of their users. This is especially true for startups— smaller companies that gained millions of users in a short span of time and garnered significant media attention, sometimes due to alleged bullying incidents. The 14 social media companies I analyze in this book are: Facebook, Instagram (Facebook-owned), Twitter, Ask.fm, Snapchat, YouTube (Google-owned), Yik Yak, Secret, Google+, Tumblr (Yahoo! owned), and Whisper, and the digital messengers Voxer, WhatsApp (Facebook-owned), and Kik.

This choice of companies also allows for a comparison among a variety of platforms. Facebook's affordances are quite different from Twitter's and not at all similar to those of some anonymous or messaging apps. Hence these companies will face different issues and are expected to have different policies for preventing cyberbullying.

In general, however, these companies tend to offer the technological capability for a user to report an offensive post to the sites' administrators, with the promise that such content will be taken down if it violates company policy. Some companies also seek to actively educate users about cyberbullying. For instance, Facebook has created the Safety Center with "Parents Portal" and "Bullying Prevention Hub," an information clearinghouse on Facebook's platform with specific advice for parents, educators, and children who become involved in these incidents on how to handle emerging situations.

While these efforts have their merits (Family Online Safety Institute Annual Conference, 2013), some researchers have shown examples of what is perceived as the ineffectiveness of these reporting mechanisms, such as slow response to reported content (Bazelon, 2013b; Crawford & Gillespie, 2016; Van Royen, Poels, & Vandebosch, 2016). Some researchers have observed that reporting might not be enough, especially given the ability to employ various forms of AI, which enable intermediaries' managers to monitor any suspicious activity on their platforms and catch cyberbullying as it happens (Bazelon, 2013b; Greenberg, 2016). Others, however, have also pointed out that supervised machine learning would clash with freedom of speech as ensured by the First Amendment, or with privacy protections, for instance when such measures are applied to content shared among users privately. These concerns go beyond political expression in the strict sense of the word. A democratic culture, where "individuals have a fair opportunity to participate in the forms of meaning-making that constitute them as individuals" (Balkin, 2004, p. 1), can be affected when intermediaries, being private entities, decide which speech is allowed on their platforms and which should be taken down.

Some social media companies are trying to incorporate "digital citizenship"—teaching children not only how to use technology, but how to do so responsibly—into their self-organizational efforts to curb cyberbullying (Ohler, 2011; Family Online Safety Institute Annual Conference, 2013; Schneider, Smith, & O'Donnel, 2013b; Davidson, 2014). A theme that would sometimes emerge in the discourse around digital citizenship is that of "dignity" (Family Online Safety . . ., 2013; Wiseman, 2013). Contemporary scholars who write about dignity define it as an inherent worth of every human being, which is equal to all humans and, unlike respect, does not have to be earned (Fuller, 2006; Fuller & Gerloff, 2008; Lindner, 2010; Hicks, 2011). While "conflict may be inevitable, human dignity is not negotiable" (Wiseman, 2013), and teaching children about the values of dignity within digital citizenship education is an approach that could lead to effective interventions (Family Online Safety . . ., 2013). Analysis follows regarding what efforts intermediaries make to incorporate "digital citizenship" into their cyberbullying initiatives and to what extent these measures help create more dignitarian relationships among children. Dignity is what is violated when bullying and cyberbullying take place—when a child or a teen is ridiculed because of who or what they are (Fuller, 2006). Dignity theory echoes a strong emphasis on children's rights, an approach recently promulgated by leading scholars in the field of children and media (Livingstone & Bulger, 2014; Livingstone, Carr, & Byrne, 2015; Staksrud, 2013a). As I explain in chapter 2, it can facilitate a more constructive public understanding of young people's interaction with digital media than the one we have witnessed thus far.

It is worth noting, when discussing peer aggression in general, how we are prone to overlook the wider social and cultural conditions and the peer relations among adults that abound with indignities. Children's relationships do not happen in a vacuum; they are influenced by the world of adults (Durkheim, 2002) and are reflected in the media as well (Fuller, 2003, 2006; Hicks, 2011 Fuller & Gerloff, 2008). Yet rather than acting merely as passive recipients of that culture, children actively appropriate from it in the process of social positioning (Corsaro, 2005; Thornberg, 2015). Social positioning, depending on how we define the phenomena, is often a central theme in bullying and cyberbullying, another element in the constellation of issues contributing to it.

The temporality of many social media companies within the industry also deserves mention in my study. In a casual conversation at a conference in London in the summer of 2016, I told a high-ranking Facebook employee about my book. The person bemusedly (and rhetorically) wondered how many of the companies in my sample would still exist by the time the book was published. I smiled and nodded in acknowledgment. The social media industry is a dynamic one where important players often appear quickly and can gain millions of active users in the course of only several months. Yet, subject to fierce competition, not every company has the same chances of surviving in the market. This seems to be especially true for the new platforms that have been available only for a year or two and that may not yet be fully established. But this can also be the case with the well-established companies (Moscaritolo, 2014). Once a behemoth in the industry in terms of user base, MySpace's popularity and continued growth were affected by the advent of other social media companies. A similar fate befell another social media site, Bebo, especially popular among younger teens (Kiss, 2010). This is why an analysis of the kind I provide here can hardly be comprehensive. But it can purport to provide an overview of dominant industry trends in how companies address cyberbullying.

Focus, Themes, and Terms

As an overall framework, I emphasize that this work looks into bullying with a focus on children: it does not provide an analysis of cyberstalking, revenge porn, and online hate speech, which can also revolve around adults or specific groups of individuals based on their characteristics (for a discussion of these and legal remedies see, e.g., Citron, 2014a; Marwick & Miller, 2014). Trolling is also a phenomenon distinct from bullying but sometimes falls under the bullying label.[9] Although there are certainly overlapping elements between these concepts and bullying, I will reference them only if they are germane to particular companies' bullying policies. Sexting, while sometimes related to bullying, is considered to be a separate issue as well. Covering these topics would constitute too broad of a scope for a project of this kind.

The words "harassment" and "abuse" are often used in corporate documents as synonyms for cyberbullying (or umbrella terms for cyberbullying). I mention them in this work because of such circumstances. One issue with bullying research is that the terms "online harassment" and "cyberbullying" are commonly used interchangeably but measured differently, which introduces confusion into what is being measured and the frequency of occurrence, as well as the consequences (Mitchell, Ybarra, Jones, & Espelage, 2016, cf. Jones, Mitchell, & Finkelhor, 2013).

In chapter 2, I look into the circumstances under which online risks, such as digital bullying, can generate exaggerated concerns over youth use of technology and the consequences for different stakeholders. The chapter places such fears in the context of amplified public concerns about other types of risks. I give special attention in the chapter to wider social and cultural problems that remain less discussed in discourse on digital bullying, building the case as to why it is important to address the culture of humiliation rather than engage in simplistic binaries of finger-pointing that are so often witnessed in the aftermath of high profile incidents. I also build the case for considering digital bullying in the context of children's rights by discussing how social media companies structure policies and enforcement mechanisms around the rights to protection and participation, which are often perceived as conflicting. This fear-driven media coverage is critiqued against research about digital bullying, which draws from interdisciplinary literature in the field of media and communication (specifically children and media), education, clinical and developmental psychology, as well as criminal justice. The chapter is particularly relevant for those who need to familiarize themselves with the concept of cyberbullying from four perspectives: (1) what is known about the prevalence of this phenomenon internationally; (2) the relationship between offline and online bullying, and the role of anonymity; (3) sociodemographic and cross-cultural variables; and (4) the known physical and psychological consequences of digital bullying. I use these findings to assess the connotations behind the term "cyberbullying," which is problematic from the perspective of a number of experts, as it implies that the digital world is somehow a separate, detached space from the offline world (see boyd, 2014; Fisk, 2017). Such a connotation can create exaggerated concerns among parents and caregivers. I also present research-based evidence about the relationship between online risks and harm, emphasizing that not every risk leads to harm and that harm from digital bullying needs to be considered in context, rather than by adopting an alarmist approach.

In chapter 3, I include an overview of critical research on the increasing role of private intermediaries in regulating digital environments (DeNardis, 2014), placing this information against the safe harbor provisions of the CDA and DMCA, which ensure limited liability for online intermediaries. Those readers who are not familiar with the companies whose policies I examine in this book, or with their history in relationship to bullying incidents, can find the brief company profiles in appendix B.

In the introduction to part II of the book (chapter 4), I provide an analysis of five cases that resulted in suicides (the so-called high-profile cases): the case of Megan Meier and Rebecca Ann Sedwick in the US, Rehtaeh Parsons and Amanda Todd in Canada, and Hannah Smith in England.[10] I document pressures that companies face when such circumstances arise, the nature of the public discussion and media coverage, reactions from relevant stakeholders, and how such circumstances may result in government regulation that does not necessarily address the problem in a manner that benefits children. I also examine the consequences of similar legislation that developed in the aftermath of tragic incidents in other parts of the world, ushering in the discussion on liability protections for intermediaries and self-regulatory systems that I take up in the following chapter.

I analyze the regulatory environment in terms of digital bullying in the US and the EU in chapter 5. I intend neither this chapter nor the book to provide a comparative perspective in terms of legal differences in how individual cyberbullying cases are handled in these two locations or how they may vary based on legal requirements in the EU members states. The purpose of the chapter is rather to explain the regulatory structures that ensure limited liability for the companies. As such, the chapter should be especially useful to those readers who are not familiar with self-regulation and co-regulation. It includes explanations of relevant regulatory stakeholders, the process of self-regulation versus traditional, Command and Control regulation, and the benefits and downsides of each in the context of digital bullying. Drawing from my interviews with e-safety experts, academics, and social media companies, I explain how and why the current self-regulatory environment came into existence, the scarcity of independent evaluation, especially from children's perspective, and how such a state of affairs reflects upon children's rights.

In chapter 6, I outline the key findings of this research, policies and mechanisms against bullying on social media platforms. Relying on an analysis of texts and an examination of specific platforms, as well as on interviews with social media companies, e-safety experts, and NGO representatives, I document what is missing in the policies and discuss the implications of how these policies are worded. I further explain the companies' moderation systems, what can be known about their effectiveness, presenting the consequences of such mechanisms for child protection and empowerment on the one hand, and users' freedom of speech on the other. I address the patterns of how the policies tend to evolve and how this development can affect the perceptions of regulators.

Chapter 7 consists of an analysis of NGO-company partnerships with respect to bullying prevention and the primarily digital citizenship-based educational initiatives developed in cooperation with NGOs, which constitute an important component of the self-regulatory process. I explain the NGO landscape, relying on information about primarily US- and EU-based NGOs, examining the many important roles of these actors in policy design. I also raise important questions about transparency of this interdependent ecology and how it impacts the ability to examine the effectiveness of the self-regulatory process.

Part III, containing the final chapters (8 and 9), functions as a conclusion to the results I present throughout the book by applying the dignity framework to the findings. I place dignity theory in its broader social and cultural context; it may be a less often discussed aspect of the issue, yet it is one of key relevance to policy development. In part III I argue that the system works toward eliding public discussions about the effectiveness of the self-regulatory system, and that the debate about regulation becomes simplified and politicized to the detriment of not only children and caregivers but also companies and the wider public. Further, the simplified nature of the public debate in the countries I examine leaves stakeholders with proposals for legislation that, while perhaps politically favorable to its promulgators, fail to address the problem and can have negative implications for users' civil liberties. What the research suggests could be more effective regulatory tools than restrictive or punitive ones, such as ensuring funding for educational and bullying-prevention initiatives, or for involvement of mental health practitioners on social media, are rarely publicly discussed.

In this book I propose what a more transparent and dignity-honoring, self-regulatory framework might look like, arguing that policies and enforcement mechanisms need to be publicized and regularly evaluated. I also explore why transparency is *not* an end-goal in and of itself. The aim behind ensuring transparency *is to allow for an evaluation of the mechanisms' effectiveness from the perspective of the children involved, which could open up space for changes in policies and mechanisms in a way that works for youth.* In the final chapter I ask questions about what it means to create a culture of dignity and a policy framework that balances child protection rights with those of provision and participation.

2 Can E-safety Compromise Children's Rights?

Readers intrigued by "They Call It Bunny Hunting," the title of a September 2016 article in the *Washington Post*, may not have expected its subject to be e-safety education in the US (Gibson, 2016). The article described a class offered to tweens (11- and 12-year-olds) in Virginia, where a somber-looking sheriff deputy explained that predators and sex offenders refer to the process of luring children to communicate online as "bunny hunting." Among the scare tactics he used to inform children about the dangers lurking from an ever-proliferating number of digital devices was a warning: children could go to jail for sexting. Although he stopped short of citing cyberbullying cases that resulted in a child's suicide, or of a child killed by an online stalker, he bluntly spoke of children whose lives have been irrevocably changed because of hacking or posting photos online with geo-tags (Gibson, 2016). His message elicited gawks, gasps, and uncomfortable glances among the grim-faced students.

It is perhaps difficult to imagine that such educational practices were still taking place in 2016, three years after the US Department of Justice saw the results of its commissioned evaluation of e-safety curricula published, which recommended reducing reliance on "dramatic statements and scare tactics" (Jones, Mitchell, & Walsh, 2013, p. x; see also Jones, Mitchell, & Walsh, 2014). (I revisit this topic in chapter 7.) Despite what I saw as an ironic, or, at the very least, bemused tone of the *Washington Post* article, a cursory glance at Twitter revealed retweets that seemed to take the messages seriously—even urging parents not to hesitate to engage in similar scare tactics with their children—because "internet predators don't care" (publicly shared anonymized tweet).

This precarious attitude toward technology and the urge to protect children in the face of its real and perceived dangers is most certainly not new. Communication scholars have observed that in the past "each new media technology brought with it great promise for social educational benefits, and great concern about children's exposure to inappropriate and harmful content" (Wartella & Jennings, 2000, p. 31; see also Livingstone, 2009a). Digital technology can likewise become an easy scapegoat for competing agendas of policy makers and interest groups, and in the frequently simplified media coverage of complex issues such as cyberbullying. Much coverage of the internet and youth in general has focused on online pornography, the "stranger danger" of internet predators, as well as digital marketing "scavengers" (Montgomery, 2007).

This tendency to use new media as scapegoats for societal ills was perhaps best exemplified in the coverage of the Columbine incident in 1999, where two teenagers murdered their classmates in a shooting spree. Media emphasized these teens' tendency to play murder games and post hateful comments on websites (Montgomery, 2007). But social science researchers with a critical attitude toward predominant cultural values emphasize that the roots of the problem can be found in socialization patterns that neglect compassion and human dignity while encouraging meanness, competition, and even aggression—and that this state of affairs predates the advent of digital media (Klein, 2012).

Media coverage of cyberbullying incidents rarely examines these factors, especially coverage of the ones often labeled "high-profile cyberbullying incidents" or "bullycides," those with tragic results, ending in suicides (Bazelon, 2013b). Research indicates that a complex set of factors must come together for bullying and cyberbullying to actually result in suicide: an outcome of this kind tends to involve preexisting psychological vulnerabilities, either combined with or apart from unique social circumstances (Herba et al., 2008), and sometimes with self-harming tendencies (Lereya et al., 2013). In other words, while bullying and cyberbullying have been found to be associated with suicidal ideation and attempts (Geoffroy et al., 2016), not all cases of bullying and cyberbullying are likely to result in suicide, nor is suicide a monocausal phenomenon. Not every child who is bullied will develop anxiety or depression, even though repeated victimization can increase the odds of such an outcome (Connolly & Beaver, 2016, cf. Arseneault et al., 2010). I do not mean to propose here, or even suggest, that bullying should be seen as "a right of passage" or "a minor problem." But it is significant to mention that this level of nuance rarely finds its way into media coverage and a portrayal of the bullying-suicide relationship as one of cause-and-effect can misleadingly stoke fears of parents and caregivers.

In public debates around cyberbullying that can emerge in the aftermath of such cases, where media coverage is driven by sensationalism—and policy makers fight for votes of concerned parents and caregivers, while social media companies strive to secure polices that would allow them a degree of latitude in self-organization, children can become an excuse for policies that do not apply solely to them. "Making children the focus of claims often provides a powerful means for pressing emotional buttons and commanding assent even when the target is much broader" (Buckingham, 2011, p. 8). If socially harmful influences are seen as affecting children most especially, then the argument for controlling such influences appears stronger (Buckingham, 2011; Staksrud, 2013a). Philip Jenkins (1992) illustrates this tendency with the example of "moral entrepreneurs" who instigated the panic concerning child abuse that spread through Britain in the 1980s (Buckingham, 2011). Campaigns "against homosexuality" were reframed into campaigns "against pedophiles," and campaigns "against pornography" into campaigns "against *child* pornography," while "campaigns against 'immorality' and 'Satanism' became campaigns against 'ritualistic *child* abuse'" (Buckingham, 2011, p. 8 [emphasis added], cf. Jenkins, 1992). As some of the high-profile cases in chapter 4 demonstrate, laws resulting from cyberbullying incidents can reach well beyond their attempts to regulate harmful effects on children; as some experts observe, those efforts often fail, leaving behind implications for civil liberties and the rights of adults.

The concept of moral panic and its special cases, the media panic and technopanic (which I discuss below), can provide some background for understanding so-called high-profile cyberbullying incidents.[1] As a term that originated in the field of sociology, "moral panic" has been widely (and generically) used among scholars to refer to an exaggerated social reaction in response to a phenomenon or to activities of a social group, and media tends to play an important role in amplifying these concerns (Cohen, 1972; Goode & Ben-Yehuda, 1994; Staksrud, 2013a). In their influential essay on moral panics, Erich Goode and Nachman Ben-Yehuda (1994) outlined "five crucial elements" (p. 156) that define moral panic: "concern, hostility, consensus, disproportionality and volatility." Moral panics are characterized by the "heightened concern" that the behavior "of a certain group" poses for the remainder of the society (p. 157). They provoke an "increased level of hostility" (p. 157) toward people or a group engaging in certain behavior; they are seen as "deviant" and as a threat to the values or morals of the rest of society. Demonizing children who were the so-called perpetrators in high-profile cyberbullying incidents not only violates the dignity of these children, as I argue in chapter 4, but it can also misleadingly simplify the problem of bullying and cyberbullying. As such, it can be counterproductive in finding constructive solutions to the problem.

Moral panic does not require a majority consensus in a society, however, to deem the "wrongdoing of group members" as a "real" or "serious" a threat (Goode & Ben-Yehuda, 1994, p. 157). Moral panic can result in "disproportionality," meaning that the "concern is out of proportion to the nature of the threat" or "considerably greater than that which a sober empirical evaluation would support" (p. 158). This may be the case when media coverage exaggerates cyberbullying prevalence rates or the connection between being bullied and the likelihood of dying by suicide (Underwood, Rish-Scott, & Springer, 2011; Olweus, 2012). High-profile bullying cases may not meet the criteria of moral panics, however. *And although the goal here is not to examine to what extent they do or do not*, it is important to stress that bullying cases can elicit similar reactions, especially because of the outcome: "the consequences of a moral panic are normally changes in the law or its enforcement," (Critcher, 2008, p. 1130). Some of the cases discussed in chapter 4 provide examples.

A type of moral panic where the focus of concern is media itself (usually fears over a new medium) is referred to as "media panic" (Staksrud & Kirksæther, 2013 cf. Drotner, 1999). If concerns center on technology, it's referred to as "technopanic." Technopanics tend to coalesce around a variety of internet-related issues. Nonetheless, they can share similar traits, as the scholar Alice Marwick explains in her comparison of the cyberporn panic of 1996 and the panic over predators on MySpace social media platform more than a decade later:

The technopanic over 'online predator' is remarkably similar to the cyberporn panic; both are fueled by media coverage, both rely on the idea of harm to children as the justification for internet content restriction, and both have resulted in carefully crafted legislation to circumvent First Amendment concerns. (. . .) However, my research demonstrates that legislation proposed—or passed—to curb these problems is an extraordinary response; it is misguided and in many cases masks the underlying problem. (Marwick, 2008, abstract)

In this book I stand in strong opposition to overly risk-averse and harm-emphasizing approaches to children's involvement with contemporary media and technology. A more constructive view of children's experience with digital technology has already been proposed by scholars: "children must learn for themselves how to navigate the wider world, including learning from their mistakes, and recovering from accidents, for 'resilience can only develop through exposure to risk or stress'" (Staksrud & Livingstone, 2009, cf. Coleman & Hagell, 2007, p. 15). The importance of this proposition can hardly be overstated and was repeatedly emphasized by the e-safety experts I interviewed for this book. Yet the media coverage and public debates that have emerged around the cases I discuss in chapter 4 do not lead to such conclusions.

Risk and Harm in Context

Cyberbullying is frequently conceptualized as an "e-safety" or "online safety issue" (Katz, 2012), or an "online risk" (EU Kids Online, 2014) along with other types of risks such as child pornography, exposure to violent and sexual material, grooming (i.e., luring or enticing a child to engage in online communication), sexting, and so forth.[2] With a growing use of technology, recent research by EU Kids Online and its sister project Net Children Go Mobile shows that exposure to some of the risks is increasing. For instance, in comparison to 2010, children in 2014 were more likely to be exposed to hate messages (from 13% to 20%), pro-anorexia sites (from 9% to 13%), self-harm sites (from 7% to 11%) and cyberbullying (from 7% to 12%) (EU Kids Online, 2014).[3]

But despite the rising trend, EU Kids Online researchers caution against panic by placing their findings in context: not all the risk results in harm (Livingstone, Mascheroni, & Staksrud, 2015). On the other hand, curbing access to online spaces may indeed lower risk, but it may also cut access to opportunities. "The more children use the internet, the more online activities they undertake, the more digital skills they gain, (and thus the higher it is likely they climb the ladder of online opportunities to gain the benefits)" (Livingstone, Mascheroni, & Staksrud, 2015, p. 9). Likewise, "less engaged, skilled or supported children gain fewer opportunities or risks" (p. 9). Hence, the positive correlation between risks and opportunities should be acknowledged.

Whether risk will result in harm depends on a number of factors, which raises a key question: Under what circumstances does risk result in harm rather than in coping? Important variables that can affect the likelihood of risk resulting in harm include, but are not limited to: children's psychological and sociodemographic characteristics, family circumstances, support available at the community level (e.g., school policies and regional and country-level policies regarding e-safety education), and cultural differences (see, e.g., Strohmeier, Yanagida, & Toda, 2016). EU Kids Online research has found that online and offline vulnerability are interrelated: "children with more psychological problems suffer more from online as well as offline risks" (d'Haenens, Vandoninck, & Donoso, 2013, p. 1). In addition, more resilient children, those who were "higher in self-efficacy," employed more proactive coping strategies, such as talking to someone or attempting to fix the problem (e.g., by blocking, reporting, or deleting an offensive message). More vulnerable children, however, resorted to fatalistic or passive coping, by hoping for instance that the problem would go away on its own, or by stopping their internet use (d'Haenens et al., 2013). Taking an extended break from the internet could be helpful when children felt bothered by some risks, but it also included missing out on online opportunities and not building resilience, which is why it was not considered to be a favorable strategy.

It is important to repeat the point I made above in the discussion about media coverage of high-profile cases: although peer victimization is a risk factor for suicide among adolescents, and cyberbullying can contribute to suicidal thoughts or be in some way related to suicidal attempts (Hinduja & Patchin, 2010; van Geel, Vedder, & Tanilon, 2014) *not all bullying and cyberbullying is likely to result in self-harm or suicide, nor is suicide monocausal—on the contrary.* Consider the results of EU Kids Online and Net Children Go Mobile research in the UK showing that 21% of internet-using children ages 9 to 16 have experienced either online or offline bullying and 18% of them overall (less than a fifth) reported being upset by what happened (Livingstone, Haddon, Vincent, Mascheroni, & Olafsson, 2014). Nonetheless, cyberbullying has been found to have negative effects on school performance and children's self-esteem, and to contribute to anxiety, depression, and even to suicidal ideation (Mitchell, Ybarra, & Finkelhor, 2007; Subrahmanyam & Šmahel, 2011; Patchin & Hinduja, 2012; Kowalski et al. 2014).

A complex set of socioecological factors on individual, community, and national levels surround cyberbullying (Görzig & Macháčková 2015). Many variables mediate this particular outcome (see Bauman, Toomey, & Walker, 2013). But specific circumstances need to exist for cyberbullying to result in suicide, as shown by some cases I discuss in chapter 4. Girls are particularly vulnerable; so are children with psychological difficulties and socially disadvantaged children (Görzig & Macháčková, 2015). A certain amount of exposure to risk is necessary to develop resilience. Hence, without looking into an individual child's circumstances and the context of use, blanket denial of access to online spaces in order to prevent cyberbullying is hardly a research-based recommendation.[4]

Consider, for instance, that according to recent European research, adolescents' offline and online risk experiences were driven by the same general propensity to risks (Görzig, 2016). Such findings suggest that so-called new technologies do not bring a new type of risk propensity to the nature of digital environments (Görzig, 2016). It is therefore important to go beyond alarmist claims about technology and to examine how the context of children and teens' internet use results in either harm or benefits. The scholar Whitney Phillips explains how trolling is embedded in a wider mainstream culture (Phillips, 2015), just as cyberbullying is a problem that transcends e-safety, and as long as we see it *only* as an e-safety problem, it will remain difficult to design effective solutions. Further, I propose a dignity-based framework to foster an understanding of bullying as part of the wider culture; such an approach can focus the public debate on alternatives to overreactive measures and legal solutions that fail to achieve their stated ends (as I discuss in chapter 4).

The technological and cultural environment in which today's children grow up is significantly different from the environment of the pre-internet era (Livingstone, 2009a; Livingstone, Görzig, & Haddon, 2012; Bazelon, 2013b; boyd, 2014). Social relations and patterns of interaction among youth that existed in the so-called analogue age are now taking place in rapidly changing online venues.

Technological developments happen very quickly and the platforms where social interactions were taking place only a couple of years ago may no longer exist or be as relevant to youth as they used to be. Technological affordances of these platforms provide venues where youth's lives unfold and thus also shape their social interactions. Social media companies, only slightly over a decade old, fueled a new business model based on data collection and accumulation of social capital through sharing culture (van Dijck, 2013).

This new environment creates additional challenges for dealing with bullying and harassment. Although name-calling is not new, being labeled "a slut" or "a faggot," for instance, now has the potential to reach a different dimension. As some authors point out (Bazelon, 2013b), the meanness of spoken words can be ephemeral and fade, whereas online messaging that proliferates and remains visual can even become viral on social networking sites. The amplification of harassment through online sharing that takes place within the developmental process of social positioning can have more insidious consequences than harassment confined to a school or playground. Hurtful social positioning now leaves a trace, as exemplified in cyberbullying, perhaps providing a unique opportunity for the public to understand the extent of a problem that used to be largely untraceable, for example, when limited to verbal slurs on a bathroom wall.[5]

The cultural climate, at least in the US and the European countries that this book focuses on, seems to have become more attentive to bullying. It tends no longer to consider this phenomenon as "a rite of passage" but rather as a behavioral problem to be reckoned with. As some authors point out, awareness of bullying may have been influenced in part by shooting rampages in schools, such as the well-known 1999 Columbine incident in the US (Klein, 2012; Bazelon, 2013b).[6] Not all the children who showed such aggression had been bullied, but this and similar incidents may have put the issue into the limelight of public attention. Laws against face-to-face bullying have been adopted in US states since 1999, and with an increasing number of high-profile cyberbullying incidents, some states began to adopt laws against cyberbullying, too (Sacco et al., 2012). Similarly, the situation is changing for youth minorities, such as the LGBTQ population, who are disproportionately affected by harassment because of their sexual orientation. For instance, the word "fag" was once a commonplace term of belittlement for boys with an effeminate affect, and used without much question of whether it was right or wrong. Today's LGBTQ youth, however, are "caught between the closet and acceptance"; they have cultural support as exemplified by celebrities such as Lady Gaga and Pink, for instance, that doesn't correspond to the rejection they may still experience in their day-to-day lives (Bazelon, 2013b, p. 65).

Despite a greater recognition in the culture that these minorities need additional protection from harassment, LGBTQ youths nonetheless remain strongly impacted by cyberbullying as their personal development and coming out take place in these ever-changing technological environments. The complexity of this process is perhaps best exemplified in the case of Tyler Clementi, a Rutgers University student who died by suicide after being secretly filmed and derogated by his roommate on Twitter because of his sexual orientation (Foderaro, 2010). This story received significant media attention and also led to a wider recognition as to the extent of the impact that cyberbullying can have, especially for youth minority populations.

Cyberbullying Defined from a Research Perspective

The literature on bullying, cyberbullying, abuse, peer harassment, peer and relational aggression, and victimization among young people is vast. Rather than purporting to provide a comprehensive review of the topic, I attempt in the following very brief overview to draw attention to some of the key themes from research about cyberbullying that are relevant for this book.

Cyberbullying is not easily defined and measured (Vandebosch & Van Cleemput, 2009; Tokunaga, 2010; Mishna, 2012; Corcoran, Guckin, & Prentice, 2015). It involves the use of electronic communication technology as a means to embarrass, harass, socially exclude, or threaten (Mishna, Saini, & Solomon, 2009). It can include making offensive remarks, deceiving someone by pretending to be someone else, spreading gossip via digital media, excluding others from an online community, or taking part in voting on a defamatory site (Vandebosch & Van Cleemput, 2009). Some researchers include flaming (online fighting), harassment (for instance, exemplified in repetitive offensive messaging or discrimination based on minority status),[7] and cyberstalking (following someone online and sending repetitive threatening messages) under the umbrella of cyberbullying (see Kowalski et al., 2014). Others study these as distinct phenomena from cyberbullying (e.g. Navarro et al., 2016). Online harassment can include one-off instances that do not necessarily meet the criteria of bullying unless they are related to offline targeting in schools or in other interpersonal peer relationships (Wolak, Mitchell, & Finkelhor, 2007). Yet online harassment can nonetheless happen within a wider pattern of bullying and cause harm, such as distress, to the victim (Mitchell et al., 2016).

Similarly to offline bullying, cyberbullying can be defined as "willful and repeated harm inflicted through the use of computers, cell phones and other electronic devices" (Hinduja & Patchin, 2009, p. 5). This act, as some authors emphasize, also involves a form of power imbalance between the so-called perpetrator and the victim (Olweus, 2012). There does not seem to be an academic consensus on how many times an instance of cyberbullying needs to happen in order to qualify as "repeated": cyberbullying varies from case to case and the nature of interactions in digital environments can make it difficult to apply the criteria of face-to-face bullying. By "willful," researchers refer to "intent" in bullying—to act purposefully in this manner—and hence they distinguish bullying and cyberbullying from the cases where emotional harm may be inflicted when children use words or actions without realizing they may be hurting someone. However, once a case occurs it may be difficult to classify and determine if it meets the definitional criteria of cyberbullying (Nocentini et al., 2010).

Some findings show that face-to-face bullying and cyberbullying tend to co-occur—those who have bullied others offline do so online, too. And those who have been victimized offline have had this experience online as well (Görzig & Macháčková, 2015; cf. Hasebrink et al., 2011). Furthermore, perpetration and victimization was also shown to co-occur—those who have been on the sending side have found themselves on the receiving end (Görzig, 2011; Hasebrink et al., 2011; Lampert & Donoso, 2012; Görzig & Macháčková, 2015). This is particularly interesting from a dignity framework perspective; humiliation seems to beget more humiliation.

Much like the term *"cyber*space," even the concept of *"cyber*bullying" can be problematic (Rey, 2012; Fisk, 2017). A theme emerging from my interviews with e-safety experts addressed how "cyber" can somehow imply that the so-called online world is separate from the offline world, whereas these worlds are intertwined. Children do not necessarily distinguish between "online" and "offline" (Livingstone, 2016, p. 10); their lives take place in both—seamlessly (see boyd, 2014). And so "cyber" can add a mysterious connotation to online spaces, even implying a lawless "Wild West" that remains unconnected to reality. This is why "online bullying," "digital bullying," or "relational aggression" might be better terms, indicating that the problem is bullying, regardless of the medium. It is worth noting that some research uses "online bullying" to denote bullying that happens on the internet but that excludes mobile phones, whereas they use "cyberbullying" to refer to bullying over the internet and mobile phones as well (Livingstone, Haddon, Görzig & Ólafsson, 2011).

Some scholars argue that cyberbullying is merely an extension of face-to-face bullying and that it is a less prevalent phenomenon than its offline predecessor (Olweus, 2012), but other European research has shown that cyberbullying has increased in recent years and may actually be more prevalent than face-to-face bullying (Livingstone, Haddon, Vincent, Mascheroni & Olafsson, 2014, p. 5). Some find that partly due to the peculiarities of digital communication, it may be difficult to apply the criteria of face-to-face bullying onto types of abuse taking place in online spaces, such as bully-victim and bystander labels (see Kofoed & Ringrose, 2012). Others propose that the term "cyber-aggression" may be more appropriate (Corcoran, Guckin, & Prentice, 2015).

Furthermore, in some cases cyberbullying may be hard to distinguish from "online drama," and what to adults may seem like "cyberbullying," teens may identify or dismiss as "drama" (boyd, 2014; Marwick & boyd, 2014). Based on a study with American teens, the scholars danah boyd and Alice Marwick defined drama as "performative, interpersonal conflict that takes place in front of an active, engaged audience, often on social media," explaining that "the emic use of drama distances teens from practices conceptualized by adults as bullying or relational aggression" (Marwick & boyd, 2014, p. 1187). Many cases of drama lacked clear bully-victim roles and teens preferred not to identify as either "bullies" or "victims" because such labels jeopardized their social status, and the concept of bullying was perceived as juvenile. Furthermore, bullying, much like drama, can be about social positioning—perceived popularity and social capital (Thornberg, 2015). Company representatives and e-safety experts I interviewed for this book would sometimes label cases of one-time friends falling out with each other and being mean to each other one day, just to become friends again the next day, as examples of "drama." The terms "bullying" and "cyberbullying," on the other hand, were reserved for what they perceived as more serious cases of continuous taunting, often with clear bully-victim roles. Yet the lines between these roles can be blurred, and drama can be very hurtful even when it is part of a normal growing-up process. Because of these difficulties in defining and operationalizing cyberbullying, some companies prefer to use what they see as broader and less specific terms in their policies, such as "abuse" or "harassment," rather than "cyberbullying." I discuss these nuances in chapter 6.

The prevalence of cyberbullying differs greatly from study to study in three aspects: (1) because of the way cyberbullying is defined and measured (e.g., if children are asked whether they have been bullied in the past two or six months, or a year, or ever in their life); (2) because of differences in age studied and location; and (3) due to differing frequency rates of incidents used to classify whether one is a victim/perpetrator (e.g., at least once, more than once, or several times a week) (see: Kowalski, Giumetti, Schroeder, & Lattanner, 2014). It is also difficult to say if cyberbullying is on the rise by analyzing research based on self-reporting and indirect measurement (Vandebosch & Van Cleemput, 2009). Some recent studies in different countries show an increase in frequency of cyberbullying across various age groups (EU Kids Online 2014; Livingstone, Mascheroni, et al., 2014). Estimates of cyberbullying prevalence vary significantly from study to study, from as little as 6.5% to as much as 72%, depending on how and where it is measured (Tokunaga, 2010; Kowalski et al., 2014). While media reports frequently assert that there is a "cyberbullying epidemic" (see McGraw, 2015; Waldman & Clementi, 2015), there is little academic research to support such a claim.

Individuals' ability to remain anonymous online is a technological affordance that researchers single out as a distinct feature of some cyberbullying cases (Ybarra & Mitchell, 2004; Hinduja & Patchin, 2009; Vandebosch & Van Cleemput, 2009; Katz, 2012). Yet children frequently know who bullies them and cyberbullying can happen within close relationships as well (Mishna, 2012). One-time friends can fall out and start cyberbullying each other. The fact that the digital record of cyberbullying may not easily go away, combined with the ability for taunting to continue after school and on a variety of platforms, making it ubiquitous, are other traits described as peculiar to cyberbullying (Katz, 2012).

Unwillingness to identify as a "bully" or as a "victim" (Marwick & boyd, 2014) or to speak of cyberbullying to parents (Slonje & Smith, 2008) can pose challenges to intervention and prevention. While cyberbullying increases in middle school, some authors suggest it reaches a peak, a so-called "perfect storm" period (Katz, 2012) at age 14 to 15, which suggests that this phase should be anticipated (Katz, 2012, p. 71).[8] Some studies indicate that boys and girls have equal chances of becoming offenders and victims (Ševčíková & Šmahel, 2009), while others find that girls are more likely to be victimized by harassment (Wolak, Mitchell, & Finkelhor, 2006; Görzig & Macháčková, 2015). In traditional bullying, however, boys are more likely to be perpetrators, especially when bullying is physical and studies suggest that this might be the case because cyberbullying involves relational aggression (e.g., being mean to each other), which is preferred by girls, rather than physical aggression, which boys are more prone to (Subrahmanyam & Šmahel, 2011).

Young people who identify as LGBTQ experience higher levels of victimization than their peers who identify as heterosexual (Kosciw, Greytak, & Diaz, 2009; Robinson & Espelage, 2012). This minority group was also found to be at a greater risk of harm associated with victimization. A number of authors emphasized the importance of ensuring that schools introduce not only generic anti-bullying policies, but also anti-bullying policies that specifically protect LGBTQ youth. Contrary to this research-based policy recommendation, however, some US states even enacted bills that explicitly prohibit discussions of victimization in relation to sexual orientation (Robinson & Espelage, 2012). Scholars conducting discourse analyses explained how the public discussion of safety, which also includes online safety, works toward establishing e-safety as "a commodity that is unequally distributed across identity groups," arguing that "the discourses of safety require a person to acquiesce to normative race, gender and sexual identity performances as a pre-requisite for unconditional safety" (Pritchard, 2013, p. 339). Such a discourse places LGBTQ youth as well as racial and ethnic minorities in a particularly vulnerable position where the public outrage over cyberbullying incidents that happen to these children, even when they end in suicide, does not reach the same proportions as in the case of non-minority children. Furthermore, this public discourse fails to acknowledge the instances when adults working with children are hostile to diversity or "anything they deem non-normative" (Pritchard, 2013, p. 337).

A compounding factor is the ubiquity of technology ownership and children's ability to access it unbeknownst to parents and caregivers. For instance, in the US, according to nationally representative data from the Pew Research Center published in 2015, 92% of teens reported going online daily, 24% reported going online "almost constantly," and nearly three quarters of them reported either having or having access to a smartphone (Lenhart, 2015). According to an EU Kids Online survey from 2010, 93% of internet-using children aged 9–16 in 25 European countries went online at least weekly and 60% of them reported doing so every day or almost every day; by 2014, EU Kids Online reported that compared to 2010, children were going online more often at younger ages, and that access was diversifying (EU Kids Online, 2014). There are significant research gaps about digital access, opportunities, risk, and harm from less developed countries or what is sometimes called the Global South (Livingstone & Bulger, 2014). Nonetheless, where data is available, they tend to suggest a growing access to digital technologies. An EU Kids Online study in Brazil showed that regardless of their socioeconomic status, over two-thirds of Brazilian children consider themselves to be more knowledgeable about the internet than their parents (Barbosa et al., 2013).

The Dynamics of Bullying and Cyberbullying

Several theoretical frameworks purport to explain causes behind bullying and cyberbullying, such as theories that focus on the individual, aggressive attribution theories, social and moral cognition theories, theories of mind, and dominance theories (Mishna, 2012). Bullying can be regarded in the context of unequal power among children. A more powerful child can be one that is more popular or physically stronger, and the very act of aggression can fuel popularity (Adler & Adler, 1998; Bernstein & Watson, 1997; Mishna, 2012). This theme of "social positioning" also emerges from teenagers' accounts of how and why bullying happens (Thornberg, 2015). Bullying can be a way for those who want to be "cool" to achieve their goals (Frisen, Jonsson, & Persson, 2007; Frisen, Holmqvist, & Oscarsson, 2008), and the school culture where social hierarchy is valued, and formation of cliques tolerated as normal, can contribute to this process (Swart & Bredekamp, 2009). Hence, those who are victims for a long time can fall to the bottom echelons of social hierarchy, while those who successfully bully could achieve higher status. *In dignity terms—such culture is regarded as non-dignitarian* (Fuller, 2003, 2006; Fuller & Gerloff, 2008).

This kind of social dominance means that individuals have resources that signify power, which can depend on the developmental stage—for example toys with younger children and sex in adolescence (Long & Pellegrini, 2003). This quest for dominance can be especially present when new groups form or when new members are added to the existing groups as they compete for dominance, suggesting that bullying and cyberbullying may be particularly likely when children switch to high school or into different classes, and which can be explained by socio-ecological theories as well (Swearer & Espelage, 2011).

Other reasons that emerge from individual student accounts are that the victim is socially constructed as "different" within a peer group or that the bully has psychosocial problems (Thornberg, 2015). Literature does not seem to be conclusive on this point—some authors suggest that children who bully have trouble processing social information. Others, however, find that children who are really good at processing social information, typically extroverts, are more likely to bully (Mishna, 2012 cf. Bukowski, 2003, Hawley, Little, & Card, 2007). It is worth pointing out, though, that the most recent findings about cyberbullying, which suggest an overlap between so-called perpetration and victimization (Görzig, 2011; Hasebrink et al., 2011; Lampert & Donoso, 2012), might bring a different interpretation about why and how cyberbullying happens. Perhaps rather than attributing cyberbullying to aggression and deviance within individuals, cyberbullying can be conceptualized as a relational pattern within social positioning, one that unfolds differently on various platforms depending, to a degree, on a variety of their affordances (Kofoed & Ringrose, 2012).

Intervention and Prevention Approaches

Most bullying and cyberbullying prevention and treatment programs focus on school-age children, are frequently school-based, and seek to engage parents, schools, teachers, and bystanders in the incidents. (Because the volume of literature on intervention and prevention surpasses the limits of this book, what follows is a brief but important overview.) While some call for legislation—and as I explained in chapter 1, some laws have already been enacted—others point out that such laws could clash with freedom of speech; and that new laws can introduce further legal confusion, as there are already plenty of defamation and other laws that could apply to cyberbullying incidents. Most importantly, legislation could fail to eradicate the problem, which often originates offline and is relational in nature (Ruedy, 2008; Popkin, 2009). In her piece on similarities between bullying and hate crimes, Elizabeth Englander, a cyberbullying scholar and the director of the Massachusetts Aggression Reduction Center, draws parallels between the two. While Massachusetts has both hate crimes and bullying laws that include cyberbullying, she proposes that instead of focusing on punishment, the similarities between hate crimes and bullying should be used to inform prevention efforts emphasizing tolerance of differences, promotion of positive attitudes toward diversity, and reduction of negative attitudes toward hate-based victimization of children outside of the mainstream (Englander, 2007).

These kinds of intervention and prevention mechanisms often reflect "ecological systems theories" in which "bullying dynamics are seen to extend beyond the children who bully or who are bullied" (Mishna, 2012, p. 38; see also Swearer & Espelage, 2011). Rather, "bullying is recognized as unfolding within the social context of the peer group, classroom, the family, the school and the broader community and society" (Mishna, 2012, p. 38). Therefore, intervention and prevention programs try to take many of these factors into account. Some research that looked specifically into the extent to which face-to-face bullying intervention and prevention strategies could assist with cyberbullying, emphasized the importance of systematic whole-school approaches (Pearce, Cross, Monks, Waters, & Falconer, 2011).

But it is not entirely clear to what extent the existing bullying intervention and prevention mechanisms in schools are effective (Vreeman & Carroll, 2007; Ttofi & Farrington, 2011). Some of this inconclusiveness can be attributed to methodological downsides in the evaluation process, such as uncontrolled design (Ttofi & Farrington, 2011).

Some authors are proposing social-emotional learning (Cohen, 2006; Durlak, Weissberg, Dymnicki, & Taylor, 2011) as a strategy to build overall resilience, which can then be helpful when bullying or drama occur. Such programs involve developing interpersonal skills, emotional management, goal achievement, and teaching empathy, and were shown to be successful in reducing victimization when applied to school settings (Payton et al., 2008). Teaching empathy and active listening could assist in building a school culture where children value each other's dignity.

Dignity and Children's Rights

The concept of dignity is slowly beginning to find its way into discourse on children and digital technology, such as in the work of the internationally recognized parenting author Rosalind Wiseman (Family Online Safety Institute Annual Conference, 2013; Wiseman, 2013, 2015). Its application is still limited, but its full potential and usefulness when discussing cyberbullying in particular is significant. Taking account of the importance of dignity in our lives can help us understand power imbalances that contribute to bullying, cyberbullying, and harassment not only among children, but also among adults. Consequently, the principles of dignity can foster solutions to these power problems that could in turn help to transcend discourse that veers toward moral panic, over-simplification, and blame-gaming by ushering in a discussion about wider cultural and social forces that set the stage for bullying behaviors. Dignity theory, in concert with a strong emphasis on children's rights recently promulgated by leading scholars in the field of children and media (Staksrud, 2013a; Livingstone & Bulger, 2014; Livingstone, Carr, & Byrne, 2015) can facilitate a more constructive public understanding of young people's interaction with digital media than the one we have witnessed thus far, and thus move public perception and media coverage toward a more informed, constructive discourse.

Dignity has been written about by an interdisciplinary group of scholars and practitioners from the fields of political science and education (Fuller, 2003, 2006; Fuller & Gerloff, 2008), conflict resolution (Lindner, 2010; Hicks, 2011) and clinical psychology (Hartling, 2010). Some have assembled around a research network called Human Dignity and Humiliation Studies (Human Dignity, n.d.), led by the scholars Evelin Lindner and Linda Hartling. Dignity signifies that a being has an innate right to be valued and receive ethical treatment; it is an inalienable right, which, unlike respect, does not have to be deserved or earned (Fuller, 2003, 2006; Lindner, 2006, 2010; Fuller & Gerloff, 2008; Hicks, 2011). Dignity is sometimes conceptualized as an absence of humiliation (Hartling & Luchetta, 1999; Hartling, 2010).

In their book *Dignity for All: How to Create a World Without Rankism*, Robert Fuller and Pamela Gerloff explain the concept as follows:

It's recognizing that you and everyone else have a right to be here, and that you belong. It means valuing your own and others' presence and special qualities. It means honoring who you are and what you have to offer. It means creating a culture in which it is safe for everyone to contribute their own gifts and talents. Dignity. It's a need so strong that people will give up their freedom to have it met; an inner drive so insistent that it can move people to shocking acts of revenge when the attempt to achieve it is thwarted. (Fuller & Gerloff, 2008, p. 2)

Fuller (2003, 2006) describes the key problem in dignity violations as "abuse of rank" or what he terms "rankism." There is nothing wrong with "rank" per se—rank is a necessary unit in human organization because some people are better suited by their characteristics or qualifications to take certain positions than others. Rank per se is not a problem, then, it is *the abuse of rank or abuse of power imbalance* that creates the problem of indignity (Fuller, 2003; 2006).

People tend to ignore or overlook their need for dignity when they come to accept undignified treatment as "just the way it is"—for example by telling themselves there is nothing they can do to escape it, or by rationalizing their own offensive behavior by insisting that the other person did something to deserve it (Fuller & Gerloff, 2008). Examples of dignity violations can be found in personal and professional relationships: for instance, when a supervisor harasses an employee, when an adult verbally abuses a child, or when a prison guard torments an inmate. But such violations also occur in international relations, as when a more powerful nation pressures a smaller one to commit to a loan that will negatively impact its economy (Fuller & Gerloff, 2008). Examples of subtle rankism exist in small behaviors that devalue other people, such as when your ideas are ignored by your supervisor—whereas when your colleagues come up with the same suggestion, it is adopted with praise—or when your name is left off email announcement lists (Fuller, 2003, 2006).

Bullying is an excellent example of a dignity violation (Fuller, 2006, p. 80), as is the broader behavior of everyday meanness among children and teens: when a child is deliberately excluded from a closed group on social media where all her friends congregate, when gossip is spread about a child, or when a social media page is created to mock him or her, and so forth. In Rosalind Wiseman's 2009 book *Queen Bees and Wannabes*, she aptly describes the so-called mean-girls culture, filled with indignities, in which girls vie for power as they learn to navigate social positioning and cliques during growing-up process. The dynamic of "drama" (see Marwick & boyd, 2014) is similar to this process.

The experience of indignity due to maltreatment by another person is not limited to those at the bottom of the hierarchy. The wealthy, the famous, and the beautiful suffer indignities, too, which fuel cycles of humiliation (Fuller, 2003, 2006; Fuller & Gerloff, 2008; Hicks, 2011). By thinking that success, money, or socially constructed standards of beauty and power will earn them a lasting sense of dignity, they base their assumption on a framework of social positioning that revolves around such achievements. This is what the dignity scholar Donna Hicks calls false dignity: "the belief that our worthiness comes from external sources" (Hicks, 2011, p. 116).

When we lose sight of the fact that we are inherently valuable, that our worth is not dependent on external validation; and that we matter as human beings, we let our true dignity slip through our own hands. (Hicks, 2011, p. 116)

Adopting a dignity perspective could help illuminate why punishing or stigmatizing those who engage in bullying without examining what lies at the heart of the problem may not lead to lasting solutions. "Rankist" behavior leads to cycles of humiliation and shame, which can in turn result in a desire for retaliation, leading to more rankist behavior. Hence, it becomes a never-ending cycle. While rankism can stem from an unconscious misuse of power, it can also occur because the perpetrator feels "better than" someone else and believes this position of superiority gives him or her the green light to diminish another person's dignity (Fuller & Gerloff, 2008). Snobbery falls into this category, just like racism, sexism, classism, and other "isms" (Fuller & Gerloff, 2008, p. 9). Fuller (2006) argues that the word "rankism" goes to the heart of all "isms," and can be used as an umbrella term for all of them.

Approaching bullying and cyberbullying prevention with an understanding of dignity and rankism may help inform more effective solutions to these problems. For example, teaching individuals how to recognize "warning signs of rankism" (Fuller & Gerloff, 2008, p. 46) could empower them to stand up to instances of rankism they detect. Dignity training could be part of this proposed solution, with the aim to train people to detect instances of rank abuse and teach dignity-supporting behavior (Fuller & Gerloff, 2008). Hicks proposes a framework of ten essential elements of dignity, which could create an environment that sustains dignity:

1. Acceptance of identity: approaching people "as being neither inferior nor superior to you."
2. Inclusion: making "others feel that they belong, whatever the relationship" (e.g., family, community or organization, or even nation).
3. Safety: putting "people at ease at two levels—physically, so that they feel safe from bodily harm, and psychologically, so that they feel safe from being humiliated."
4. Acknowledgment: giving "people your full attention by listening, hearing, validating and responding to their concerns, feelings, and experiences."
5. Recognition: "being generous with praise" and validating others' "talents," "hard work" and "thoughtfulness."
6. Fairness: treating people "without discrimination or injustice."
7. Benefit of the doubt: starting with the premise that people are "trustworthy."
8. Understanding: implies believing "that what others think matters."
9. Independence: means encouraging "people to act on their own behalf so that they feel in control of their lives."
10. Accountability: taking "responsibility for your actions" and apologizing when you feel that you have offended another's dignity. (Hicks, 2011, pp. 25–26)

The concept of dignity can be viewed as akin to "positive youth development," an "approach that grew out of dissatisfaction with a predominant view of youth that underestimated the true capacities of young people by focusing on their deficits, rather than their developmental potentials" (Damon, 2004, p. 13; see also Lerner, Fisher, & Weinberg, 2000). Positive youth development shifts the focus from "curing" or "correcting" "risks," "deficits," or "maladaptive tendencies" to "understanding, educating, and engaging young people in productive activities" (Damon, 2004, pp. 15 and 20). It also sees the child as an essentially prosocial being, having "emotional dispositions biologically hardwired into our species," with "adverse reactions to inhumane or unjust behavior" (Damon, 2004, p. 18). Furthermore, this idea can be found in discussion about fostering good citizens and e-citizens/digital citizens (Larson, 2000; Montgomery, Gottlieb-Robles, & Larson, 2004). A "good citizen" is the one who "helps those in need during times of crisis" (Montgomery et al., 2004, p. 108) and the overall goal of civic education is to prepare young citizens to hold "moral and civic virtues, such as concern for the rights and welfare of others, social responsibility, tolerance and respect, and belief in the capacity to make a difference" (Montgomery et al., 2004, p. 111).

An increasing number of works today discuss not only the concept of citizenship and what it means in the digital era, but also youth activism and the ability of young people to participate in civic life (Bennett, Wells, & Freelon, 2011). If the citizen is defined as "a member of a community with civic, political, and social rights" (Staksrud, 2013a, p. 152, cf. Marshall 1950; Tsaliki, 2007), then "digital citizenship" can refer to "membership of an online community, affording you civic, political, and social rights— rights coinciding with the UN human rights and rights of the child" (Staksrud, 2013a, p. 152). I critically examine the concept of digital citizenship as defined here, against how it is used in social media companies' policies and in the context of the Children's Online Privacy Protection Act of 1998 (COPPA) in the US and General Data Protection Regulation (GDPR) provisions in the EU, in chapters 3, 8 and 9.

This section in particular and this book overall examine digital citizenship narrowly—concerning how the concept has been applied in e-safety education and specifically in reference to cyberbullying. Educators who advocate the introduction of digital citizenship into school curricula argue that "the most important job before us is to help students understand issues of digital responsibility and to do so at school as part of a digital health initiative" (Ohler, 2011, p. 26). Jason Ohler, the author of *Digital Community, Digital Citizen,* asserts that trying to solve cyberbullying by restricting access to technology or by punishing students who break the rules, does not solve the issue but merely "address[es] the symptoms" (Ohler, 2011, p. 26).

Balancing Protection, Provision, and Participation

In recent years a concentrated group of scholars around the world who specialize in children and the media have begun to propagate an important approach related to digital citizenship, one of "children's rights" (Livingstone & Bulger, 2014; Livingstone, 2016). As I demonstrate in this book, I strongly favor the recognition and support of children's rights as an overall framework for discussing company responsibility. The international experts Sonia Livingstone, John Carr, and Jasmina Byrne write in their report for the Global Commission on Internet Governance:

It is vital that internet governance organizations recognize that around one in three internet users is aged under 18, and so assumptions about users (for example users' awareness, understanding, abilities, needs or rights) should acknowledge and address the fact that an estimated one in three internet users are children. (Livingstone et al., 2015, p. 16)

The authors argue that internet policy makers seldom recognize children's rights, and when children are given consideration, it is usually to the extent that they have the right *to protection and safety*, but the rights to *provision and participation* tend to be neglected (Livingstone et al., 2015, p. 1). Livingstone argues that even scholars who study youth and digital media shift the focus to risks, perhaps unwittingly, when they choose to frame their research in terms of "media effects" rather than choosing to focus on "rights" (Livingstone, 2016).

Provision and participation are strongly embedded in the idea of a youth's digital citizenship, and digital citizenship is an important policy adopted by social media companies, as an educational tool frequently developed in collaboration with NGOs, to address bullying. In thinking about rights of protection versus rights of participation it is helpful to analogize "positive and negative freedoms" (Livingstone, 2016, p. 9, cf. Berlin, 1958), whereby protection rights are akin to negative freedoms (freedom *from*) and participation to positive freedoms (freedom and ability *to*) (Livingstone, 2016). While children have the right to be protected from bullying on social media they also have the right to participate in these spaces, as they can offer opportunities for the social-emotional, educational, and civic development of young people, in addition to their leisure and entertainment.

Protection rights "receive widespread support" as it is "uncontentious that children should be free from sexual or violent abuse and that protection is required online as well as offline" (Livingstone, 2016, p. 9). The same argument can be made for protections against cyberbullying. Participation rights, on the other hand, may be more difficult to address: "Who are we, critics ask, to assert that children have the right to live not merely without fear or harm but according to a late-modern vision of participatory democracy?" (Livingstone, 2016, p. 9). Ensuring the entire spectrum of rights implies not curbing participation at the expense of protection and vice versa. A relevant question is: To what extent are social media companies honoring these rights? And some ask, to what extent are they obliged and able to ensure these rights having in mind that they are commercial companies with private interests?

Provision includes, for instance, "opportunities for creativity, exploration, expression online and with digital media" or "expanded array of entertainment and leisure choices online" (Global Kids Online, 2016, pp. 7–8), all of which could be found in children's participation on social media. Participation rights could entail: "Take[ing] up of enhanced connections and networking opportunities, user-friendly fora for child/youth voice and expression, child-led initiatives for local and global change, and peer-to-peer connections for entertainment, learning, sharing, and collaboration" (Global Kids Online, pp. 7–8), all of which could, arguably, take place on social media platforms.

These rights are guaranteed to children under the UN Convention on the Rights of the Child (UNCRC), which was adopted in 1989.[9] The "substantive rights," according to the convention, "are commonly divided into three Ps": (1) "rights to provision, concern the resources necessary for children's survival and their development to their full potential"; (2) "rights to protection concern[ing] the wide array of threats to children's dignity, survival, and development"; and (3) "rights to participation enable children to engage with processes that affect their development and enable them to play an active part in society" (Livingstone et al., 2015, p. 8).

Child rights advocates agree the most important contribution of the UNCRC has been to change the public perception of children from "passive objects of charity" to "independent holders of rights" (Livingstone et al., 2015, p. 9, cf. UNICEF, 2014, p. 40). Although the UNCRC was drafted before "mass adoption of the internet," it is very much applicable to the digital age and "it is the yardstick by which any and every action taken by states *or private sector actors* can be judged" (Livingstone et al., 2015, p. 9, emphasis added). Social media companies, as private-sector actors, can also be judged by these benchmarks (see also Lievens, 2016).[10]

While this brief section of the chapter cannot go into discourses about cultural construction of childhood (see Prout, 2005; Livingstone, 2009a; Facer, 2012), it is important to recognize that children have long been predominantly constructed, in what might be called the public imagination in an economically developed world, as "vulnerable," "innocent," and "in need of protection" (Livingstone, 2009a; Facer, 2012; Staksrud, 2013a). On the other hand, a competing construction of children emerged with their growing use of the internet—that of savvy early adopters of digital technology or so-called "digital natives" (Prensky, 2001). Adults were then framed as "naïve incompetents" struggling to manage online risks, resulting in "increasing public anxiety about how children's participation in digital spaces might be managed" (Facer, 2012, pp. 401–402). Such a discourse naturally favored protection. As the scholar Keri Facer aptly observes:

We need to recognize that any debate in this area will be inadequate if it is framed around an idea of the child only as innocent, vulnerable, and biddable. We need to confront the reality of children's sexuality and exploration of risk; we need to recognize the limitations of parental oversight (many parents, not simply negligent parents) and we need to have richer conversations with younger people themselves about what it means to participate in public space and the risks, the powers, and the consequences of such participation (Facer, 2012, p. 410).

Facer concludes that current strategies of doing so, which are based on "building children's awareness of risk and developing their resilience if they experience difficult situations" are only the beginning in shifting the focus away from risk (Facer, 2012, p. 410).

Perhaps, most importantly, if the support from the state at the level of policies and education and other internet governance bodies (including those of social media platforms) are wanting, then it may be "unrealistic" to assume that "parents are available and competent in all matters regarding their children's internet use . . . especially given the internet's complex, cross-border nature" (Livingstone et al., 2015, p. 9). The communications scholar Elisabeth Staksrud pertinently applies Ulrich Beck's and Elisabeth Beck-Gernsheim's Theory of Individualization to the field of policy regarding children and digital media (Beck & Beck-Gernsheim, 2001). Staksrud explains how an "outsourcing of the functions of public institutions" to the European Commission, and via its self-regulatory initiatives to the industry and NGOs, might have left parents and caregivers with a plethora of advice, yet at a fundamental loss as to which advice is authoritative enough to follow (Staksrud, 2013a, p. 123).[11]

In the late 1990s—when media already seemed to pervade every aspect of a child's development—there was a growing recognition that the UNCRC needed to do more to address the impact of media and communications (Livingstone, 2009a). These communication-related points set forth by the UNCRC "include children's rights to express their views freely in all matters affecting them (Art.12), . . . freedom of association and peaceful assembly (Art. 15), protection of privacy (Art. 16), and to mass media that disseminate information and material of social and cultural benefit to the child" (Livingstone, 2009a, p. 210). This "free flow of information" should be "driven by human needs *rather than commercial and political interests*" (Livingstone, 2009a [emphasis added], cf. Hamelink 2003, p. 1; Livingstone, 2009b).

All of these issues covered by the UNCRC point to a growing recognition of the need to honor children's *digital citizenship*, and consequently children's participation and provision rights. But they also urge the pubic and policy makers alike to critically examine the ability of social media platforms to enable children's rights in the context of their commercial interests as private companies. Adopting a rights-based approach that honors the full spectrum of children's rights perhaps makes it easier to see why indiscriminately curbing access to online spaces is not a solution to the problem. They also advocate a shared responsibility for ensuring children's rights, which applies to online intermediaries as well. Further, they can help sort out why an overwhelming focus on risks, of which cyberbullying is an example, can result in favoring protection to the detriment of participation and provision.

Ensuring that social media companies' policies and mechanisms will balance rights of protection, participation, and provision is far from straightforward, however, and I take up the subject in the policy solutions section of this book. Ensuring provision rights is perhaps the most difficult task, and should the companies take it seriously it can require them to go beyond their business models by paying attention to children and teens, not only in the context of advertising revenue, and not only in terms of ensuring basic protections from harms such as bullying, violent content, or sexual abuse. Rather, it prompts them to think very carefully as to which content or technological affordances allow young people to develop their full potential.[12] One can perhaps legitimately wonder whether there is a place for provision rights that go beyond what is stipulated in the law and beyond what the platforms already design as part of CSR, given that these private corporations are primarily accountable to their shareholders.

E-safety Approaches to Honor Children's Rights

By examining cyberbullying in the context of academic research on the subject of e-safety, as well as on coverage of e-safety in the media and the fears that emerge in the public concerning young people's use of so-called new technologies, it becomes increasingly clear how such discourses of fear and technopanic can overwhelmingly focus on risks, often to the detriment of participation and provision rights. A dignity theory approach could help drive public debate beyond risk-driven narratives and elucidate broader social and cultural factors at play, rendering the discourse less alarmist. Thus I propose a framework for assessing the social media companies' part in addressing bullying in the context of honoring the entire spectrum of children's rights.

3 Shaping Company Responsibility: Privatized Public Sphere

Offline bullying, once primarily considered a school-based occurrence, also tended to be traditionally thought of as a problem for the school to handle, whether by managing existing incidents or attempting to prevent future ones. With digital communication, however, bullying has spread "beyond the schoolyard" (Hinduja & Patchin, 2009), making it less clear as to which individuals and institutions are responsible for what aspects of the issue. Although most of the literature on cyberbullying discusses the roles of actors such as parents, bystanders, and schools, the actual digital platforms where cyberbullying incidents frequently happen are less discussed.

In this chapter I briefly illustrate the increasing role of private platforms in regulating online spaces and examine its implications for freedom of speech and privacy (DeNardis, 2014; Crawford & Gillespie, 2016). I also provide a very brief description of available legal tools in cyberbullying cases, and how they relate to companies' liability and the Communications Decency Act (CDA). (I provide a more elaborate explanation of regulatory environments in the US and the EU, together with the historical context behind self-regulation, in chapter 5.) In appendix B, the reader can find profiles of the companies whose policies I examine in this book together with an explanation of their technological affordances, which can affect the nature of bullying that takes place on their platforms.

Privatization of Digital Public Sphere

In September 2016, when Facebook decided to remove a photo posted by a Norwegian author, the move caused an international outcry. "While we recognize that this photo is iconic, it's difficult to create a distinction between allowing a photograph of a nude child in one instance and not others," the company explained (Levin, Wong, & Harding, 2016, para. 3). This was not *any* iconic photo, but the Pulitzer Prize-winning picture of "a naked,

9-year-old girl fleeing napalm bombs during the Vietnam War, tears stream-
ing down her face," an illustration symbolic of "the horrors of modern war-
fare" (Scott & Isaac, 2016, para. 1). Following an intense few days' debate
in the global media, Facebook decided to retract its decision and allow the
photo on the platform after all, recognizing that its historic significance may
well trump the company's nudity policy. The incident yet again gave rise to
concerns about the extent to which online intermediaries were assuming
the roles of news organizations and publishers—questioning their intermediary status (Preston, 2016)—but also regarding cultural sensitivity of their
policies. It may be difficult to agree on the same nudity standards among
European countries, or as compared to the US, let alone globally.

Social media companies are corporations that delineate the boundaries
of what content is allowed on their platforms or which user behavior is
permitted through end user agreements such as Terms of Service (TOS), privacy policies, or community guidelines/standards. Of particular relevance
to the scope of this book is the body of work that discusses the increasing
privatization of the digital public sphere, and the consequent implications
of such privatization for civil liberties. As the internet governance scholar
Laura DeNardis observes: "This private ordering, rather than (or in addition
to), laws, norms, or governments determines the conditions of freedom of
expression in the public sphere" (DeNardis, 2014, p. 158). Another well-
known illustration of this process can be found in Facebook's decision to
allow users to post breastfeeding images, which had previously not been
allowed because of nudity concerns (Facebook, 2015b). Nonetheless, childbirth images that explicitly depict female body parts are still being removed
by the company's moderators, if discovered (Hill, 2014; June, 2016).

What remains unclear, however, is the extent to which the platform's
professed editorial values and economic interests inform its decision-making
processes. Neither is it clear how pressure groups and the media, or the platform's perceptions of user preferences, influence its policies. Likewise, when
companies decide which content contains bullying or is offensive, they regulate free speech on their platforms, often using their own criteria. While
one's privacy and reputation are protected by content removal, this can signify a limitation of another's free speech (Solove, 2007; DeNardis, 2014).

Censorship can take place at different levels. For instance, a number of
app companies whose policies I analyze in this book, including Instagram,
Kik, Voxer, Secret, WhatsApp, Yik Yak, and Snapchat, are primarily designed
for use on mobile phones. In order for users to access them, they first
need to download the app either from the Apple App Store or Google Play.

Gatekeeping can take place at this checkpoint as well at the behest of the app store. For instance, some explicitly or implicitly political apps have not been allowed for distribution by the Apple App Store, having gone through an approval process that can be characterized as opaque and arbitrary (Hestres, 2013). A similar type of gatekeeping will be particularly relevant when discussing the blocking of the app Secret in Brazil, later on in the book.

Violent content matter on these platforms can provide a testing ground for the decision to allow or to censor. Company decisions about which content glorifies violence can have important implications for access to information in the context of civil liberties. Consider the following case that illustrates this process against the backdrop of the Black Lives Matter movement in the US. When an African American young woman posted videos of her standoff with the police on Facebook-owned Instagram, people began to live-comment on her video, which the police said had helped embolden her to turn violent on them (Victor, 2016). The police then submitted a request to Facebook to deactivate her account so that it did not interfere with the standoff, and Facebook complied—temporarily deactivating her Instagram and Facebook accounts. The woman had pointed a shotgun and fired at the police and was subsequently killed in the standoff (Victor, 2016).

The increasing influence of private companies over the online public sphere is well illustrated in those cases where, by invoking their private policies, they defy government preferences and resist government pressure to remove contentious content. Google-owned YouTube refused to remove the movie *Innocence of Muslims*, even after the US government urged the company to analyze its content as a possible violation of its TOS and remove the video accordingly. After Google determined that the video did not constitute a violation, it decided to keep it on the platform and only temporarily blocked access to the video in Egypt and Libya. Google explained that the company had a bias toward freedom of speech, and acknowledged the difficulty of making such decisions on a platform that spans cultures and languages (DeNardis, 2014).

These private companies' policy decisions have well-documented implications for end users' privacy as well (Solove, 2007, 2013; Vaidhyanathan, 2011; Cohen, 2012; DeNardis, 2014). While social media companies offer their services for free, they embed online advertising strategies into their platforms, which allow them to target users based on their characteristics in an effective manner, and to sell data to third parties. What is not always clear, however, is the interplay of companies' economic incentives and decisions regarding censorship and content removal, including in connection to bullying.

The regulation of content on the internet often becomes intertwined with peripheral institutions such as media companies and politicians, whose leveraging of internet infrastructure to accomplish their goals can conflict with the rights of individuals (DeNardis, 2012). In the area of international copyright, for instance, rights owners and media content industries in cooperation with law enforcement are implementing measures that regulate copyright infringement by gradually terminating internet access to individuals who commit violations, or by blocking access to infringing websites or slowing down the bandwidth (DeNardis, 2012, p. 5). Domain-name seizures are also employed to this end. These policies are often exercised in complete disregard of the principle of fair use (Aufderheide & Jaszi, 2011).

In a similar fashion, politicians frequently invoke protecting "innocent children" from risks when trying to make a convincing argument for introducing legislation that also challenges the human rights of adults (Staksrud, 2013a, see chapter 12) or use it as an excuse for enforcing policies that do not even concern or help children. (I elaborate on this topic in chapter 4.) For instance, stopping child pornography is not uncommonly cited as a rationale for regulating copyright infringements (Staksrud, 2013a). Since child pornography is a concern that politicians understand and could capitalize on, anti-piracy groups can leverage this issue to get public office holders to block file-sharing sites or work with intermediaries to block infringing content (Masnick, 2010).

The publishing of sensitive US government correspondence in 2010 by WikiLeaks prompted another turn to intermediaries for content regulation. A number of private intermediaries such as EveryDNS.net (a company providing domain-name related services), Amazon (providing web hosting), as well as financial intermediaries like Visa, MasterCard, and PayPal, which enabled financing for WikiLeaks, all terminated their services to WikiLeaks. All of these private intermediaries had their rationales for these decisions—primarily referring to their TOS, which did not allow for WikiLeaks to publish the material that did not belong to it, any materials that may put people in danger, or that constituted an encouragement of illegal activity. The companies denied that they had been pressured by the US government and insisted they had done so solely based on the violation of their private policies (DeNardis, 2012). In reprisal for denying services to WikiLeaks, the hacker group *Anonymous* mounted distributed denial of services (DDoS) attacks on their websites, disrupting the websites of EveryDNS, MasterCard, Amazon, Visa, and PayPal. Such dynamics illustrate the complexity involved in the decision making of these private companies, which are not always transparent and well understood. Similar complexities can be observed in the context of companies' decision-making processes in reference to cyberbullying, which I detail in chapters 4 and 6.

How the Use of the Terms "Platform" and "Sharing" Reflect a Company's Business Model

Of particular relevance for this book are works that analyze how these private companies conceptualize sharing and human connection, how they use language and terminology to position themselves, and how all of this relates to transparency of social media companies' business models. Most of the companies I discuss in the book prefer to use the word "platform" to describe their ethos and activity. In his influential piece on the politics of platforms, scholar Tarleton Gillespie analyzed the discursive deployment of the word "platform" to demonstrate how these companies use it strategically to frame their services in a way that allows them to "both pursue current and future profits, to strike a regulatory sweet spot between legislative protections that benefit them and obligations that do not, and to lay out a cultural imaginary within which their service makes sense" (Gillespie, 2010, p. 348; see also Gillespie, 2015; Crawford & Gillespie, 2016). As Gillespie points out, using the example of YouTube:

YouTube must present its service not only to its users, but to advertisers, to major media producers it hopes to have as partners, and to policy makers. The term "platform" helps reveal how YouTube and others stage themselves for these constituencies, allowing them to make a broadly progressive sales pitch while also eliding the tensions inherent in their service: between user-generated and commercially produced content, between cultivating community and serving up advertising, between intervening in the delivery of content and remaining neutral. (Gillespie, 2010, p. 348)

Throughout this book I analyze the implications behind companies' provision of cyberbullying policies, which are germane not only when discussing the tension between cultivating a community and ensuring advertising revenue, but also for understanding decisions to intervene in the content instead of remaining neutral. Crawford and Gillespie (2016) raised issues about the effectiveness of companies' flagging mechanisms and how these can leave users with few options while limiting companies' responsibility for content moderation through its positioning terminology.

In her critical history of social media, *The Culture of Connectivity*, scholar José van Dijck explains how coded structures engineered by these platforms alter the nature of our connections and interactions (van Dijck, 2013). The crucial by-product of sharing culture on these platforms is valuable behavioral and profiling data that companies monetize through advertising. She explains:

Under the guise of connectedness they [platforms] produce a precious resource: connectivity. Even though the term "connectivity" originated in technology, where it denotes computer transmissions, in the context of social media it quickly assumed the connotation of users accumulating *social* capital, while in fact this term increasingly referred to owners amassing *economic* capital. (van Dijck, 2013, p. 16)

As van Dijck (2013) stresses, platform owners tend to call for more transparency and openness from their users, which ensures "maximum sharing and frictionless online traffic" (p. 21) while failing to apply the same transparency standards to their own practices and business models (p. 17).

Corporate Social Responsibility

Within the dynamic of cultivating a community while remaining profitable, a company's corporate social responsibility (CSR), a type of self-regulation incorporated into its business model with the goal of ensuring its ethical behavior, can be a fulcrum in the balance. Cyberbullying policies are included in the range of business practices that can be addressed under CSR (Haigh, Brubaker, & Whiteside, 2013).

Corporate social responsibility is invoked in the context of duty of online service providers to protect minors who use their websites, raising the question of whether companies are doing enough (O'Neill, 2013). In its strategy on corporate social responsibility, the European Commission describes CSR as corporate actions that are "above" their legal obligations toward society and environment (European Commission, 2016). The commission also lists "improving self and co-regulatory processes" as part of its strategy on CSR. This is particularly important for the information communications technology (ICT) sector in the context of e-safety (O'Neill, 2013, p. 253). Therefore, if companies are not legally obliged to comply with specific provisions about bullying on their platforms, developing anti-bullying provisions in corporate documents and subsequent enforcement mechanisms can be considered as part of their CSR or self-organizational effort or their private regulation (for differences between private regulation and self-organization vs. self-regulation, see chapter 5).

The importance of getting social media companies to understand protecting and empowering young users as an investment into their business models that can yield high returns, rather than a necessary evil or liability (see Lievens, 2016), is an intended by-product of CSR and self-regulatory initiatives. In its CSR strategy, the European Commission has promoted ensuring e-safety for children, including abuse reporting, as a children's human right (Lievens, 2016, cf. Shift & the Institute for Human Right and Business, 2013). The importance of transparency and accountability of such efforts is emphasized in the Council of Europe's Guide to Human Rights for Internet Users, which also calls on companies to ensure that users have easily accessible tools to report their rights infringements (Lievens, 2016).

Perhaps in an effort to make the public perceive their platforms as ones that put safety first, most companies prefer not to describe their anti-bullying efforts as CSR. Rather, they describe cyberbullying policies and enforcement mechanisms as an integral part of what they do, as part of their ethos, and not something imposed on the company. While they may not describe it as CSR, companies (especially if older and established) seem to understand all too well the performative component of their e-safety efforts (as I discuss in chapters 6 and 7).

Limited Liability for Intermediaries

In the following sections I briefly outline some of the legislation in the US and EU that exists or is proposed regarding bullying and cyberbullying. These pieces of legislation neither contain provisions regarding social media companies nor specify which mechanisms social media companies need to develop in order to address bullying on their platforms.

As bullying and cyberbullying started to gain prominence in public discourse, sometimes as a result of high-profile incidents (Bazelon, 2013b), US states began to adopt laws against bullying which sometimes have a "cyberbullying" or an "electronic harassment" component. All states have anti-bullying statutes and tend to require an implementation of school policy (Stopbullying.gov, 2014; Hinduja & Patchin, 2016). They typically mandate investigation of bullying incidents, consequences for children who bully, and reporting systems for schools to districts or to states' departments of education (Sacco, Silbaugh, Corredor, Casey, & Doherty, 2012).

Efforts which hold school districts accountable for addressing bullying can nonetheless perpetuate a bully-victim dynamic because they fail to capture the complexity of bullying incidents and require schools to fit the information on these incidents into simplified reporting forms (Gilden, 2013, p. 397). In light of evidence from research that cyberbullying cases can be "messy" (Kofoed & Ringrose, 2012), and that there is an overlap between victimization and perpetration (Kowalski, Giumetti, Schroeder, & Lattanner, 2014; Görzig & Macháčková 2015), laws and policies that demand fitting children into neat "bully-victim roles" may be doing them a disservice.

These laws also exhibit a tendency to focus on symptoms and not on root causes behind bullying. For example, as of 2012, few states referred to funding sources that would enable schools to implement prevention-related education (Sacco et al., 2012). If limited only to reporting and punishing individuals—without introducing educational programs aimed at character development (Ohler, 2011)—such measures do not target wider behavioral patterns that can result in bullying.

In a 2012 review of state anti-bullying legislation, Dena T. Sacco and colleagues at the Berkman Klein Center for Internet and Society further found that these laws differ in their level of specificity in addressing bullying; they observed that "most of the laws go well beyond research-based definitions of bullying to encompass a wide range of behaviors, often borrowing and modifying language from legal definitions of harassment" (Sacco et al., 2012, p. 4). Such definitions of bullying open doors to conflation with harassment despite the fact that harassment tends to be defined as being motivated by distinctive characteristics of the victim (Sacco et al., 2012). Small differences in language can significantly change how specific behavior is legally defined: for instance, determining whether these laws refer to motivation of the perpetrator or whether the act needs to be "overt" (U.S. Department of Education, 2011; Sacco et al., 2012) can cause additional confusion.

Also, it is notable that as of January 2016, according to the Cyberbullying Research Center, 18 states had criminal sanctions as part of their bullying laws and a number of others had proposed such measures (Hinduja & Patchin, 2016). This trend toward "criminalization of certain bullying behaviors" (Sacco et al., 2012, p. 9, cf. U.S. Department of Education, 2011) may be another indicator of an overall focus on punitive measures surrounding bullying and cyberbullying, which I address in chapter 4.

While among social science and legal scholars "the merits of criminalizing bullying behavior are up for debate" (Iowa Supreme Court, 2015, p. 2065, cf. Christensen, 2009; Tang, 2013; Albertson, 2014; Bulger, Burton, O'Neill, & Staksrud, 2017), such practices as well as shaming of so-called perpetrators go against dignity framework and restorative justice approaches I embrace in this book. Applying dignity-based solutions could involve leveraging educational initiatives and addressing root causes of the problem by teaching children empathy and stressing the fact that every human being has an inherent worth, rather than stigmatizing perpetrators or merely punishing them.

US federal laws on cyberbullying have not been adopted, and some of the proposed ones, such as the Megan Meier Cyberbullying Prevention Act, have followed high-profile cyberbullying cases and generated significant controversy, as I further explain in chapter 4. Proposed federal bills do not contain provisions regarding responsibilities of social media companies or online intermediaries.

The First Amendment presents a challenge to cyberbullying legislation (King, 2010) as does the Fourth Amendment and the Due Process Clause of the Fourteenth Amendment (Goodno, 2011; Sacco et al., 2012). Marwick and Miller observed in 2014: "As of yet, there is no consensus on whether or not the speech that constitutes 'cyberbullying' is protected by the First Amendment" (Marwick & Miller, 2014, p. 26, cf. Zetter, 2010; Yellin, 2013). These amendments limit the ability of public schools to punish specific speech, to apply their provisions to off-campus events, or to search student computers and smart phones when conducting investigations. Even so, as one legal scholar perceptively observes in the *Berkeley Technology Law Journal*: "Even if the statutes did not have potential constitutional issues, the statutes would not address the root of the cyberbullying problem. A more lasting solution would be to educate children on moral and ethical internet use" (Chang, 2010, p. 520).

In the EU, the European Data Protection Legislation can be applicable to issues of cyberbullying and harassment in cases where a person engaging in cyberbullying discloses personal information of the alleged victim (Confederation of Family Organisations . . ., 2013). "While there is no EU legal framework regarding violence in schools" (Eighth European Forum . . ., 2013, p. 4), some member states may have laws that could be applied to specific forms of bullying. States could also have laws on harassment, stalking, and defamation that could be used in cyberbullying cases (Confederation of Family Organisations . . ., 2013). In the UK law, for instance, a number of existing laws such as Protection from Harassment Act 1997, Defamation Act of 2013, or Malicious Communications Act of 1988 (Legislation -gov.uk, n.d.c, n.d.a, n.d.b, respectively) can be applicable in cyberbullying incidents (Cybersmile Foundation, 2015).

Issues Regarding Intermediary Liability

In 1996 the Communications Decency Act became the first large-scale attempt of the US to control pornographic content on the internet. Section

230 of the CDA, which in that context was protective of freedom of expression and innovation, includes the following provision especially relevant to the responsibilities of online intermediaries:

Immunizes providers and users of "interactive computer services" from liability for information "provided by another information content provider." In other words, where an entity has provided a forum for online speech, that entity shall not be held liable for tortuous speech of others who may use the forum for harmful purposes. (Lipton, 2011, p. 1132; see also Communications Decency Act, 47 U.S.C., Section 230; Lipton, 2013)

Some legal scholars suggest that such a state of affairs should be changed, as the victims may be left without legal remedies for harassment acts, especially in cases where anonymous perpetrators cannot be found: "Section 230 has had the practical effect of preventing courts from engaging in meaningful discussions of the standard of care that might be expected of these service providers absent the statutory immunity" (Lipton, 2011, p. 1132; see also Leither, 2010; Levmore, 2010).

Some authors propose that social networks' liability should be increased as compared to other online intermediaries because of the large amount of personal information that users reveal on these websites (Monaghan, 2011).[1] Introducing "a heightened standard of care" for intermediaries, which would include "traceable anonymity," in the form of logging users' IP addresses, employing screening software that would limit the amount of harmful materials on their websites, and some form of duty to monitor content depending on the size and nature of the intermediary, are among some proposed solutions (Gilden, 2013, p. 389; see also Citron, 2014a). I address some of these initiatives, many of which already exist as part of companies' private self-organization, in chapter 6.

Some legal scholars who address issues concerning online communication and social media recommend introducing measures similar to a provision in the Digital Millennium Copyright Act (Stalla-Bourdillon, 2009; Poole, 2013).[2] The procedure would be executed in the following way, according to an article in the *University of San Francisco Law Review*:

When cyberbullying adversely affects teens and preteens, service providers should have a duty to act. . . . Section 230 of the CDA should be amended to require ISPs [internet Service Providers] and websites to remove bullying and defamatory content about children. The least imposing way to do this would be to implement a notice and takedown system similar to the Digital Millennium Copyright Act (DMCA). . . . When an ISP or a website is notified that a child . . . is being bullied or attacked on their site, the service provider should be obligated to remove the offending post and/or cut off the offender's access to the site. The notifier should have to certify that he or she is either the person or a parent of the person being bullied and that the content being requested for removal is bullying, defamatory or intentionally causes emotional distress. The service provider will then have a reasonable amount of time, perhaps 48 hours, to remove the material. (Poole, 2013, p. 250)

The author of the article also proposes that a "good faith" exemption should be granted to ISPs who did not take all of the content down because they could not locate all the copies of the bullying content on their platform. In the concluding chapters of the book I discuss the usefulness of this proposition in light of findings and other surveyed research.

This approach could be useful for some types of bullying such as blatant, persistent bullying or what companies might perceive as harassment, when it is apparent that such abuse is taking place and content removal or blocking would make it stop (at least on that particular platform and at least online), while making a point that humiliation is not sanctioned and socially acceptable. It may, however, be less effective in cases of relational bullying where social positioning and power imbalances play a role, situations that I elaborate further throughout the book. Also, based on the findings I later present, it is highly unlikely that the self-regulatory environment, either in the US or EU, would favor such an approach, especially in light of the availability of blocking and reporting mechanisms provided by the companies, which purport to do just that (the effectiveness of which I examine and critique in subsequent chapters).

In response to the article I excerpt above (Poole, 2013, p. 250), I would add that the person who posted the allegedly bullying content would need to be notified and given the right to complain (as with similar provisions of the DMCA), which would put the company into the difficult position of making decisions about torts that are "notoriously ambiguous" (Chang, 2010, p. 522).[3] But that's not all: it would add another layer of bureaucracy that could provide the incentive for companies to just keep the content down or the user blocked—unless such takedowns (especially if they become pervasive) negatively affected the company's business model (as I examine in chapters 6 and 8). The negative impact on the business model could happen through users' dissatisfaction, for instance, by limited access to content as a result of removals, which could turn them away from the platform. Such restrictive actions could also potentially and negatively affect "frictionless sharing" and data collection for advertising purposes.

Hence, such a measure could have speech implications—companies being private entities whose interests may not be aligned with public interest would have an incentive to take even constitutionally protected speech down to avoid liability. Additionally, it is questionable to what extent parents and caregivers (who could request such removals) are in the position to make informed and constructive choices in such situations, which also illustrates the difficult task of striking the balance of children's rights to protection versus participation (as I discussed in chapter 2), and issues of privacy.

Anonymity of the perpetrator is another issue with prosecuting cyberbullying cases. In a well-known case, Liskula Cohen, a celebrity model, sued Google to obtain information about an anonymous harasser who published defamatory information about her. She argued that the content posted about her "impugn(ed) her chastity and negatively reflect(ed) on her business as a professional full-time model" (Wolf, 2012, p. 604).

Cohen could not sue the anonymous blogger for the content because she did not know who he/she was; the court eventually ordered Google to reveal the identity of the blogger on the grounds that the content was defamatory. However, while "statements of factual nature are considered defamatory under tort law, mere expressions of opinion, no matter how insulting, abusive or negative, are not actionable" (Wolf, 2012, p. 605). Cyberbullying often involves precisely such hurtful statements that are opinions and not facts, which—in the US at least—may not be actionable under defamation law. Another tort that may apply to cyberbullying cases, "intentional infliction of emotional distress," was also characterized as difficult to prove.

Children have been prosecuted in the past on cyberstalking accounts. The case of Megan Meier (see chapter 4) may have brought an increase in legislative activity whose goal was to make "cyberbullying" a crime (Delta & Matsuura, 2013). In another case, two teenagers from Florida were arrested after posting doctored images of their classmate on a fake Facebook page created in her name. One photo showed the classmate's head on a nude girl's body with a teasing caption. Subsequently, a judge sentenced the girls to 21 days of home detention on cyberstalking charges. Yet another example involved two girls in Texas, one 12 and another 13, who were arrested on felony charges for online impersonation for creating a fake Facebook page of a classmate and then using that account to bully other students (Delta & Matsuura, 2013). Specific disciplinary actions may be supported by research in such circumstances. But labeling children as criminals and punishing them without adequate educational initiatives can hardly be considered as a research-based recommendation.

Despite limited liability, there have been attempts to sue social media companies on grounds of cyberbullying. In *Finkel v. Facebook*, the plaintiff sued for defamation and negligence (Digital Media Law Project, 2009a, 2009b) after a private Facebook group was created about a teenager whose authors "asserted or implied," among other things, that she had "contracted the HIV virus" and was "of dubious morals." The complaint alleged that Facebook should be held liable for publishing defamatory content because the company "should have known that such statements were false and/or have taken steps to verify the genuineness of these statements" (Digital Media Law Project, 2009a).

The plaintiff argued that Facebook's TOS, which grant the company "ownership interest" in what was described as "defamatory content," made the "CDA 230 inapplicable" (Digital Media Law Project, 2009a). (Note that the impact of ownership interest is worth examining when thinking about a company's intermediary status.) Parents of the children who posted this defamatory content were accused of negligence, having failed to supervise their children. The court dismissed the case, deciding the company was nonetheless immune from liability under the Section 230 of the CDA. It is perhaps worthwhile to observe that the complaint did not state whether the bullied teenager (or someone on her behalf) had reported (flagged) the allegedly defamatory content to Facebook and whether Facebook responded in due time (thus raising concerns about Facebook's reporting tools, which are a component of the company's private anti bullying enforcement mechanisms) (Digital Media Law Project, 2009b).

Children's Online Privacy Protection Act (COPPA)

A number of social media companies stipulate in their TOS that children under the age of 13 are not allowed to use their platforms. While social media companies report not to approve of underage use, and to move swiftly to remove detected unauthorized users, this issue nonetheless remains a significant problem (O'Neill, 2013) because age is self-reported and can be falsified.

While some companies have 17 or 18 as their minimum age, the reason why 13 is the most commonly used cut-off age is the Children's Online Privacy Protection Act (COPPA), a US law that puts company responsibility into perspective, and the model for Article 8 of the European General Data Protection Regulation (GDPR Regulation EU 2016/679).[4] COPPA, which took effect in 2000, passed amid much controversy around children's internet use (Montgomery, 2007), and applies to "operators of websites or online services directed to children under 13 years of age and operators of other websites or online services that have actual knowledge that they are collecting personal information online from a child under 13" (Federal Trade Commission, n.d., Rule Summary). The law essentially prohibits such sites to collect personal information from children under the age of 13 unless parental consent is given. Rather than allow children under 13 to access the sites and seek parental consent, most social media sites ban access to children under 13 altogether.

During the sign-up process most social media sites then ask users to state their age—a requirement that can easily be circumvented by children. Research has shown not only that children tend to do so but also that parents actively help them in this process (boyd, Hargittai, Schultz, & Palfrey, 2011; Livingstone, Ólafsson, & Staksrud, 2011), making the law largely ineffective for these purposes, at least when implemented in this manner. Platforms not based in the US also need to comply with COPPA if their services are directed to children in the US (Federal Trade Commission, 2015). Even though a number of children under 13 can be found on social media sites, the companies, then, tend to publicly deny "actual knowledge" of having such children on their sites. Revised COPPA rules came into effect in 2013 and expanded the definition of "personal information" to include geolocation and cookies, among others (Federal Trade Commission, 2013).

A correlative consequence of this age limit puts underage children in the position where they remain invisible for platforms not only in terms of personal data collection, but in general (they are not the platforms' "digital citizens")—they do not have *any* rights (see chapter 2 and the discussion of "illegal digital aliens" in chapter 9, cf. Staksrud, 2013a, p.156) and platforms are under no obligation to cater to or innovate for them (boyd, 2015).

Another relevant question here in the context of children's participation rights is the extent to which parents or caregivers are able to make constructive decisions about children's participation in specific online spaces. Are parents or caregivers informed enough about specific digital environments, or about COPPA/GDPR and why the age limit is 13 (boyd et al., 2011)? What about those cases when children suffer from abuse at home or would like to participate in sites that cater to, for instance, LGBTQ communities, without coming out to their parents (see e.g., boyd, 2015)?

But should companies also be asked to do more in order to *not* collect personal data from those under 13 or, as some would argue, teens in general (Montgomery, 2015)? And if this is a public policy goal, should the regulators have the responsibility to design and enforce a law that is more than a pretense of a working legislation? This is a complex set of questions. I revisit the debate on protection rights on the one hand, versus participation and provision rights on the other (and whether they need to be pitted against each other) throughout the book.

Social Media Companies and Affordances

Here I provide a brief overview of the type of companies whose policies and anti-bullying mechanisms I analyze in this book. Individual platform or app profiles are located in appendix B, including: Facebook, Instagram, Twitter, Ask.fm, YouTube, Yik Yak, Secret, Google+, Tumblr, Snapchat, Whisper, Voxer, WhatsApp, and Kik. Relying on the concept of "technological affordances," or "actions or uses a technology makes easier" (Earl & Kimport, 2011, p. 32), I've categorized the selected companies based on the user actions they allow for.

Social Media versus Digital Messengers

Digital messengers enable private communication among two or more people, similar to SMS or group chat, which happens online. But not all digital messengers necessarily consider themselves to be "social media." On the contrary, some strive to build their reputation based on *not* being "social media."

Within the industry, social media companies can be perceived as particularly conducive to cyberbullying because of their affordances, which allow for instantaneous content sharing with a large number of people. Affordances of digital messengers, on the other hand, which primarily enable private communication between two or several people, are not perceived as favorable to cyberbullying. A representative of one company compared social media to radio broadcasting and pointed out the difference in using the company's platform:

You're broadcasting and that may be to all of your friends or to the entire world, you're like a radio station . . . as opposed to when you make a phone call to someone. That's private communication, that's not broadcasting, that's having a conversation with someone. That's why cyberbullying typically occurs in social networks / social media and particularly those that enable individuals to be anonymous. We don't have any attributes or characteristics of those types of apps and platforms that enable those types of behaviors. (Anonymous, personal communication with the author, November 6, 2014)

Social media platforms provide users with an ability to share content simultaneously with multiple friends or followers. Followers differ from

Table 3.1
Social media versus private communication (digital messengers)

Social media	Digital Messengers	Both
Facebook	WhatsApp	Snapchat
Instagram	Voxer	Kik
Twitter	(Note that many platforms that are in the "social media" category on the left, also provide some form of direct messaging capacity, e.g. one can send a private message on Twitter and Facebook has its Messenger app).	
Ask.fm		
YouTube		
Google+		
Tumblr		
Whisper		
Secret		
Yik Yak		

friends because one user can "follow" another user's profile and see posts (content as in text/photos/video) from that person in his or her own news-feed, but that person does not see posts from the follower without follow-ing him or her back. To "friend," on the other hand, implies a symmetrical relationship, in the sense that "friends" typically follow and receive posts and updates from each other.

Digital messengers, on the other hand, are primarily intended to provide for communication (via text, photos, or video) between two people or a closed group of several people. While Snapchat and Kik used to be primarily messengers, they have added functions that allow users to receive updates from other people in their networks (similar to "newsfeeds"), which is why it could be said that they could be classified as both. This classification is relevant because different functions or affordances might call for different cyberbullying policies and prevention measures, and they also affect how platforms position themselves in relationship to cyberbullying (see table 3.1).

True Identity, Pseudo-anonymity, and Anonymity

The platforms surveyed here allow for varying degrees of anonymity; those that allow users to be anonymous can be perceived in the industry as espe-cially favorable to bullying. Asking users to go by their real-life names on the platform is sometimes put forward as an especially safe feature that allows transparency and is less likely to encourage bullying. The literature on cyberbullying and anonymity indicates that while this may be true on some occasions, it is not always the case; a number of victims report to know who "the perpetrators" are (Mishna, 2012; Kowalski et al., 2014). Cyberbullying can also happen among friends who used to be close but then fell out.

Facebook requires users to go by their real offline names in order to create their online profiles, a guideline that users can nonetheless violate. Google+ used to ask for the same, but at the time of this research, it allowed pseudo-anonymity, which means that users can create profiles under names they do not use in their real lives. Facebook does not allow impersonation, while Twitter allows parody accounts as long as they are clearly labeled as such.

Some platforms that label themselves or are labeled within the industry as "anonymous apps" allow for sharing without having a name or a pseud-onym attached to the content being shared. For instance, on Whisper, one could share the following text written over a photo of a gun: "I was just diagnosed with severe bipolar and depression . . . my parents bought me a gun for graduation" (Dickey, 2013). Such a post might then be shared either with random people who are also using the platform or with peo-ple's contacts in their phonebook or with users in the geographical vicinity (or with some algorithmic combination thereof). The point is that no one should know who is saying what, which is why they are called "anony-mous" platforms. Yik Yak, for instance, started off this way but later moved to another model (see table 3.2).

Table 3.2
Degrees of anonymity

True/Real/Authentic Identity	Pseudo-identity	Anonymous
Facebook	Instagram	Secret
	Ask.fm	Whisper
	YouTube	Yik Yak (initially anonymous, and as of March 2016 introduced usernames)
	Yik Yak	Ask.fm
	Twitter	
	Google+	
	Tumblr	
	Snapchat	
	Kik	
	WhatsApp	
	Voxer	

The anonymous apps included in this study did not consider themselves to be places where users come to post "deep and dark secrets." Some of these platforms are primarily "mobile applications" or "apps"—software applications designed for use on mobile devices such as smartphones and tablets. Platforms that had been initially designed for use on desktop or laptop computers can also have their mobile app versions. In the case of platforms that are primarily designed for mobile use, however, users typically need to download them from Google Play or the Apple App Store. This is why, for those platforms that are primarily apps, the descriptions in the appendix refer to them as such.

Civil Liberties and Liabilities

The increasing role of private companies in regulating cyberbullying raises key questions concerning civil liberties in online spaces on the one hand and the limited scope of social media companies' liability for cyberbullying incidents on the other. A brief description of the platforms I surveyed in this book, which the reader can find in the appendix B, shows how their technological affordances are relevant to their handling of cyberbullying. All of this lays the groundwork for chapter 4, where I show that despite the tendencies toward limited liability of online intermediaries, high-profile incidents can result in the public perception that these companies are or should be liable for cyberbullying. That in turn influences changes in their self-organizational measures, as I explain in chapter 6.[5]

II   Vagaries of Self-Regulation

4 Perils of Politics-Driven Regulation

In this chapter I offer analyses of several cyberbullying incidents that were related to suicides. Cases like these, often labeled "high-profile" cyberbullying incidents, have received significant media attention in their respective countries, and internationally as well. They illustrate and provide additional context for a discussion in this chapter about the dynamics between media, policy makers, companies, and other stakeholders that have contributed to the current regulatory culture and social media policies.

Imprecise Use of the Term "Cyberbullying"

In chapter 2, I discussed how scholars find it difficult to arrive at a precise and comprehensive definition of cyberbullying. A number of the cases I describe in this chapter exemplify how "cyberbullying" is similarly used in the media in an imprecise manner. For instance, "cyberbullying" is a term that primarily refers to peer conflict and peer aggression, but it was used in the media to label conflicts in which cyberbullying may have only been a component or where the primary issue was sextortion.

For instance, in the case of Hannah Smith, the presence of cyberbullying was impossible to prove by a posthumous police investigation. And consider that the case of 13-year-old Megan Meier in 2006, which brought significant attention to the concept of "cyberbullying" not only in the US but internationally, was not entirely based on peer conflict. It involved an adult, a mother, who pretended to be a boy on the MySpace social network, and under such guise interacted with the young girl. She committed an act of deception that was frequently labeled as "cyberbullying" in the media even though, arguably, cyberbullying was only a component of her behavior. Amanda Todd, a 15-year-old girl from Canada, committed suicide after her nude photos were exposed online, followed by bullying and slut shaming. She was led into exposing her breasts on a webcam to a 35-year-old man, who was the principal actor in this case. Although this case clearly involved an online predator, and cyberbullying per se was not at the heart of this issue but rather a consequence, the incident was frequently labeled by the media as a "cyberbullying case." The case of Rehtaeh Parsons began with an alleged gang rape, which was photographed with a phone, only to result in cyberbullying and slut shaming after the photos were shared on social media. While cyberbullying played an important role in this case, as the girl was humiliated and harassed by her peers once the photos began to spread, the case originated as the crime of sexual offense.

Interrelated Themes in "Cyberbullying" Cases

Several interrelated themes emerged from these cases; all of them are important for understanding the context in which cyberbullying policies of social media companies are created. They all indicate what can be described as the simplified nature of the public debate around these cases and, subsequently, the punitive regulatory measures introduced to address what is sometimes imprecisely characterized as "cyberbullying." (My research-based evidence in previous chapters argues against such approaches and instead stresses the value of educational measures aimed at cyberbullying prevention.) A number of these cases drew significant public attention to social media companies, both in general and to the platforms specifically involved; this resulted in pressures from the public and often ad hoc initiatives from dispersed regulators and policy makers, which in turn contributed to the shaping of the self-regulatory environment. In addition, social media companies have sometimes engaged in conducting investigations, such as in the case of Amanda Todd. Such examples further demonstrate an increasing role of private companies in these processes. Finally, a number of laws resulting from these cases were seriously questioned in the media coverage on the grounds of impinging on end users' civil liberties and were sometimes characterized by legal experts as "misguided legislation."

Summaries of the Cases

In the five cases I examine here—the death by suicide of Megan Meier and Rebecca Ann Sedwick from the US, Amanda Todd and Rehtaeh Parsons from Canada, and Hannah Smith from the UK—the themes I mention above surfaced against the backdrop of exaggerated fears over children's use of digital technology, dignity, and children's rights, all being topics I focus on in part I. Perhaps most importantly, these cases (especially as I present them in the context of their aftermaths) demonstrate the mechanisms that can propel social media companies into revamping their policies, just as they can strengthen the public perception that the companies are or should be liable, which can in turn influence changes in their self-organizational measures.

Megan Meier

One of the early cases that received widespread media attention, and was primarily labeled in the media as "cyberbullying," was the case of Megan Meier, a 13-year-old girl from O'Fallon, Missouri, who committed suicide in October 2006, after interacting with her friend's mother, Lori Drew. Drew had pretended to be a teenage boy on the social networking website MySpace (Steinhauer, 2008). Megan appeared to be an emotionally sensitive girl, who had struggled with self-esteem and weight issues and had been on anti-depression medication before the incident took place (Maag, 2007; Megan Meier Foundation, n.d.b). A person representing herself as a boy named "Josh" added Megan as a friend on MySpace and started talking to her. Megan liked the boy from the photo, even though she never talked to him over the phone or in person throughout the month of what Megan's mother described as "innocent flirtation" (Maag, 2007). Josh told her he was home-schooled and had no phone access.

Megan's mother, Tina Meier, who later founded the Megan Meier Foundation to address bullying, appeared in the US mainstream media to discuss her daughter's case (Megan Meier Foundation, n.d.a). In a previous school her daughter had attended, Tina said, Megan had tried "desperately" to join popular girls, but she was teased about her weight (Maag, 2007).

Megan had been a friend of Lori Drew's daughter, but the two had a falling out (Megan Meier Foundation, n.d.b). As the *Guardian* reported, Drew had been upset that Megan was "spreading lies" about her daughter and wanted to "expose her" (Glaister, 2008). The families knew each other, and Lori Drew allegedly knew Megan had been emotionally sensitive and was on medication; but once Megan switched schools, she got a new group of friends, joined the volleyball team, and lost weight, which, according to her mother, helped her become accepted in the new community (Megan Meier Foundation, n.d.b).

A germane observation in the context of dignity framework can be made about the public discussion surrounding this case. Rarely did it adopt a critical stance toward the proposition that a girl (in this case Megan), women, or people in general should derive their self-worth from their looks and popularity status. That a perceived improvement in one's looks should result in a rise in social status is a premise that all too often remains unquestioned in the public and even an individual's mind. According to dignity framework, every human being has dignity or internal, inherent value that does not have to be earned. Striving for social status, social influence, or ways to improve one's appearance as a source of dignity is a classic example of what the dignity author Donna Hicks characterizes as "false dignity" (Hicks, 2011, see also chapter 3).

Motivated by apparent peer conflict between her daughter and Megan, Lori Drew opened an account under the name of "Josh Evans" on MySpace, and according to the prosecutors she "bragged" about "the prank" (Michels, 2008). Drew's daughter, her 18-year-old employee, and another girl from the neighborhood helped her maintain the false MySpace account (Michels, 2008; Collins, 2008).

The Meier family reported that the FBI was looking into the matter after Megan's suicide and the story was kept private, outside of media coverage, for a year. The FBI, however, according to the family's account, could not retrieve the last message Megan had received from Josh Evans, which her parents reported to have seen by logging into the account after the suicide: "Everybody in O'Fallon knows how you are. You are a bad person and everybody hates you. Have a shitty rest of your life. The world would be a better place without you" (Megan Meier Foundation, n.d.b). When the investigation determined that Drew's actions may have been cruel but did not break any laws (Collins, 2008), Megan's parents decided to go public and talk to the media about the story.

Amanda Todd

Amanda Todd died by suicide in October 2012, a month after posting a nine-minute YouTube video called "My Story: Struggling, Bullying, Suicide and Self-harm." Using flash cards, she silently described the events that resulted in her situation and followed with a plea for help (ChiaVideos, 2012). While her mental health was affected by cyberbullying, this case also involved child pornography and sexual extortion.

In 2009 and 2010, Amanda used a video chat platform to meet new people online, where she received compliments on her looks. One of the people she spoke to asked her to flash for him on camera, which she eventually did (Riley Huntley, 2012).[1] According to the story Amanda tells in the video, he later found her on Facebook and threatened that he would send the photo of her bare breasts to her teachers, classmates, and family if she did not perform for him on camera again. Furthermore, he said he knew Amanda's address, which reportedly made her increasingly anxious. Once the anonymous assaulter revealed her photos, Amanda received a notice from the police that her naked photo, constituting a criminal offense of child pornography, was circulating on the internet.

Bullying and cyberbullying ensued, not only from her classmates but also from anonymous people who had seen the photo. She transferred to a different school but then got involved with drugs and alcohol, which reflected that she'd been psychologically affected by the situation. When the assaulter resurfaced, asking for another session of nude exposure, he threatened to reveal the photo in her new school environment if she did not comply. Furthermore, he made a Facebook page, where the photo of Amanda's flashing was the profile photo. In the confessional YouTube video, Amanda reported that she lost respect from her new classmates and was bullied, after which she started cutting herself. When she moved to yet a different school, she got involved with "an old guy friend" while his girlfriend was on vacation (Riley Huntley, 2012). Only a week later, the "old guy friend," his girlfriend, and a group of other people came to Amanda's school and verbally and physically abused Amanda. Bystanders captured the incident on digital cameras, resulting in yet another round of bullying and cyberbullying.

Amanda then attempted the first suicide by drinking bleach but was rescued and taken to the hospital. Her classmates and some other people ridiculed her suicide attempt on Facebook. After that, she moved to another city to live with her mother (her parents had been separated). She was cutting, was on anti-depressants, and attended counseling. A month after she posted the video on YouTube where she had told her story in silence, using flashcards, Amanda killed herself, allegedly by hanging.

Rehtaeh Parsons

Rehtaeh Parsons committed suicide at the age of 17 two years after being photographed while reportedly being raped and later bullied when the photos were disseminated to friends in school and the community. This case, which took place in Nova Scotia, Canada, received significant media attention, and was also one in which cyberbullying was conflated with child pornography. Although Rehtaeh's parents reported the case while the girl was still alive, the Royal Canadian Mounted Police concluded that they had insufficient evidence to press charges, and media coverage to a great extent revolved around the issue of responsibility or blame of individuals involved in the incident (see e.g., "Rehtaeh Parsons, Canadian Girl . . .," 2013). Following the suicide, however, the case was reopened, and the police reported to have found new information by conducting investigations into the rape allegations and the distribution of child pornography ("Rehtaeh Parsons case . . .," 2013). The incident resulted in criminal prosecution of minors and in a new cyberbullying law in Nova Scotia. The online "hacktivist" and social justice group called Anonymous, which threatened to reveal the identity of the young men involved in the cyberbullying, may have contributed to the reopening of the case (Omand, 2015).

Rebecca Ann Sedwick

Rebecca Ann Sedwick committed suicide in September 2013. According to the Polk County sheriff, Rebecca jumped from an abandoned factory in Lakeland, Florida, after being bullied; *AbcActionNews* quoted him as saying, "At the end of the day, it wasn't a school yard fight that led to the demise of this young girl. It was bullying online" (Raiche & Williams, 2013). Months later, CNN reported that the police file raised questions about evidence for the alleged bullying in this case, citing an expert who had reviewed the police files and could not find any evidence of bullying for the seven months leading to the suicide; the case had by then "garnered national and international attention" (Wallace, 2014). As has been apparent with victims in other high-profile suicide cases, according to the *New York Times*, Rebecca had been experiencing psychological difficulties and had been cutting herself; she would share those cutting images on digital platforms on which she would also receive mean comments in reply (Alvarez, 2013b). The day she ended her life, Rebecca changed her username on Kik messenger into "That Dead Girl" (Alvarez, 2013b). About a month after her death, the sheriff charged two girls, 12-year-old Katelyn Roman and 14-year-old Guadalupe Shaw, with "aggravated stalking"; they were characterized as Rebecca's "chief tormenters" (Almasy, Segal, & Couwels, 2013; Wallace, 2014). Following the suicide, two politicians from Florida introduced "Rebecca's Law" which would make bullying a crime (Dahl, 2014). "The bill would make in-person and online bullying a misdemeanor that would carry a year-long prison sentence on the second offense," while bullying involving threats would constitute a felony (The Stream, 2014, para 4). The charges were dropped after a highly problematic set of sheriff's actions and investigation, which I describe later in this chapter.

Hannah Smith

Hannah Smith, from Leicestershire, England, was 14 when she committed suicide after what her family described as "months of torment" on Ask .fm (Robson, 2013). In the weeks before she took her life, Hannah allegedly received messages on Ask.fm that criticized how she looked and urged her to kill herself ("Hannah Smith: Ask.fm 'happy to help police,'" 2013). Her father had tried to keep her away from Ask.fm after Hannah's school warned parents against allowing their children to use Ask.fm, but she continued to use the site (Rudd, 2013a). Ask.fm agreed to cooperate with the police in determining the cause behind the girl's death and in revealing the identities behind the usernames, which the coroner had obtained from Hannah's computer and mobile phone ("Websites could be made to reveal . . .," 2013; Hannah Smith death . . .," 2013).

A year after the suicide, however, the police investigation revealed that the girl had been sending "vile" posts to herself prior to the incident; the coroner, looking at messages and their IP addresses, found no evidence that the girl had been exposed to online bullying (Davies, 2014; "Hannah Smith inquest . . .," 2014). Her father nonetheless reported that she had been bullied, especially after being attacked at a party by a girl who used to be her friend and that her head had been "smashed against a wall" (Davies, 2014). Hannah's teachers reported that she was also involved as "a bully," and the coroner concluded there was no evidence that the school and family could have known about her intention to kill herself (Davies, 2014). This suicide case is the one that put Ask.fm, a social networking website, in the spotlight of UK public attention.

Simplistic Binaries of Finger Pointing

Despite the abovementioned caveat that Megan Meier's suicide was not a typical case of bullying, the extensive coverage of the case in the mainstream media, and the public outrage that followed, led to what can best be described as the vilification of Lori Drew, an adult, as "the bully" (Celizic, 2007; Zetter, 2009). This is not to excuse Drew's misguided actions for their undoubtedly devastating consequences, but merely to suggest that the coverage seemed to perpetuate the bully-victim narrative, with little recognition of the fact that the relationship between bullying and suicide is not at all straightforward and that a suicide tends to result from a complex set of factors, such as depression and anxiety, which bullying can exacerbate. Consider the ABC online news article, "Parents: Cyberbullying Led to a Teen's Suicide" (2007), based on statements made by Meier's parents, who were convinced that their daughter's death was the result of a "cruel cyber hoax." The title not only cements the cause-and-effect relationship between bullying and suicide, but it also makes the article itself sound like a warning message to all parents rather than the report of conclusion arrived at by Meier's parents. Although coverage of the case often recognized that Megan had suffered from depression, this evidence was frequently used in conjunction with the suggestion that Drew had known about the girl's depression and hence, should have known better not to engage in "bullying," again shifting the focus away from cyberbullying complexity and onto blame. The neighbors soon turned against the Drews, resulting in fear of backlash assaults, as it was described in the media, which in turn made it difficult for Lori Drew to run her business and continue living in the area. She was harassed online as well (Hamilton, 2007). Mounting accusations from the media and the public confirmed and continued to cultivate the bully-victim narrative.

After Amanda Todd's suicide, her case, too, received significant mainstream media attention, not only in Canada but internationally. The Canadian Broadcasting Corporation (CBC) aired two news documentaries analyzing the details behind the case and the subsequent investigation as part of its series *Fifth Estate*: "Stalking Amanda Todd: The Man in the Shadows" (Kelly, 2014) and "The Sextortion of Amanda Todd" (Kelly, 2013). Extensive media debate was frequently focused on the punitive aspects of the issue, raising questions of who should be held responsible for not assisting Amanda prior to the suicide, and the blame was often placed on the failure of the police to thoroughly investigate the case—as well as on the school system and educators for failing to address systematic bullying and cyberbullying. Mainstream media coverage of cyberbullying in the US is frequently limited to questions of responsibility to the detriment of capturing the complexity behind cyberbullying as a phenomenon (Milosevic, 2015b). For instance, questions such as whether these incidents may display a culture-wide pattern of meanness in children's social relations, or how meanness in popular culture may be providing a negative model for youth behavior, are rarely examined. All of these could have been raised in reference to the bullying and cyberbullying that took place from Amanda's peers after her nude photos had been exposed. Interestingly enough, questions of whether Amanda tried to report abusive photos and comments to Facebook or YouTube in an effort to have the companies remove such content were difficult to find in media coverage.

The overall punitive orientation of the public debate seemed to culminate when the hacker group called Anonymous set out to find the offender on their own. As *Slate* and *The DailyDot* reported, Anonymous had identified a wrong man and exposed his name and address, resulting in subsequent threats to and bullying of this individual (Morris, 2012; Murphy, 2012).

According to some media reports, Amanda's mother had seen the messages that the sex offender had sent to Amanda, blackmailing her by asking to perform for him on camera. She had reported the case to the Royal Canadian Mounted Police (RCMP) while Amanda was still alive, but they were said not to have taken any action, advising her daughter to stay away from the Web and to take caution ("Amanda Todd suicide," 2013). The e-safety experts interviewed emphasized two common points as being problematic when engaging with law enforcement officials about cyberbullying-related incidents involving minors: the first involves not taking these cases seriously until they have resulted in a tragic outcome; the second concerns an insufficient understanding of social media technologies and how pervasive online harassment can be. Even in those countries where cyberbullying is not defined by the law, harassment-related provisions or other legal acts could apply to cyberbullying cases. Furthermore, advising teens to stay off the internet is hardly a viable solution to the problem (d'Haenens, Vandoninck, & Donoso, 2013). Nonetheless, it is often the question of whether the law enforcement is ready to become involved in such incidents. Finally, the question of whether punitive actions are able to solve the issue at all is rarely examined in public discourse around cyberbullying.

Much like Amanda Todd's case, the incident involving Rehtaeh Parsons resulted in a criminal prosecution, of minors in this case. While the names of the alleged offenders had not been revealed in the media because they were minors at the time when the reported rape occurred, Anonymous hactivists once again attempted to take justice into their own hands by trying to find and reveal the names of the perpetrators. In an attempt to prevent the blame-gaming rally, Rehtaeh's family urged the group not to reveal the boys' identities, and Anonymous temporarily withheld them ("'Anonymous' won't release names," 2013). By January 2015, two men tried in the case who admitted to creating child pornography were sentenced to probation (MacDonald, 2015). According to the Canadian law, Rehtaeh's name should not have been disclosed in the media either, but the family insisted that this ban be lifted because they wanted her name to be known.

With Rebecca Sedwick's case, the sheriff revealed the names of the two girls accused of bullying even though they were minors, because this felony charge required that the names be made public. But according to media reports, only a month later the charges had been dropped due to the lack of evidence necessary to establish a stalking case. CNN quoted cyberbullying expert Nancy Willard, who described the case as "yet another example of law enforcement and the media being quick to make a judgment that bullying caused a suicide when other factors might have been at work" (Wallace, 2014). According to Rebecca's mother, who spoke to the *New York Times*, Rebecca had been bullied for months prior to her suicide, and her mother had complained to school officials, whom she said did little to alleviate the situation. She then moved Rebecca to a new school, allegedly closed her Facebook page, and took her cell phone away. The *New York Times* reported that the girl was using social media unbeknownst to her mother (Alvarez, 2013b). The charges were dropped when the State Attorney's office, "after weeks of investigation" and "an analysis of thousands of Facebook messages" (Alvarez, 2013c), could not provide enough evidence to support the charges.

The girls accused of bullying Rebecca were treated in a less than dignified manner and in complete disagreement with research-supported evidence that no actors in this process should be stigmatized (Morrison, 2002; Ahmed & Brathwaite, 2006). Such treatment also obscured the complexity of the case as presented to the public. The two girls' lawyers said it was "outrageous" that the sheriff had arrested them and dragged their names and images into the media coverage while failing to provide the evidence to back criminal charges. Some of those who criticized such actions raised concerns that sheriff had been driven by a personal agenda (Alvarez, 2013c; Bazelon, 2014). Katelyn, who appeared on NBC's *Today Show* to tell her side of the story (Stump, 2013) was expelled from school, and her family was threatened and insulted. The girls had been labeled as bullies while the investigation found no evidence of bullying for seven months leading to Rebecca's death (Wallace, 2014).

The time following Rebecca's suicide was difficult for Katelyn, who reported feeling self-doubt and guilt even though she did not bully Rebecca during the year before the suicide (Pesta, 2014). Katelyn's mother also recounted how difficult it was to see her daughter's face all over the media and the internet as she was accused of being "a bully"—a digital footprint that would not easily go away. Katelyn underwent counseling as a result of post-suicide events (Pesta, 2014).

Some media outlets pointed out that cyberbullying did not directly cause, but may have only contributed to, the girl's suicide, and that she did suffer from depression and self-harming tendencies, part of it resulting from her family situation. However, with such actions of the sheriff, it was nonetheless difficult to avoid the "bully-victim narrative," where the alleged bullies were vilified, and the complexity behind the alleged bullying case unjustifiably simplified. Such narratives were well documented in Emily Bazelon's analysis of cyberbullying cases, which sought to give voice to all the participants involved in the selected high-profile incidents that she investigated (Bazelon, 2013b). Her study described how the complexity of peer relations during adolescence tends to be reduced in sensationalist media coverage; and how the behavior that could be addressed using educational efforts is increasingly criminalized, a factor that does not necessarily help address future bullying cases (see Suski, 2016, cf. Bradshaw, 2013).

Social Positioning: The Problem of Oversimplified
Bully-Victim Narratives

The story of Rebecca's suicide told from the perspective of one of the accused girls, Katelyn, provides more nuance to the media-told narrative that revolved around the arrests. Her story, which she narrated to the popular women's magazine *Cosmopolitan*, reveals an aspect of such incidents that tends to get lost in media coverage: how cyberbullying can be a part of social positioning, power imbalances, and the resulting complexity of adolescents' everyday lives and social relations (Pesta, 2014).

According to this article, Katelyn and Rebecca had been good friends in the fifth grade. In the sixth grade, Katelyn became friends with Guadalupe, the other girl who was arrested in the case, whom the article described as a "queen bee," an expression used to refer to a popular girl in a group (Wiseman, 2009). Guadalupe grew up with her father, saw her mother infrequently and sometimes had to take care of her siblings; her lawyer described her less-than-model upbringing as one of struggle. Guadalupe happened to be interested in a boy who used to be Rebecca's boyfriend. Worried that he still had feelings for Rebecca, Guadalupe managed to turn about a dozen girls against her, although Guadalupe's lawyer said that she denied those charges (Pesta, 2014). Katelyn appeared to succumb to the peer pressure as well; everyone around her, she said, was calling Rebecca a liar, and she didn't know what to do.

The pressure on Katelyn became so strong that she was forced into physically fighting Rebecca at school one day. The teachers eventually broke up the fight. Around the time of the fight, which, according to Katelyn happened a year before the suicide, the girls exchanged a couple of heated text messages but their communication did not resume after that. When in the summer before she died, Rebecca texted Katelyn, asking her to be friends again, Katelyn gave her a polite no. After the suicide, the police used one piece of exchange between "the bullies"—Katelyn and Guadalupe—as a proof of their complicity. The girls wrote to each other that they felt guilty and they wished it had been them instead of Rebecca. However, another, allegedly Guadalupe's post, said she did not care that she had bullied Rebecca and that the girl died (there is evidence that Guadalupe did not write this and that her account had been hacked). Katelyn, in a separate exchange with another girl, expressed feeling guilty, implying it was her fault (Pesta, 2014).

Such complexity and nuance of youth social relations and the role of other factors (such as family circumstances) fail to come across in simplified "bully-victim" narratives. Most importantly, omission of this aspect of the story in the public discussion can result in failing to invoke solutions that may actually help children build necessary resilience and adopt a more dignified way of treating each other.

How Blame Gaming Influences Policy

While some cases resulted in blame gaming of the individuals involved in cyberbullying, in others, the limited narrative revolved around blaming social media companies. Such public narratives may have more lasting effects than the immediately observable consequences for one social media company. They can influence the development of a set of preferred self-organizational policies and company narratives industry-wide.

After Hannah Smith's death had garnered a significant amount of media attention for Ask.fm, large advertisers on the social networking website pulled their ads, Vodafone and Save The Children being among the organizations to do so (Robson, 2013). UK prime minister David Cameron called Ask.fm a "vile" site and invited users to boycott "websites that allow cyberbullying [so as] to help prevent more deaths of young people" (Cushing, 2013). Such public pressure forced the website "to order an independent review of the site's safety features" by a law firm (Best, 2013); the details as to how the review was executed were not publicly accessible.

This instance of the cancelation of advertising is perhaps good evidence for what Douglas Leeds, the CEO of the company that purchased Ask.fm in 2014, meant when he said that "safety is good business" (Magid, 2014). In order for a social media company to ensure its legitimacy and to be publicly considered as an acceptable venue for teens, it needs to put safety and the perception of safety as its primary value (Magid, 2014). Furthermore, users will only keep coming back to a platform if they enjoy their experiences there, and bullying, the argument goes, is not conducive to a pleasant experience (an argument I revisit in chapter 8). The Latvian owners signed non-disclosure agreements with Ask.com after the company purchased the site and were therefore not available for an interview. This case illustrates how social media companies can become easy targets in this "blame-gaming" process. Some of the e-safety experts I interviewed observed that in high-profile cases, e-safety issues have the potential to become politicized. Taking the strong stand against Ask.fm adopted by Prime Minister Cameron, then, can also be analyzed from the perspective of securing support and votes of parents and caregivers, who are particularly vested in ensuring the safety of their children.

How Privatization of the Digital Public Sphere
Affects Personal Freedoms

The involvement of social media companies in police investigations can further illustrate the implications of corporate actions for civil liberties. In cases related to child protection, while companies should assist law enforcement when provided with lawful requests, such actions should nonetheless take into account children's privacy—which was not the case when investigating Rebecca Sedwick's death. The following account also draws attention to how such cases can increase the involvement of private corporations in processes that are normally in the domain of law enforcement.

Consider the role of one social media company, Facebook, on the investigation process that followed the case of Amanda Todd's suicide. In May 2014, almost two years after the suicide, a suspect was caught in the Netherlands. His lawyer told the Canadian newspaper the *Globe and Mail*: "I don't think the police made this case. I think Facebook made this case. They put it all together" (White, 2014a). He also added, "Who is to say that Facebook did this investigation correctly? We will have to go over all their work." Facebook declined to comment on its involvement in this case except to state that it followed strict guidelines for working with the police to deal with child pornography cases (White, 2014a). The investigation and prosecution benefitted from a constellation of efforts involving Facebook, who provided the IP address to law enforcement (Surbramaniam & Whalen, 2014). Collaboration among international agencies resulted in the arrest of a Dutch man of Turkish descent, Aydin Coban, who was charged with "extortion, internet luring, criminal harassment and the possession and distribution of child pornography" ("Amanda Todd: police alerted . . .," 2014).

The means used to incriminate and arrest the alleged perpetrator were characterized in the media coverage as controversial from the standpoint of civil liberties. Once they decided to investigate, the covert Dutch police broke into the suspect's bungalow and installed tracking software onto his computer. The *Globe and Mail* reported, "While the tracking software—called 'a keystroke logger'—is common among investigative arsenals in other countries, its use is rare and contentious in the Netherlands" (White, 2014b). The investigators had nonetheless received a court approval prior to installing the software. This move produced evidence of Coban's blackmailing

Amanda and a number of other victims. The Canadian RCMP sought his extradition to Canada.

The increasing role of the companies in this process seems evident in Rebecca Sedwick's case as well. The girl was allegedly bullied on Ask.fm, Kik, and Voxer (Alvarez, 2013b). According to CNN, the sheriff's office quit trying to obtain the data from the companies once the state attorney declined to file charges (Wallace, 2014), which is especially interesting considering that initially the sheriff had placed the primary blame for Rebecca's death on online bullying (Raiche & Williams, 2013). In the interview with Voxer, another app through which Rebecca was allegedly bullied, the company representative explained that the app was probably not related to the bullying incident and it likely just happened to be on her phone. Rather than absolving companies from responsibility when cyberbullying cases actually happen on their platforms, the discussion here serves to underscore that cyberbullying is complex both in its causes and in its manifestations.

The investigators did analyze Facebook posts, one of which allegedly came from Guadalupe Shaw, the girl charged with aggravated stalking, and it read: "Yes ik I bullied REBECCA and she killed herself but IDGAF" (Alvarez, 2013a; Pesta, 2014).[2] Guadalupe claimed she did not post it herself, that her account had been hacked (Wallace, 2014). According to the sheriff's investigation of Rebecca's phone as reported in the *New York Times*, she had received messages such as "why are you still alive?" and "you're ugly!" (Alvarez, 2013b).

In light of evidence that the charges against the girls had been unfounded and largely exaggerated, the manner in which the case was handled, by retrieving the girls' private messages and publishing them in the media, reflects an attitude on behalf of the authorities that does not take into account youth privacy. In terms of social media companies' responsibility, this case is also important since Rebecca Sedwick was 12 at the time she used these platforms, and according to the TOS on a number of platforms, children under the age of 13 are not allowed to access them.

Another important point to acknowledge is the difficulty of designing policies and mechanisms on these platforms to assist children in resolving the cases that arise as a consequence of the complexity and volatility of their social relations. While a button to report bullying may be a minimum requirement, social media companies are engaging a number of other mechanisms I describe in the following chapters. Despite protection under CDA 230, which is based on not getting involved with content, social media companies are nonetheless forced to find ways to become involved with content in order to address bullying.

In the Aftermath: Ad Hoc Actions by Regulators and Policy Makers

Prime Minister Cameron's actions regarding Ask.fm (in the Hannah Smith case), as well as the sheriff's handling of the investigation in the case of Rebecca Sedwick, point to the ways in which personal and political agendas can get in the way of shaping effective social media policy. But the best examples of what a number of scholars and interviewees for this book would characterize as largely misguided regulatory actions took place in the aftermath of the Megan Meier, Amanda Todd, and Rehtaeh Parsons cases.

In the Megan Meier case, after a local investigation determined that Lori Drew did not commit a crime, Thomas O'Brien, the US attorney in Los Angeles, in what the *New York Times* labeled as "a highly unusual move" prosecuted the case himself (Steinhauer, 2008). Although O'Brien was not a state attorney general, in the US, state attorneys general have exhibited a tendency to initiate actions against social media companies in the context of high-profile incidents. Attorney generals in specific states may act individually (Bodley, 2014) or they can join together to investigate activities of individual social media companies. MySpace was the focus of one such combined action in 2008 (Proskauer, 2008) at the time when the case of Megan Meier received significant attention in the media and around the time when MySpace found itself in the center of a "technopanic" (Marwick, 2008) concerning online predators. Social media companies and the concept of Web 2.0 were new at the time, and once several high profile internet safety-related incidents emerged, the policy makers reacted to the public pressure.

In November 2008, a federal jury issued "what legal experts said was the country's first cyberbullying verdict" (Steinhauer, 2008) in the Meier case. The charges were reduced from felonies to misdemeanors based on violation of the Computer Fraud and Abuse Act, which had been amended several times since being enacted in 1986. The decision was considered problematic because the use of the act was broadened to apply to new technology with wider implications (see Steinhauer, 2008). Under these guidelines, Drew was found guilty of accessing a computer without authorization—because she signed into her account using a fake name, and thus violated the site's TOS. Hence, this was the first time that a federal act used to address computer crimes was applied in the prosecution of TOS violations. If Drew were to be found guilty, the case could open doors to social media-related litigation at a large scale. Consider, for instance, that numerous minors violate TOS on a daily basis by lying about their age and accessing social media websites even when they are under 13 years of age, which many websites do not allow (boyd, Hargittai, Schultz, & Palfrey, 2011).

In 2008 Lori Drew filed motions to dismiss the indictment on the grounds of "failure to state an offense, vagueness, and unconstitutional delegation of prosecutorial power" in *United States v. Drew* (Digital Media Law Project, 2008). The Electronic Frontier Foundation and the Berkman Klein Center for Internet and Society at Harvard University filed amicus briefs to dismiss the case. The public pressure around this case was perhaps evidenced by the fact that the judge, while allowing evidence of Megan Meier's suicide on trial, had to emphasize to the jurors that Drew was not charged with causing the suicide. Eventually, in July 2009, in the light of all the concerns around setting a precarious precedent, Drew was cleared of all charges.

This case resulted in a legislative effort as well, of the kind that was critiqued previously for its punitive orientation. Representative Linda Sanchez (D-CA) proposed a piece of legislation called the Megan Meier Cyberbullying Prevention Act (2009) that stipulated up to two years in prison for electronic speech whose aim was "to coerce, intimidate, harass or cause substantial emotional distress to another person." *Wired* reported the bill "was met with little enthusiasm" by the House Judiciary Committee (Kravets, 2009) and it never made it into law. Bipartisan fears around the bill, expressed in a hearing on September 30, 2009, conducted by the Subcommittee on Crime, Terrorism and Homeland Security, included the danger to constitutionally protected free speech. An opinion in response to the hearing submitted by the American Civil Liberties Union (ACLU) read:

Criminalizing free speech online is unconstitutional and will be ineffective. Harassing speech will either continue online in violation of the law, or it will simply shift to other spheres within which it simultaneously exists. Moreover, the scope of "bullying" speech is likely to fall short of the constitutional standard requiring the existence of "a true threat.". . . The focus should be on the bullying and harassing behavior and not on the means by which it is communicated. (American Civil Liberties Union, 2009)

Such concerns over civil liberties, and questions as to whether criminalizing the internet as a means of communication is effective in solving problems that frequently originate or persist offline, illustrate perils that emerge in attempts to regulate cyberbullying. This reference to "true threat" is a good example of the difficulty of enforcing such regulation. In a number of cases the Supreme Court has stated: "The government cannot punish violent words—even 'vehement, caustic' or 'unpleasantly sharp attacks'— unless they are 'true threats.' The problem is identifying what, exactly, counts as a 'true threat'" ("What is a true threat on Facebook?," 2014).

Consider how a recent online harassment case that garnered significant media attention exhibits this dilemma (Dewey, 2014). In December 2014, in a hearing of *US v. Elonis*, the Supreme Court weighed whether posts that Anthony Elonis posted on Facebook in the form of a rap song, in which he threatened his ex-wife with death, amounted to the standard of "true threat" (Citron, 2014b). More specifically, the jurors were struggling to determine if the standard for assessing whether such speech amounts to a "true threat" should be based on the speaker's subjective intent to harm the person, or if a reasonable listener would interpret the threat as a serious intent to harm (Citron, 2014b).

The opinion expressed by the ACLU in reference to the Megan Meier Cyberbullying Prevention Act coincided with the opinions of a number of e-safety NGO representatives and e-safety experts, some of whom participated as expert witnesses in this congressional testimony, such as Nancy Willard, at the time the director of the Safe and Responsible Internet Use in Eugene, Oregon, who attached a statement of opposition to the bill that had been signed by "all of the nation's leading authorities on the issue of cyberbullying" ("Digital media safety . . .," 2009). The letter stated that "trying to make this a federal criminal offense is ludicrous." Another expert witness on the issue explained that criminalization would not help in effectively addressing the issue of cyberbullying for children.

Bill C-13: Protecting Canadians from Online Crime Act

Another piece of legislation whose grounds have been critiqued from the civil liberties point of view is Bill C-13, which was largely brought about by the Amanda Todd case. The bill was proposed by the Conservative government and was sometimes labeled "Conservatives' cyberbullying legislation" (Boutilier, 2014). The essential underpinning of Bill C-13 was to update the lawful access provisions of the Criminal Code, which allow the state to obtain access to electronic communication. It creates a new criminal offense for nonconsensual distribution of intimate images. The bill is also relevant from the standpoint of privatization of digital public sphere theory, however, as it allows telecom, internet, and social media companies to "voluntarily" disclose data on user information without a court order, and grants them immunity from criminal and civil lawsuits for such disclosures; it also increases police authority in data access and search (Geist, 2013).

The meaning of "voluntarily" was debated in the media, but there would still have to be a warrant from the police for a company to reveal the data (Dyer, 2014). Critics of the bill pointed out that it resembled another bill (Bill C-30) that had failed in 2012 due to surveillance concerns, and which allowed for "warrantless mandatory disclosure of basic subscriber information" (Dyer, 2014). *Toronto Star* labeled Bill C-13 as having "little to do with cyberbullying, the bill's proposed target" (Austin, Stewart, & Clement, 2014).

With "reasonable suspicion" police authorities could now access "transmission data" (including deep packet inspection) and "tracking data" using new types of warrants. These new warrants, critics said, "fall below the usual requirements for a search warrant" (Austin, Stewart, & Clement, 2014). Furthermore, they argued, the amount of data that could be accessed in this manner surpassed in scale personal information about the suspect and could constitute surveillance of people other than the suspect. Even Amanda Todd's mother expressed concerns about "provisions that allow warrantless access to Canadians' personal data," which are executed in the name of her daughter and other victims in similar cases (Boutilier, 2014).

Nova Scotia Law

Similarly, the *Toronto Star* labeled the Nova Scotia law, which took effect in August 2013, as "inspired by Rehtaeh Parson's suicide"; the law allowed people "to sue or seek a protection order from the courts if they or their children are being cyberbullied" ("Cyberbullying law inspired . . .," 2013). It also allowed victims to seek assistance from an investigative unit that would help them identify the perpetrator, in the case of an anonymous one, and research the case; in event of a lawsuit, parents could be held liable for damages if the perpetrator was a minor (Bill 61: An Act to Address and Prevent Cyberbullying, 2013). The *Globe and Mail* editorial spoke out against the law ("Nova Scotia Cyberbullying Law goes too far," 2014). According to the newspaper, the law was unnecessary because in many similar cases the victim could seek a restraining order or rely on libel provisions. Furthermore, because the law would cover a single phone call that distressed the accuser in the same manner as if the harassment were repetitive, it was said to define cyberbullying too broadly. Also, because the accused did not have to be a named person, charges could be pressed against an internet address, and any device capable "of connecting to it" (for instance, the phone or computer of an accused teen's parent) could be confiscated permanently and disposed of, the law was even more problematic from a civil liberties standpoint.

The first application of this law attracted significant media attention and it involved adults, much to the surprise of even the victim in that case, who had thought that the law had been principally designed to protect minors; in this case, the female victim reported a man who was posting "negative and threatening comments about her and her family on Facebook" (Judge orders end to Facebook cyberbullying . . .," 2014). The investigative unit conducted research on the subject and determined that cyberbullying took place. A Nova Scotia judge then "granted a cyberbullying prevention order" that required the perpetrator to cease all future cyberbullying and take down comments that had already been on the site, in addition to paying $750 in court costs. From the standpoint of research findings on cyberbullying, these laws define cyberbullying broadly and employ punitive measures of which alleged effectiveness is not necessarily supported by research. The Nova Scotia law has since been struck down by the Supreme Court of Nova Scotia, which called it "a colossal failure" (Ruskin, 2015).

An incident similar to those of Rehtaeh Parsons and Amanda Todd happened in California to a girl named Audrie Pott, who was also allegedly raped while passed out at a party; the photos were then posted online and the girl was severely bullied, after which she died by suicide ("US teen's death . . .," 2013). Audrie's family pressed charges against three US teens who were then arrested for sexual battery ("Three US teens arrested . . .," 2013). The boys received sentences of 30 to 45 days and the case resulted in a state bill that stipulated stricter punishment for juveniles committing sexual assault but no anti-bullying law was relied on in the case ("Lawmaker modifies . . .," 2014).

International Consequences for Social Media Companies

The pattern of events that includes bullying, cyberbullying, slut shaming, and prosecution of minors seems to be taking place more frequently all around the world, which will no doubt elicit further legal responses as various countries and continents address who can be accountable for those acts. At the time of this writing, the US, Canada, and the EU did not have legislation that would specify the mechanisms that social media companies need to have in place to address cyberbullying incidents, outside of cooperating with law enforcement when investigating individual cases. This means that (outside of the provisions specified above) companies are not legally required to proactively monitor content on their platforms in an attempt to prevent bullying. They are also not legally obliged to take down content that users report to them as "bullying," although companies can decide to do so if they determine that the reported incident constitutes "bullying" in their view and thus goes against their TOS; and they do not face penalties if they do not respond to users' requests in a timely manner.[3]

Similar high-profile incidents in Australia, however, may have contributed to creating a piece of legislation that specified the responsibilities of social media companies in addressing cyberbullying ("Charlotte Dawson's death . . .", 2014). In December 2014, the Australian government introduced a bill into the Parliament that would appoint a Children's E-safety Commissioner who would have the power to order large social media companies to remove offensive material posted online (Lannin, 2014). Under the bill, which has since been adopted, titled "Enhancing Online Safety for Children Act" (Parliament of Australia, n.d.), if the commissioner determines that a post should be taken down and a social media company does not do so, it faces a fine of $17,000 per day, while individuals face prosecution under criminal law.[4] Parents can file a report on behalf of their children. Microsoft and Google opposed the law, and so did the Australian Human Rights Commission, citing freedom of speech concerns (Lannin, 2014). At the time of this book's writing, Yahoo!, Facebook, Facebook-owned Instagram, and Twitter would also be affected; however, what were described as "smaller" social media companies that did not have local offices and employees in Australia, such as Snapchat, would not (Vaas, 2014). One reason, according to the Australian Parliament Secretary for Communications, was the impossibility of enforcing laws against overseas firms ("Snapchat not covered . . .," 2014).

Several e-safety experts interviewed stressed that governments internationally were reluctant to introduce demanding regulation on social media and the technology industry for fear of stifling technological innovation and driving away technology-associated investments. This concern was particularly important for start-ups and less established media companies. I discuss the tension between the impulse to introduce Command and Control regulation and the support for self-regulation in chapters 5 and 6.

Toward a Greater Dignity-Based Policy Debate

As the cases I examined here indicate, the shaping of cyberbullying policies of social media companies can take place in a context where this complex social and psychological phenomenon is unduly simplified and reductive regarding questions of responsibility and blame (Bazelon, 2013b; Milosevic, 2015b). In case of Rebecca Sedwick, law enforcement's decisions to arrest minors contributed to the creation of a largely fabricated bullying narrative cast in a bully-victim binary.

High-profile cyberbullying incidents can be politicized in nature, and can contain elements of technopanics, resulting in laws that can misconstrue cyberbullying and raise significant concerns for individual freedoms. Such policy-making practices seem to do little in the way of helping youth navigate complex processes of social positioning and building resilience while growing up. This conclusion has been voiced by e-safety NGOs and experts in some of the congressional testimonies referenced here, but also by a number of respondents in this book's sample as well. Mob vigilante actions reinforce and perpetuate these binaries.

Such situations open doors to the process of privatization of the digital public sphere as exemplified in social media companies' cyberbullying policies, sometimes leaving these companies with little guidance and oversight as they struggle to do their best to protect children but also to deflect negative publicity and regulatory actions against their businesses. As I show in the case of Ask.fm, once companies face public pressure, safety policy becomes as much an ethical issue as a prerequisite to staying in the social media business.

These blame-gaming narratives fail to honor the dignity of every actor in this process and thus miss a valuable opportunity to address the heart of the problem. Perhaps most importantly, by neglecting to raise questions about how contemporary culture normalizes humiliation, these public debates fail to examine larger societal issues at play. For instance, rather than blaming technology for the problem of cyberbullying, a more dignity-oriented debate might ask: *What makes the culture of humiliation so popular? What are humiliation patterns that youth adopt (sometimes by modeling adults and media) and reinforce in their own behavior—and consequently in digital environments where their lives unfold?*

5   Industry Self-Regulation in the US and in the EU

High-profile incidents and their influence on the development of anti-bullying mechanisms may misleadingly overemphasize the reactive nature of regulation and policy developments. In this chapter I look at how the concepts of alternative regulatory instruments (ARIs) such as self- and co-regulation (Lievens, 2010, 2016) apply to social media companies' cyberbullying policies; I provide an overview of regulatory and historical circumstances in which a preference for self-regulation emerged in the US and Europe, and end the chapter with a description of self-regulatory initiatives relevant to cyberbullying in the US and EU.

Traditional regulation in the US and at the level of the EU does not oblige these companies to develop anti-bullying policies and enforcement mechanisms. But companies nonetheless develop them on their own, or as a consequence of policy makers' initiatives and encouragement, in an effort to exhibit responsible behavior toward their users, parents, educators, and other stakeholders. The term "self-regulation" broadly covers these initiatives in the context of cyberbullying.[1] The historical context in which these initiatives emerged, and the rationales behind choosing self-regulation over relying on traditional regulation to make the companies develop such policies, are important for understanding the design of anti-bullying policies and for assessing their effectiveness.

By no means in this brief chapter can I address the extensive range of policy documents that concern protection of minors from harmful content online in the EU and the US.[2] Nor do I claim to provide a comprehensive recount of differences in self-regulatory efforts in the field of e-safety and child protection online in these locations. Rather, I refer only to those developments and documents of most immediate relevance for understanding cyberbullying policies of social media companies.

The Promise of Technological Innovation and Investment

Forms of self- and co-regulation that fall under the category of "alternative regulatory instruments (ARIs)" (see Lievens, 2010) or "alternative modes of regulation" (Latzer, Just, & Saurwein, 2013) have become more widespread since the mid-1990s, as galloping Internet development tested the limits of traditional regulation (see Lievens, 2010). For instance, consider (among many possible examples), that speech deemed illegal in one country can be hosted on a website in another where it is legal, thus undermining the ability of countries to enforce their national laws in an effective manner or to address the problem of editorial responsibility (Newman & Bach, 2004). The Vietnam War–era photo that I used to introduce chapter 3 well illustrates the relevance of editorial discretion.

A preference for self-regulation in the field of child protection online can hardly be understood outside of the context of the stated intent to protect digital innovation—self-regulation that serves the industry while meeting policy goals. The introduction of safe harbors for online intermediaries, such as CDA 230 and similar provisions in the European eCommerce Directive, as well as DMCA notice and takedown procedure in the US, were born out of the same concerns for innovation.

Historical Context

The historical context behind opting for self-regulation in matters regarding free speech and the protection of children from harmful content online started to take shape in the early to mid-1990s, with court cases that forced regulatory authorities to grapple with changes brought forth by digital environments. These changes were outlined in the influential Bangemann Report (1994), a study commissioned by European Council and conducted by experts, which urged the EU to "put its faith in market mechanisms as the motive power to carry us into the Information Age." The report signaled a peril frequently voiced in e-safety-expert circles: new digital technologies have the potential to render existing regulatory measures obsolete. Also decisive, as Elisabeth Staksrud and Sonia Livingstone write, was the reasoning that the industry knew its technology best, as parents did their children (Staksrud, 2013a, p. 90, cf. Staksrud & Livingstone, 2009). This increasing delegation of the burden of responsibility onto parents and caregivers, whose often questionable understanding of technology may undermine their ability to support their children's best interests, may be problematic.[3] I further examine parental roles in children's use of technology in the upcoming chapters of part II as well as in part III.

In a 1995 high-profile case, the Bavarian government prosecuted CompuServe, a major Internet service provider at the time, for its role as a third-party host of pornography, which was in violation of German obscenity law. The case further prompted the European Commission, fearful of the specter of "potentially incompatible" national frameworks regulating the Internet in Europe, to call for EU-wide solutions that would empower consumers by allowing them to filter out undesired content on their own (Newman & Bach, 2004, p. 400, cf. Commission of the European Communities, 1996).

United States v. Thomas in 1994 could be seen as the US counterpart to the Bavarian case, which saw prosecution of a couple in California that ran an online adult bulletin board (Newman & Bach, 2004). Congress then stepped in with the Communications Decency Act (CDA, see chapter 3), which came into force in January 1996 only to be struck down by the Supreme Court a year later, in *ACLU v. Reno*. The full act defined the concept of indecency too broadly, and the reversal served as an alert against overly stringent government intervention, leaving only CDA 230 in place.

Although regulation may be difficult to define specifically, it can be said to refer to "various means of achieving public policy objectives" (e.g., reducing children's experience of bullying) (McLaughlin, 2013, p. 77). These means may include Command and Control regulation (commonly defined as the regulation of an activity through legislation that states what is legal and what is not and specifies sanctions, and also referred to as "classical" or "traditional" regulation) or various forms of ARIs such as co-regulation and self-regulation (Lievens, 2010).[4] It is, in essence, a function of corporate policy and practice development to ensure that the way a company conducts its business is within public policy parameters.

Limitations of Traditional Regulation

In light of the challenges of constantly evolving technology, Command and Control regulation is said to run the danger of not only being "rigid" but also "suffering from a knowledge gap" (McLaughlin, 2013, pp. 78–79), as it provides little space for input from non-state actors (such as NGOs, consumers and citizens, and independent experts). If the industry agrees on a public policy objective, then there is a greater likelihood of compliance, but also increased cost-efficiency for the state, as parts of the costs are transferred to other actors (such as industry or NGOs) (de Haan, van der Hof, Bekkers, & Pijpers, 2013). Robert Madelin, the former director-general of the European Commission, who has extensive experience in self-regulation, cites the successful self-regulatory efforts in the food advertising industry, whereby provision of nutrition labeling was the desired goal:

There was a stage at which some of the very big [industry] players decided to give nutritional information—product by product—and they did this thing, which public health groups [e.g., NGOs and independent experts] were asking for, faster than the legislator could create a legal obligation to do so. So that, for me, is the proof of [the] concept [of effective self-regulation]—if you get the right way to get the consensus, companies are able to do this thing for which there is an agreement [public policy objective] faster than the law could do it. (Madelin, personal communication with the author, September 5, 2016)

"International forum shopping" is another limitation of traditional regulation; it refers to "ascertaining the jurisdiction with the most favorable legal regime for a particular activity and the anchoring of that activity within that particular regime" (McLaughlin, 2013, p. 79). Hence, in theory, if a country had a cyberbullying law with negative implications for online intermediaries, companies could escape it by anchoring their activity elsewhere. Consider that the Australian cyberbullying law (mentioned in chapter 4), which demanded that companies take down cyberbullying content upon request from the Children's E-safety Commissioner, was said to apply only to companies that had "Australian employees or advertising revenue" (Vaas, 2014, para. 3). This is why developing a set of industry-wide standards and getting the industry to agree on them is seen as a more effective approach.

While these views on the downsides of Command and Control regulation may not be entirely agreed upon (see, e.g., Svantesson, 2005), they seem to have opened up the space to a preference for self-regulation when it comes to the social media industry.

Differences in the US and the EU Self-Regulatory Environments

Some authors argue that the tension between different government branches in the US (namely judicial and legislative) leads to a form of "regulatory uncertainty," a term that can be seen as a defining feature of the self-regulatory system in the US (Newman & Bach, 2004, p. 401). For instance, while the striking of the CDA resulted in a preference in the executive branch toward industry solutions and filtering—which had been pursued in the EU—the legislative branch in the US responded with another set of restrictive regulations—the Child Online Protection Act (COPA, struck down in 1998, and which was the precursor to Children's Online Privacy Protection Act) and the Children's Internet Protection Act (CIPA) of 2000. CIPA is still in place, and it mandates all US schools and libraries that wish to receive funding from specific federal government programs to use online filtering aimed at protecting children online (Federal Communications Commission, 2016).[5]

Hence, despite a seeming agreement in both the EU and US that ARIs were necessary, the approach to implementation of these differed. In the US, some authors suggest, self-regulation became largely reactive and enacted "through the threat of stringent formal rules and costly litigation, should industry fail to deliver socially desirable outcomes"—resulting in "legalistic self-regulation" (Newman & Bach, 2004, p. 388). On the other hand, in Europe, the public sector (through the voice of the European Commission) engaged proactively with the industry through meetings and agreements on "a joint course of action," or so-called "coordinated self-regulation" (p. 391). While Europeans might interpret self-regulation in the US as laissez-faire, to Americans self-regulation in Europe may appear as government intervention (p. 406). However, rather than intervention, the EU approach may be better seen as "a guided or directed legal framework which actively fosters and encourages self-regulation" (p. 176). This look at the disparities of implementation of otherwise agreed-upon principles of regulation further illustrates the complexities of developing viable regulatory policies for the global social media industry.

In the EU, self-regulatory initiatives in the area of child online safety (which encompass cyberbullying) were actively fostered and convened by the European Commission (EC) via programs such as Safer Internet for Children, while such standing convening initiatives in the US were, to a great extent, wanting. Thus the EC actively fostered the creation of the several initiatives and coalitions: the Safer Social Networking Principles initiative; the CEO Coalition (even the description of the initiative said that the EC vice president and the companies agreed to "cooperate—not compete—for a Better Internet for Kids") (Digital Single Market, 2014); and the ICT Coalition (all discussed later in the chapter). These were all efforts to convene major industry players not only from the EU but also from the US—given that this was where the leading social media companies came from—such as Google (YouTube) and Facebook.

In the US, on the other hand, such convening initiatives can only be found in few examples. One is Online Safety and Technology Working Group (Collier & Nigam, 2010) at the Department of Commerce in 2010.[6] Another is the Internet Safety Technical Task Force at the Berkman Klein

Center for Internet and Society in 2008, which was convened pursuant to investigations revealing that MySpace had inadequate safety measures in place (Berkman, 2008, 2010; National Association of Attorneys General, 2008). Hence, in the US, self-regulatory initiatives relevant to cyberbullying regulation tend to be more sporadic and reactive—resulting from investigations or threats of legal interventions—whereas the EU has what could perhaps be described as a more unified regulatory voice (i.e., the EC) whose aim is to bargain for consensus. In the US, attorneys general (AGs) may investigate individual companies on their own and the Federal Trade Commission (FTC) can also initiate actions (at least when privacy is concerned) (Bodley, 2014; Maryland Attorney General, 2014; New York State Attorney General, 2014). Nonetheless, as some authors observe, the FTC is "severely limited in its ability to manage business practices proactively" relying on "reactive strategy" designed to "produce large cost for firms that take the wrong step" (Newman & Bach, 2004, p. 405).

Legalistic Self-Regulation: The Case of Facebook

Consider that in 2007, the AG of New York State reached a settlement with Facebook (then only a three-year-old company), which provided guidelines for the creation of some of the mechanisms discussed in chapter 6 (Mathews, 2007; McMillan, 2007). The office of the AG was investigating the company based on allegations that it had failed to meet the claims made to the public about protecting minors. Facebook denied any wrongdoing.

While this action did not seem to take place specifically in response to cyberbullying or a high-profile cyberbullying case, the provisions reached as part of the agreement address, among other issues, abuse and harassment on the platform. The company pledged to make its safety efforts publicly available on its website, to address complaints of harassment via links and email designated specifically for that purpose, and to handle complaints in 72 hours.

Most importantly, the AG was to approve a third-party office called the Independent Safety and Security Examiner whose purpose was to evaluate complaints in reference to Facebook's handling of abuse reports, but I could not find the evidence of the work that this body produced.

What could be described as a robust abuse reporting and community management system (see also chapter 6), has gradually emerged and significantly developed at Facebook since 2007. As the company became more established, its relationship with regulators moved toward a more collaborative one, with fewer investigative instances of this kind. With Maryland's attorney general it proposed to launch a pilot project called the Educator Escalation Channel in

2012, when Facebook was an eight-year-old, more established company; the project can be seen as a particularly good example of how established companies can develop a more collaborative relationship with regulators.

Established Companies: Toward More Collaborative Patterns

As a pilot project the Educator Escalation Channel was designed to work with schools to "streamline reporting of potential cyberbullying occurrences on Facebook that may not be resolved through Facebook's normal process or [which may] demand more immediate attention" (Maryland Attorney General, 2013). According to an informant from the AG office in Maryland, at the time of its proposed launch in 2012, the Educator Escalation Channel was not a response to perceived ineffectiveness of Facebook's reporting tools; rather, Facebook officials felt that their systems and processes in place for cyberbullying reports were already strong. Whether Facebook initiated the move, or the AG did, was not clearly specified.

This project would allow schools the opportunity to "escalate" a case to the company's attention.[7] Every school system in Maryland identified one point person, whom all schoolteachers should be familiar with, to be responsible for direct communication with Facebook. If the schoolteachers noticed a case of cyberbullying, they were first urged to report it to Facebook using its regular reporting service for abusive content. If the issue was then not resolved within 24 hours, they could contact the designated point person for their school district who could then escalate it to Facebook. Facebook was testing this project in Maryland and, according to a representative from the attorney general's office, the company intended to implement it throughout the country. The project had no government funding; Facebook covered all costs, which were described as minimal.

The project could result in a faster resolution of those subtle bullying cases in which the company may not have sufficient evidence to establish it as one that constitutes cyberbullying. For instance, if throughout a bullying incident a number of students call their classmate a "cow," and then several of them write "Moo" on the classmate's wall, Facebook may not be able to establish that such a seemingly benign comment represents bullying. However, a teacher witnessing bullying on school premises may trace its connection to the incident on Facebook, and use the Educator Escalation Channel to try to ensure that the content is taken down.

Nonetheless, there did not seem to be any evidence to suggest that the company launched this project in an effort to avert legislation or a lawsuit, although when the Educator Escalation Channel was in the development stage, online bullying and harassment appeared to be an important area of concern for the AG, particularly in 2012.

In 2013, a cyberbullying law called Grace's Law, which stipulated that bullying someone under the age of 18 could lead to a fine of up to $500, or up to one year in prison (Ames, 2013), was passed in Maryland in response to the bullying case of 15-year-old Grace McComas, who committed suicide in April 2012. This high-profile incident might have put the public pressure on regulators in the state to take action, thus providing additional, political incentives for the development of the Educator Escalation Channel in order to demonstrate to the public that the regulators were indeed doing their best to address future suicides. At this time, Facebook had been considering opening up their site to children under 13 (Troianovski & Raice, 2012). Although the company had nonetheless decided not to pursue that option, word of it might have drawn further attention to the company. The AG reported being in close conversation with Facebook at the time (Communicators with Doug Gansler, 2012).

It appears that, rather than resulting from potential confrontation, the company partnership with the regulator was very cooperative, illustrating an evolutionary pattern in industry-regulator relationships as companies became more established—away from adversarial and toward more collaborative patterns.

The project characterized Facebook's effort to make the reporting of abusive content on the site more effective by personalizing it (by providing schools with direct personal contact with the company). But, if direct communication with Facebook had been an option available to all teachers, rather than to just the point people designated as "escalators," the company may have been flooded with reporting requests, the opposite effect of what had been intended with the project.

Language that reflects the benefits a company offers its users—expressed in terms like "personalization" and "intimacy"—helps to ensure the effectiveness of a company's enforcement policy, just as it serves the additional purpose of making the work of the company more streamlined and efficient. In chapter 6, I examine the relationship between a company's policy effectiveness and its efficiency.

Protecting Online Intermediaries from Liability—Ensuring Innovation

Several pieces of legislation enacted from mid-1990s to the early 2000s in the US and EU reflected the recognition that technological development and market competitiveness needed to be protected by shielding online intermediaries from liability, thus providing various forms of safe harbors for online intermediaries. I discuss two of them below.

Electronic Commerce Directive (E-Commerce Directive)

The European E-Commerce Directive[8] provides liability protections for online intermediaries in the way the CDA 230 does in the US: on the grounds of companies being intermediaries only, having no knowledge of illegal content, and when given awareness or knowledge, promptly removing it (Directive 2000/31/EC of the European Parliament and of the Council).

However, as the legal scholars Urs Gasser and Wolfgang Schulz argue, unlike Section 230, the protections that the E-Commerce Directive ensures are limited. The system does not cover injunctions, for example. And there is a degree of uncertainty about how to apply exemptions which in turn relates to uncertainties about how to classify various social media companies, given that the Directive specifies only "abstract prototypes," such as "caching providers" or "host providers" (Gasser & Schulz, 2015) or as a "mere conduit" (Angelopoulos, 2013) for others' content. These circumstances resulted in a degree of fragmentation in applying liability exemptions (Gasser & Schulz, 2015).

Most of the companies I analyze for this book, however, originated in a non-EU or "third country" (i.e., the US) and are established there, which would imply that the E-Commerce Directive does not apply to them (Wauters, Lievens, & Valcke, 2016, p. 40). But if the companies "provide their services in the EU market," and "operate in the EU," and "have their offices and personnel in the EU," then they "could possibly fall under the scope of the E-Commerce Directive" (Wauters, Lievens, & Valcke, 2016, p. 240).

The E-Commerce Directive provides basic guidelines for illegal content. It does not explicitly regulate liability for content that can be harmful to minors (and online bullying can be an example of such content). For the content that can be harmful to minors, the Directive encourages, *but does not make obligatory,* "codes of conduct for the protection of minors and human dignity" (Wauters et al., 2016, p. 242). Although social media companies can voluntarily introduce "editorial control" in the form of filters, for instance, some scholars argue that such actions are "risky" because companies can then "be assumed to be active instead of passive players and may consequently lose their exemption from liability" (Wauters et al., 2016, p. 242, cf. Lievens, 2010, p. 361). One can legitimately wonder to what extent companies are editorializing already with various examples of decisions I discuss in this book, and numerous content-related interventions I outline in chapter 6.

Digital Millennium Copyright Act (DMCA)

The Digital Millennium Copyright Act in the US implemented two 1996 treaties of the World Intellectual Copyright Organization (WIPO) and criminalized circumvention of technologies designed to protect digital copies of copyrighted materials (software, music, or video). This gave rise to numerous high-profile lawsuits against young people and their caregivers (Montgomery, 2007).

DMCA Section 512 shields intermediaries from liability for copyright infringements on their networks as long as they "promptly" (Civic Impulse, 2016) block or remove infringing content once notified. They need to do so "without trying to assess the lawfulness of the contents at stake," and yet they must provide content creators with an opportunity to complain, "unless copyright holders file an action seeking a court order" (Stalla-Bourdillon, 2009, p. 156); this dynamic is sometimes referred to as "mandatory self-regulation."

Types of ARIs—Pros and Cons

One might be hard-pressed, as the legal scholar Eva Lievens has noted, to find an agreed-upon definition for the terms "self-regulation" and "co-regulation," but the numerous options contain similar elements. Bearing in mind these definition-related difficulties, Lievens made a useful suggestion for overcoming such disagreements by using "ARIs" (alternative regulatory instruments), a term that captures the way self-regulation (with little or no government involvement) moves in a continuum toward co-regulation with increasing government intervention (Lievens, 2010). Individual drafters of these instruments, and the experts who advocate them, can then explain what their specific example entails but still refer to them under the broad category of ARIs.

Some scholars, for instance, have grouped alternative regulatory instruments by the range of actions and characteristics they encompass, such as: "co-regulation," "state-supported self-regulation," "collective industry self-regulation," "single company self-organization," and even "self-help restriction by users including rankings to impose restrictions on access to content" (Marsden, 2012, p. 215, see also Latzer, Price, Saurwein, & Verhulst, 2007). In the following sections I examine the pros and cons of self- and co-regulation, as well as how they both overlap and vary.

Self-Regulation

Eva Lievens defines self-regulation as including "the creation, implementation and enforcement of rules by a group of actors, industry in particular, with minimal or no intervention by the state" (Lievens, 2016, p. 77, cf.

Lievens, 2010). But, as I mention above, scholars tend to vary their descriptions of the term's parameters.

Some emphasize that self-regulation tends to involve more than one company and thus define it this way: "collective, voluntary activity involving market participants who agree to abide by joint rules much like a club membership" (Latzer et al., 2013, p. 376).[9] Others argue that this voluntary industry self-regulation can involve *one company only* and can refer to "corporate governance and corporate social responsibility" and is sometimes called "self-organization" (Latzer et al., 2013, p. 376) or "individualized self-regulation" (Puppis, 2010, p. 141, cf. Black, 1996).

In self-regulation, the state refrains from intervening in the regulatory process "assuming that social mechanisms will ensure that the objectives of regulation are met," and that with such a broad definition, even the market "may be considered a form of self-regulation" (Schulz and Held 2004, p. 6). Wolfgang Schulz and Thorsten Held (2004) thus broadly characterize self-regulation as explicit or intentional (where one or more actors agree to observe sets of rules or define codes of conduct) and implicit (where the regulatory outcome is not a result of actors' intentions and is influenced by market and corporate culture).[10]

Not everyone would agree: ARIs in general, some authors argue, are nonetheless "distinct from pure market coordination driven by the private interests of individuals and organizations, because regulation refers to *intentional restraints* on the conduct of market players with the goal of achieving *public objectives*" (Latzer et al., 2013, p. 376, emphasis added). And so self-regulation itself may be a "misnomer" in this view, "because self-regulation by the industry only rarely exists without a contribution from the state" (p. 377).

Co-regulation
Co-regulation, on the other hand is thus conceptualized as a way to implement the law, a rather "top-down approach" whereas self-regulation is "bottom-up" as "an alternative to regulation" (Lievens, 2010, p. 169 cf. Senden, 2005).[11]

The scholars Peter Lunt and Sonia Livingstone (2012) note that in both self- and co-regulation "firms set their own standards and police their own activities as reputable firms, often under the guidance of trade associations" (p. 24, e-book edition). They nonetheless propose four characteristics of co-regulation:

1. "The system is established to achieve public policy goals targeted at social processes."

2. "There is a legal connection between the non-state regulatory system and the state regulation."
3. "The state leaves discretionary power to a non-state regulatory system."
4. "The state uses regulatory resources to influence the outcome of the regulatory process (to guarantee the fulfillment of the regulatory goals)." (Lunt & Livingstone, 2012, p. 24, citing Held, 2007, p. 357)

Lunt and Livingstone contend that under the conditions where the second and the fourth feature are not present, the system becomes self-regulatory.

Self-Regulation in the Context of Cyberbullying Policies

In the context of the cyberbullying policies and enforcement mechanisms that I discuss in chapter 6, one can observe that a number of individual companies I analyze in this book have never participated in *any explicit, voluntary, industry-wide initiative* (convened by either a government body or an industry association) either in the US or in the EU, whereby they would *explicitly* commit to agreed-upon measures to prevent bullying on their platforms. This is not to say that they have no anti-bullying policies and enforcement mechanisms—on the contrary.

Some of these companies created anti-bullying policies by learning from the more established companies, whether through existing industry good practice guides or discussions at e-safety conferences (UK Council for Child Internet Safety, 2010). Or, they were sparked by high-profile cyberbullying incidents, or, indeed, by fearing possibilities of future incidents or negative publicity in relationship to bullying. Hence, it could be said that they did so through market mechanisms because *they were pursuing their private interests as organizations* (by assuming corporate social responsibility—even when they prefer not to label their efforts as CSR) and *they never formally committed to preventing bullying on their platforms as part of a public policy goal within a self- or co-regulatory initiative.*

Only a handful of companies out of the 14 I analyze in this book participated in *any* self-regulatory initiative in the US and EU relevant to bullying (e.g., the Safer Social Networking Principles, the CEO Coalition, the ICT Coalition, or the Internet Safety Task Force). Hence, when discussing TOS and other corporate policies that refer to bullying, I use the term "private regulation" or "self-organization" rather than "self-regulation." The more established companies (see chapter 6) have been part of self-regulatory initiatives in the US and EU that formulated the first industry-wide standards for bullying intervention (e.g., reporting mechanisms), which many of the younger companies then informally adopted via corporate social responsibility efforts, rather than by formal self-regulatory initiatives.[12]

Drawbacks of ARIs

Despite the stated advantages, self-regulation and other ARIs can have several drawbacks that are particularly relevant to consider. These include insufficiently effective enforcement, limited sanctions for those that fail to abide by agreed-upon pledges, less transparency and accountability—all of which can contribute to ordinary citizens' general sense of democratic deficit and an inaccessibility to regulatory procedures (de Haan et al., 2013; McLauglin, 2013; Latzer et al., 2013).

Also, favoring private interests over public interests is a particular concern (consider this point in reference to citizen vs. consumer rights in chapters 7, 8, and 9); assigning too much responsibility to the industry, especially to key industry actors, can lead to privatized governance and the potential for having too much influence over the regulatory process (Tambini, Leonardi, & Masden, 2008; Lievens, 2010; McLaughlin, 2013).

Regulation by Raised Eyebrow and Regulatory Legitimacy

Proper monitoring and regular public reporting was an essential feature for any self-regulatory system to be effective. And that remains a central plank in the (European) Commission's doctrine on self-regulation. (Robert Madelin, Director General, European Commission DG Connect, 2010 2015, personal communication with the author, September 5, 2016)

The importance of monitoring and evaluating the success of ARIs is perhaps best illustrated by the description of self-regulation as "regulation by raised eyebrow"—meaning that when policy makers are dissatisfied with an issue they indicate in an ambiguous way the possibility of legislative intervention, which acts as an incentive for industry to improve its efforts (McLaughlin, 2013).

The European Commission outlined the following guidelines in a 2006 report:

Making public the key performance indicators will reassure public opinion that the system is working effectively. Independent evaluations carried from time to time out by external institutions to measure SROs (self-regulatory organizations) against objectives can also reinforce public opinion perception. (Report of the Round Table on Advertising, 2006, pp. 19–20)

In chapter 6, I pay particular attention to whether social media companies make their "key performance indicators," or standards of effectiveness of anti-bullying mechanisms, available to the public.

If ARIs are not transparent, and if there is little evidence of their effectiveness, then their legitimacy can come into question. "Input legitimacy" refers to how an alternative regulatory instrument embodies "democratic standards such as participation and accountability," for example of citizens, consumers, NGOs, the public.[13] (See chapter 7, where I discuss this in the context of NGO ability to provide independent voice.) "Output legitimacy" refers to whether (or the extent to which) alternative regulatory modes are able "to contribute to the achievement of public objectives," and "hence [why] performance evaluation is a central but rather difficult task for research" (Latzer et al., 2007; Latzer et al., 2013, p. 375).

In light of the professed importance of regular monitoring and evaluation, there have been surprisingly few independent evaluations of self-regulatory effectiveness (that which concerns cyberbullying) within the US and EU. A continuous independent evaluation that would assess the effectiveness of the companies' anti-bullying efforts—and how that effectiveness might be defined—does not seem to exist. Policy makers sometimes cite unavailability of funding—the issue of who would pay for evaluation when, in times of austerity, it can be difficult to gather funds for evaluating even Command and Control regulation, let alone ARIs. Some policy makers might find an evaluation of the effectiveness of a company's anti-bullying enforcement mechanisms, which company pays a third party to conduct, as an "independent audit."[14] It should be argued that a stricter criterion for independent evaluation depends on it being commissioned by a regulator and not paid for or executed by the company itself.

The European Commission raised the issue of "inconsistency" and "ineffectiveness" of self-regulatory measures in its 2011 report on the implementation of recommendations made in 1998 and 2006 regarding the protection of minors and human dignity. Although the EC maintained its commitment to self-regulation, it indicated that legislation would be considered if self-regulation failed to deliver (McLaughlin, 2013, p. 87).

Examples of Self-Regulatory Initiatives

Some examples of self-regulatory initiatives in the EU that concern digital bullying include the Safer Social Networking Principles (SSNP), the CEO Coalition, and the ICT Coalition for Children Online, with notable involvement of NGOs and e-safety experts. These initiatives typically work by pledging the signatory companies that become initiative members to uphold specific agreed-upon standards or principles regarding child or teen protection online. A number of signatory companies may not be social media companies necessarily but broadly belong to the ICT sector, such as telecoms and ISPs.

Within SSNP, the following principles were of direct relevance to cyber-bullying: "raising awareness of safety education messages and acceptable use policies to users, parents, teachers and caregivers in a prominent, clear and age-appropriate manner," "work[ing] towards ensuring that the services are age-appropriate for the intended audience," "providing easy-to-use mechanisms to report conduct or content that violates the Terms of Service," and "assessing the means for reviewing illegal or prohibited content/conduct" (European Commission, 2009).

Independent evaluation of mechanisms that social media companies provide to address bullying was conducted as part of two self-regulatory frameworks in the EU and one self-regulatory initiative in the US. As part of SSNP, independent researchers analyzed self-declaration statements and tested a number of services offered by these companies (Staksrud & Lobe, 2010). A follow-up evaluation was conducted a year later (Donoso, 2011). The goal was to examine the extent to which the signatory social media websites adhered to the principles they had signed as part of that self-regulatory effort. Of the 14 websites studied by the independent researchers—just Facebook and YouTube overlap with the 14 I analyzed for this book—evaluations overall found that the companies were slow to respond to users' complaints (Staksrud & Lobe, 2010; Donoso, 2011).

While the overall findings for Facebook concluded that the company had implemented most of these self-regulatory principles "very satisfactorily" or at least "rather satisfactorily" (Donoso, 2011), the findings also indicate that "reports of inappropriate content/contact are not answered," "the mechanisms to avoid re-registration of underage users are inefficient," "not all sections in the Terms of Service are easy for children to understand," and there was a "lack of concrete information, especially targeted at children on the consequences of breaching the terms" (Donoso, 2011, p. 24). These findings go back to 2010 and 2011, and are by now dated, especially because youth have migrated to new platforms in the meantime.

The most recent independent evaluation in the EU was conducted as part of the ICT Coalition for Children Online in 2014 (ICT Coalition, n.d.; O'Neill, 2014b). Among the signatory companies included in this sample were Ask.fm, Google (Google+ and YouTube), Facebook, and Twitter. The ICT Coalition agreed to honor six principles concerning the protection of minors using their services, among which Principle 3, "Dealing with abuse/misuse," asks companies to develop the capacity to report abusive content and ensure that they "implement appropriate procedures for reviewing user reports" (ICT Coalition, n.d., Principles, p. 2). Principle 6, among other provisions, asked companies "to provide access to information that will help educate parents, caregivers, teachers and children about media literacy and ethical digital citizenship" (ICT Coalition, n.d., Principles, p. 4), which is best reflected in companies' development of Safety and Help Centers, which I discuss in chapter 7. The evaluation of this initiative pointed to the need for improvement in reporting in reference to mobile platforms. But in this case, although the evaluation was said to provide testing and evaluation of site safety (see O'Neill, 2014b, Methodology, p. 62–63), it did not carry out actual tests on the tools provided by the companies (Lievens, 2016).

Neither was testing of the sites conducted as part of Internet Safety Technical Task Force (Berkman Center for Internet & Society 2008, 2010), which convened at Harvard University's Berkman Klein Center for Internet and Society. This self-regulatory initiative resulted from the settlement of a group of state attorneys general with MySpace (Berkman Center for Internet & Society, 2010); it is one of the few self-regulatory initiatives relevant to bullying in the US that involved some form of independent evaluation. The companies that were members of the Task Force, among them the social networking sites Facebook, MySpace, and Bebo, were asked to deliver an overview of e-safety measures they were providing on their platforms at the time, including those to prevent harassment or bullying. The Task Force concluded that all eight social networking sites that participated in the Task Force evaluation provided technological tools for users to report abusive content.

If a website reported that it was committed to handling all reports of incidents within 24 hours, however, such specific information was not tested. The results of the Task Force's study were published in the end of 2008 (Berkman Center for Internet & Society, 2008), and since that time the social media landscape has significantly changed. As of the writing of this book, there have been no other government-initiated efforts of this scope that have asked social media companies to provide a description of measures they were taking to address bullying on their platforms; and which would then *also* include an independent evaluation of these social media companies' efforts.

One of the few initiatives of this kind in the US, the 2010 Online Safety and Technology Working Group (Collier & Nigam, 2010), convened by the US Department of Commerce, did analyze the industry's e-safety efforts, but its goal was not to provide an independent evaluation of the social media companies' cyberbullying policies. The Working Group included assistance from prominent members of the e-safety NGO community in the US, some of which I interviewed for this book.

Toward Mechanisms of Value to Children and Young Users

A continuous ("standing") independent evaluation does not exist either in the US or in the EU. Two factors contribute to the lack of a sustained study. First, given the fast-paced development of technology and children's shifting preferences, a number of sites tested in the studies referenced above are no longer the most popular social networking sites for children (e.g., MySpace and Bebo), and the majority of social networking platforms that are popular with children as of this writing in 2016 and 2017—Instagram, Snapchat, or Kik, to name just a few—have never been subject to evaluation in this manner. Second, although the study produced by the ICT Coalition was relatively recent (2014), it only evaluated two of the four social networking sites or companies that provide such services (Facebook and Google), even though the other two (Ask.fm and Twitter) were listed as members at the time of this writing (see O'Neill, 2014b).[15]

Third and most importantly, the usefulness of these mechanisms has not thus far been *independently* tested *with children and young users*. Hence the issue at stake is not *only* whether the companies have the promised mechanisms in place and whether these mechanisms are doing what the companies state they are doing—although this is an important issue—but also whether young users find these mechanisms useful and effective in solving bullying issues and why this may or may not be the case.

6   Untangling the Companies' Motives and Actions

It was a sunny Sunday morning in November 2014. I was standing in front of a building in San Francisco, eyeing one of the many floors on which the start-up company I was hoping to interview should have been located. I had tweeted its representative earlier—having found no personal email addresses on the app site—and he was more than kind to answer (something that few did when contacted without a reference). He gave me his address, to which I emailed the interview questions. After several back and forth attempts and little success in setting up a mutually convenient time for the interview, the representative sent a brief message: "I should have some time on Sunday," he wrote, leaving me wondering *when* on Sunday, exactly, because that day would be the last one of my stay in the city. So, I took my chances by showing up at the doorstep of the building, semi-uninvited, thrilled to recognize the name of the company on the intercom. I rang the bell and began to explain myself after hearing a male voice at the other end. He let me in, into what I remember as a light, spacious office that belied the covert reputation the company had acquired in the media.

This story reflects substantially more availability than I experienced in my early attempts to interview people from many other companies; it seemed nearly impossible to reach the human beings behind generic contact info on websites, never mind finding a company phone number. Of course, social media representatives are too busy to talk to researchers—imagine if they had to answer dozens or hundreds of queries (or more?) from researchers daily—and I acknowledge how impractical that would be. When I was allowed in, I considered myself lucky, even when I learned very little.

The person whose kind willingness to help began to open the industry's doors for me was Sonia Livingstone, a professor at the London School of Economics and Political Science. As a well-known academic and founder of the EU Kids Online, a network of more than 150 researchers in 33 countries in Europe who research children and digital media, Livingstone reached out to some of the company representatives and e-safety experts, asking if she could put me in touch regarding the interviews.

Until then, I had not fully appreciated the extent of nontransparent behavior, perhaps best exemplified in the widespread practice of non-disclosure agreements (NDAs) that many companies would ask visitors to sign upon entering their premises, and an overall lack of perception of any obligation to explain their operational policies to the public. Several e-safety advisers to companies told me that they, too, had to sign NDAs; even they were not always privy to companies' operational policies. If the advisers were expected to provide critiques on companies' policies, they may have found it difficult to fulfill their role under such circumstances. It further appeared that this situation was accepted as the (perhaps lamentable) "way things are" in the community of e-safety experts (with few exceptions: see Carr, 2013b), NGOs, policy advisers, and regulators.

In the context of the differences between legalistic versus coordinated self-regulation discussed in chapter 5 (Newman & Bach, 2004), some policy advisers in the EU thought that just getting the US companies to the table as part of the self-regulatory effort had been a significant sign of accomplishment—given that such actions were not something that the US companies had necessarily been accustomed to. Soliciting the good will and cooperation from the industry, as one e-safety expert observed, was important for the EU's economic competitiveness. But asking US companies to provide more transparency might have been too high of a bar, especially given that they were regarded primarily as private businesses—and less as public utilities or venues where the public sphere unfolds.

As I explained in earlier chapters, each company tailors its intervention and prevention tools to its specific technological affordances, but there are no written rules or minimum standards to which every company *must* adhere. These minimum standards and sometimes very elaborate policy and enforcement mechanisms tend to emerge nonetheless as part of the self-regulatory and self-organizational efforts that I analyze in this chapter.

Broader questions I pose about this process include: What can be known about the companies' efforts to address cyberbullying and about the companies' policy enforcement mechanisms? What do companies consider as an effective policy and enforcement mechanism, and why? What assumptions about the nature and occurrence of bullying on their platforms do companies' documents and representatives make? How do they explain the rationales about the particular tools of enforcement they use and react to perceived ineffectiveness?

What Does It Mean to Moderate Content?

In the summer of 2016, YouTube came under fire when some of its popular channels accused the company of having "vague" TOS and "a selective approach to moderation" (Kiberd, 2016). (Companies use in-house or outsourced employees as moderators, whose role is to look into content reported for TOS or Community Guidelines/Standards/Rules violations and decide which action to take if the content is determined to violate the company policy.) The allegations made by the channels were elaborated in a video titled "The YouTube Rant (I'm getting banned off YouTube)," which allegedly inspired many others of its kind. The video—which had been uploaded by what a news article posted on the Vice Media platform Motherboard described as an "already infamous" YouTube "'commentary' channel" called LeafyIsHere—had at that time already gathered more than 5 million views (LeafyIsHere, 2016). According to the article, it had previously been common to see smaller channels shut down for "roasting"[1] and "occasional parody," whereas bigger channels "consistently . . . got away with it" (Kiberd, 2016). In an apparent change of policy, however, YouTube was now said to have become stricter in its moderation practices and perhaps more consistent, given the video's allegation that now even some bigger channels were receiving warnings and restrictions on their platform activity (so-called strikes) for violating its Community Guidelines (Kiberd, 2016).

The interplay of any platform's business model with its policies on taking down abusive content may be difficult to discern, and it is a particularly interesting question that seems rarely discussed in public. For instance, does the shutting down of widely popular accounts or removal of their content negatively affect any platform's commercial interests, and if so, to what extent and in which ways? I raise questions such as these throughout this chapter.

Problems regarding the ways in which moderation is put into practice with respect to abuse, harassment, and bullying are by no means peculiar to YouTube; most companies struggle with these behaviors in one way or another.

Definitions, Behaviors, and Levels of Transparency

Most social media platforms include some sort of anti-bullying, anti-abuse, or anti-harassment provisions in their TOS or other corporate documents, whether they're labeled Community Standards, Community Guidelines,

Rules, or Principles. (Some companies do not make any references to "community," however, a factor that notably emerged in my analysis.)

Such documents rarely provide a more specific or detailed level of explanation for what these companies consider to be "bullying" on their platforms. Some companies provide examples of related behaviors that they consider to be "bullying," such as "abuse" or "harassment," but these instances are less common. A company may sometimes elaborate on bullying in its Safety or Help Center, but, as I discuss later in the chapter, not all companies have Safety Centers.

Some corporate documents that did stipulate examples include the following:

Twitter: "Some of the factors that we may consider when evaluating abusive behavior include: if a primary purpose of the reported account is to harass or send abusive messages to others; if the reported behavior is one-sided or includes threats; if the reported account is inciting others to harass another account; and if the reported account is sending harassing messages to an account from multiple accounts" (Twitter, 2016d).

Facebook: "We don't tolerate bullying or harassment. We allow you to speak freely on matters and people of public interest, but remove content that appears to purposefully target private individuals with the intention of degrading and shaming them" (Facebook, 2016f).

Facebook had been updating its Community Standards to provide more specific explanations of what the company considered to be "bullying and harassment," The document explains further:

This content includes, but it is not limited to: pages that identify or shame private individuals, images altered to degrade private individuals, photos or videos of physical bullying posted to shame the victim, sharing personal information to blackmail or harass people, and repeatedly targeting other people with unwanted friend requests or messages (Facebook, 2016a).

YouTube's specified examples of "harassment and cyberbullying" include:

Abusive videos, comments, messages . . . making hurtful and negative comments/videos about another person . . . deliberately posting content in order to humiliate someone . . . revealing someone's personal information . . . maliciously recording someone without their consent . . . incitement to harass other users or creators . . . [and] unwanted sexualization, which encompasses sexual harassment or sexual bullying in any form. (YouTube, 2016)

Ask.fm specified that content containing "rude words or . . . intended to embarrass anyone" was not allowed, but this was not clustered under "bullying" in the company's policy, and "mean" content, or content intended to "harass, scare or upset," was not allowed either (Ask.fm, 2016a).

These four companies had the most specific examples to be found as I conducted my research, but they still fell short of providing guidelines as to how the companies put them into practice. What would count as "abusive"? Or, how are "purposeful targeting" and "deliberate humiliation" assessed in practice? What counts as "hurtful" or "shaming"?

Company documents did not explain whether bullying captured the concept of power imbalance among children, whether the action had to be repeated, what would constitute repetition, or how the company went about determining whether it had been repeated. "Bullying" and "harassment" were often used interchangeably. But, as I discussed earlier in this book, these nonetheless distinct terms may also carry different legal consequences in various geographic locations.

Twitter preferred to use a broader term, "abuse," rather than "bullying," a decision that the company explained as part of its effort to protect freedom of speech by not becoming involved with the content on the platform. Laying out very specific provisions for "bullying" would demand content mediation (such as removing tweets in bullying cases), an action that may infringe on freedom of speech and that the company preferred not to undertake. "Regarding the accounts whose sole purpose is to be abusive, we wouldn't necessarily want to take down tweets, we just want to remove the entire account," explained Patricia Cartes, the head of Global Trust and Safety Outreach, Public Policy at Twitter, in our personal communication. The company has other strategies, which I detail later in the chapter.

It was typically the representatives of more established companies who provided an explanation for the language found in their policies.[2] They specified that the decision not to include definitions of the word "bullying" reflected the similar difficulties of researchers: if the academic community could not arrive at a single, agreed-upon definition of what constituted bullying or digital bullying, it would not be helpful for companies to be bound to one or guided by one.

None of the interviewed companies reported to publicly disclose the guidelines that their respective (or outsourced) moderators used to determine whether a case constituted bullying (and hence whether to act on it or not, i.e. take such content down or leave it on the platform due to possible violation of the company's Terms).

As a rationale for not disclosing these guidelines, the representatives of some (especially more established) companies explained that determining whether a case constituted bullying was done case by case, and the decision was almost entirely context-dependent, which is why it was difficult to draw such generalizations. Furthermore, the guidelines for moderators were characterized as complex, extensive, and involving long training, which is why they could not be easily regurgitated into simple explanations for the public. I wondered if companies would consider a post as "bullying" even if it were *one post only* without evidence of repeated bullying communication. One representative of an established company explained that they would take into account repetition and power imbalance. But if a single post was reported, they still might consider it to be bullying and take it down; without knowing if such activity is part of offline bullying, they would prefer to err on the side of caution.

For YouTube, bullying was used interchangeably with "harassment," and a single post could qualify:

We can take it down even if it's just one comment, or one video, for instance; if it crosses that line that we consider as harassment—and this is a case-by-case situation—we don't have a clear "that word is harassment and that word isn't harassment" [policy]. It doesn't work that way. It's always case by case – who is attacking who and in which manner. (YouTube representative, personal communication with the author, November 12, 2014)

In a 2014 interview, an Ask.fm representative said they believed one mean comment would *not* be enough for the company's moderators to determine that a case constituted bullying; it would have to be repeated commenting. But two years later, in my communication with Justin Patchin,[3] a well-known cyberbullying expert who acted as an e-safety adviser for the company, I learned that in practice it was nonetheless context-dependent, and that one comment could be enough (e.g., if it was accessible to others or if someone had created a public profile about someone else and made a single post). He observed that companies in general tend to be interested not in definitions but in behaviors. Because moderation was outsourced to one or more companies, he said, specific guidelines (including those for filtering) might have been left at their discretion and there may not have been a formal, company definition of bullying. As I stated in the beginning of this chapter, very few companies provide examples of specific behaviors that they consider as "bullying."

Furthermore, under such circumstances where context was the determining factor, it became increasingly important to use *human* moderators rather than an automatic detection system (despite its levels of sophistication). Several companies that preferred not go on record provided another rationale for not disclosing their moderation guidelines: they would not want to make it easy for users who wanted to abuse the policy to circumvent the rules.

Through my interviews I learned a great deal about what companies consider to be bullying, much of it not detailed on the companies' websites. This was especially the case with smaller start-ups.

The Evolution of Self-Organizational Efforts

The more established a company was, or if it found itself at the center of a high-profile incident, the more likely it was to provide a greater degree of elaboration of its policy and enforcement tools.

In 2014, among the documents of relevance to bullying (as well as harassment or abuse), some of the surveyed companies merely had Terms of Service. Nonetheless, by 2016, they had gone on to develop more documents in the form of Principles, Community Standards/Guidelines/Rules, or Safety Centers. These further elaborated the companies' anti-bullying policies and enforcement mechanisms, or referred users to NGOs, or provided more information about bullying.

Safety Centers sometimes exhibited videos and educational texts about bullying that the companies developed with the assistance of NGOs. The companies who had such features characterized them as an important part of their self-organizational effort and as an example of an evolving company policy.

Facebook, YouTube, and Twitter seemed to lead the way: Facebook first introduced "Community Standards," YouTube had "Community Guidelines," and Twitter had "Twitter Rules." Other companies followed suit, often with remarkably similar wording. Facebook had also developed a "Bullying Prevention Hub," a section of the company's website containing information about how to prevent bullying.

From the standpoint of self-regulation, it is important to observe that the development of these online documents, Safety Centers, and enforcement mechanisms was not a self-regulatory requirement for all the companies surveyed here, as a number of them had never taken part in any formal self-regulatory initiative related to bullying. Some of the established companies may have submitted these texts and enforcement mechanisms as best-practice evidence within self-regulatory initiatives in Europe, such as ones I discussed in chapter 5 (Safer Social Networking Principles, CEO Coalition, and ICT Coalition), and in the US (Internet Safety Task Force). Consider, for instance, that Principle 6 of the ICT Coalition specifically advised the companies to provide educational provisions and "links to other sources of relevant, independent and authoritative advice for parents and carers [*sic*], teachers and for children" (ICT Coalition, n.d., p. 4), which Safety Centers illustrate. But other companies that did not participate in such initiatives could develop and adopt these provisions via informal industry-wide collaboration or simply by observing the model of the more established companies.

The Spillover of Expertise

Representatives of these younger companies attended e-safety conferences, such as the Family Online Safety Institute's (FOSI) annual conference, which brought together industry and NGO representatives as well as educators, academics, government representatives, and other interested parties to discuss relevant issues in the e-safety field. These younger companies could thus create contacts with the older companies and even hire people who had previously worked for them in a process that was sometimes described as "the spillover of expertise."

Establishing contacts with e-safety NGOs who may later advise them can also happen at these conference venues, and exemplifies how self-organization evolves. Companies could hire people who had previously worked for state attorneys general offices. Some very new platforms that offered similar types of affordances (e.g., anonymity) reported that some of their competitors were not so willing to share best practices among themselves.

A possible reason why some older companies, such as Voxer, or other companies such as WhatsApp, did not have Safety Centers at this time was that they might not have had the need to develop them, and might not have been publicly perceived as having the properties of social media. Given that their platforms were primarily enablers of private chats between two or several people, they might not have seen their platforms as conducive to bullying either. (See table 6.1.)

Technological Affordances and Varieties of Bullying

Varieties of technological affordances among these platforms can account for quite different types of bullying. Many informants observed that bullying on Facebook and Twitter tends to be subtler than on anonymous platforms, such as Ask.fm. On Facebook, children can communicate in less straightforward ways than by writing mean comments or swear words on each other's profiles; they can tag the target in a post that contains an ironic photo, for instance. Or, they can easily exclude someone by creating

Table 6.1
Presence of Community Guidelines/Principles/Rules/Standards and Safety Centers at the Time of Research

Company	Founded	Community Guidelines/ Principles/Rules	Safety Center
Facebook	2004	Yes	Yes
YouTube	2005	Yes	Yes
Twitter	2006	Yes	Yes (within Help Center)
Tumblr	2007	Yes	No
Voxer (primarily messenger)	2007	No	No
WhatsApp (primarily messenger)	2009	No	No
Kik (initially primarily messenger)	2009	Referred to but not apparent in 2014; yes in 2016.	No in 2014 but yes in 2016
Ask.fm	2010	Yes	Yes
Instagram	2010	Yes	Yes (as part of Help Center)
Google+	2011	Yes in 2014 but not apparent in 2016	Yes
Snapchat	2011	Yes	Yes (significantly smaller scale in 2014 than in 2016)
Whisper	2012	Yes (in 2014, there were Community Guidelines but not as a separate document from TOS). In 2016, there was a separate document (Whisper, 2016b)	No
Yik Yak	2013	No in 2014 but Yes in 2016. They were just called "Guidelines" rather than "Community Guidelines" (Yik Yak, 2016b)	No in 2014 but Yes in 2016
Secret	2014	Yes	No

closed groups or by ignoring that person in conversations. In all instances it might be especially difficult for a platform to discern that bullying is in fact taking place, and thus hard to take action to remove the content or block the offending user. Similar subtleties can be seen on Twitter in a practice called "subtweeting," which refers to tweeting about someone without using their handle and mentioning them, often in a mocking or derisive way.

On Ask.fm, however, swear words and openly mean questions were more common. As I discussed in chapter 2, anonymity can disinhibit users. It can be easier to bully someone online than in person, and easier still on an online platform that allows anonymity or the use of a pseudonym. This is why the affordances of anonymous apps such as Whisper, Secret, or Yik Yak are seen as conducive to what some informants characterized as more "blatant" bullying.

Delegating the Reporting to the Community

One of the functional purposes of these corporate documents was to convey the idea that e-safety is an effort of the entire community of users on a given platform. This ability of the platform to get the community to "regulate/ moderate/police itself" was understood by some informants as an "advanced or evolved" self-regulatory mechanism and cyberbullying policy. Such self-directed language also tries to convey the idea that the company does not want to interfere in free speech on the platform unless it "decides" or "feels" that it is necessary (e.g., regarding a violation of Community Guidelines), and that, when it comes to bullying, it is primarily the responsibility of the community to regulate itself rather than have the company regulate the community. Here are examples from YouTube and Facebook:

Respect the YouTube Community:

We're not asking for the kind of respect reserved for nuns, the elderly, and brain surgeons. We mean don't abuse the site. Every cool, new community feature on YouTube involves a certain level of trust. We trust you to be responsible, and millions of users respect that trust. Please be one of them. (YouTube, n.d.a).

Facebook gives people around the world the power to publish their own stories, see the world through the eyes of many other people, and connect and share wherever they go. The conversation that happens on Facebook and opinions expressed here mirror the diversity of people using Facebook. To balance the needs and interests of a global population, *Facebook protects expression that meets the community standards* outlined on this page (Facebook, 2016a, emphasis added.).

Such messages can convey that bullying is not a norm but an outlier on the platform, and that the community comprises participants who do not bully. Belonging to the community implies self-moderating by refraining from bullying:

Have Fun: The language below is meant to support this rule. It allows us to continue providing and improving our Services, and it helps ensure that *a few mean users* don't ruin the fun for everyone else. Your part in that is simple. Just use common sense—keep sending awesome Snaps to your friends and please don't send Snaps that they don't want to receive. (version of a guideline formerly on Snapchat; emphasis added) .

Newer Companies: Liability, Community, and Freedom of Speech?

When companies did not have Community Guidelines and Safety Centers—whether it was because they were in an early stage of e-safety development or just didn't see the need to develop such policies—they were more likely to provide anti-harassment provisions without making specific references to "bullying."

These provisions were typically stipulated in TOS and housed under the sections of company websites labeled "Legal." Indeed, their purpose seemed geared to outlining the legal responsibility of the company and protecting it from possible liability in case harassment took place—quite a different task than establishing a sense of community. In such cases companies may have even openly emphasized their discretional right to take action on the content they considered to be in violation of TOS.

Apps allowing anonymity faced particular pressure from media reports about the alleged severity of cyberbullying on their platforms. That is why, especially if they were newly established, they addressed the negative media attention by emphasizing that they did not hesitate to take down questionable content.

Guaranteeing freedom of speech, then, was not a rationale they used to avoid taking action in certain circumstances while gearing the company's efforts toward creating a community that can manage itself. The guidelines that these companies followed when they did take down content were not publicized either. Takedowns were resolved on a case-by-case basis, which again points to the question of the power that private companies have over the digital public sphere. But the longer the company maintained its presence on the market, and especially if its name appeared in the media in relation to bullying, the more likely it was to abandon this discretionary discourse.

Community Autonomy and Transparency

Companies that rely on the language of community responsibility appear to convey the idea that users have a voice in delineating what is allowed on their platforms. While such wording may imply user empowerment, it also appears to downplay the extent to which the companies really *are* the final arbiters on what takes place on their platforms.

Facebook, in particular, the oldest company and the one in the sample with the largest number of users, presented itself as a platform with participatory governance. It had a Site Governance Page (Facebook Site Governance, n.d.) where users could leave feedback to any announced changes to the company's TOS, which Facebook termed "Statement of Rights and Responsibilities" (Facebook, 2015f).

In this regard, Facebook behaved like a government entity that created a public debate prior to introducing a new law. Users were portrayed as having a significant amount of leverage over values and norms the company embraced—as exemplified in the debate on nudity. While Facebook had initially prohibited breastfeeding images, it changed its policy in 2014 to allow photos of mothers breastfeeding on the platform. The company posted then its decision with the following explanation:

We agree that breastfeeding is natural and beautiful, and we're glad to know that it's important for mothers to share their experiences with others on Facebook. The vast majority of these photos are compliant with our policies (Facebook, 2015b).

This suggests (perhaps much like the Vietnam War photo explanation) that the company imbues its own values as to what amounts to "natural" or "beautiful." According to a *Tech Times* article, Facebook's decision arrived only after the pressure from feminists and breastfeeding advocates, clustered primarily around #FreeTheNipple movement (Arce, 2014; Esco, Richards, & Azuelos, 2015). Whether the company acceded to the pressure from advocacy groups, or the decision had little to do with it, is not at all clear and transparent. What matters when explaining the logic behind cyberbullying policies, however, is the idea that such discourse promotes the notion of user autonomy, participation, and shared governance.

According to "Facebook Principles," a document that the TOS and Community Guidelines are based on, transparency is the cornerstone of the company's ethos:

We are building Facebook to make the world more open and transparent, which we believe will create greater understanding and connection. Facebook promotes openness and transparency by giving individuals greater power to share and connect and certain principles guide Facebook in pursuing these goals. Achieving these principles should be constrained only by limitations of law, technology, and evolving social norms (Facebook, 2016b).

This statement suggests that Facebook understands itself or wishes to be understood not merely as a corporate entity, or a brand whose purpose is to provide a satisfying product to its users, but as a platform with a mission to enhance human connection as embodied in "sharing culture" and a focus on the inherent value of "sharing," as José van Dijck aptly explains:

Facebook's business model is most certainly a contentious balancing act between stimulating users' activity and exploiting it; its success ultimately depends on customers' willingness to contribute data and allow maximum data mining. . . . Values of connectedness and community are equated with connective values, smoothly aligning business models with user interests. (van Dijck, 2013, p. 64)

Based on what social media companies publicly reveal about their moderation practices, it is difficult to tell how content moderation (e.g., taking posts down because of cyberbullying) may reflect on their business models and revenue. Might it affect user satisfaction or even the process of data collection? And how does investment in safety relate to company revenue? These aspects of the discussion are carefully elided in company discourse that focuses on user benefits, autonomy, and community empowerment. In the following chapters I return to some of the relevant points.

Enforcement: From Formal Document to Practical Operation

When it comes to enforcing policy, much like with defining terms such as harassment and cyberbullying, what is formally written in the company documents may only be a fraction of what actually takes place at the operational level. Most companies provide users with the ability to report or flag abusive content, or at least to contact customer service. The companies will only take action on reported content if the moderation process establishes that the content constitutes bullying, harassment, or abuse, thereby violating TOS / Community Guidelines (see also Crawford & Gillespie, 2016). Most companies provide their users with tools to block abusive users or posts, which can, under some circumstances, lead to an account suspension.

Some companies at one point provided a form of filtering for the words and phrases that were not allowed on the platform (e.g., Ask.fm, Secret, Whisper, Yik Yak), and some reported doing so in different languages in markets where they had significant numbers of users (although what "significant" meant in exact numbers was not necessarily specified).[4]

The companies whose discursive cornerstone was freedom of speech were reluctant to employ filtering. Companies did not disclose whether they had moderators for every language represented in their user base, how many such moderators they employed (or outsourced moderation to), or what criteria they used to decide that they needed to introduce a moderator for a specific language.

The more experienced social media companies tended to provide more elaborate explanations of their tools for enforcing the policy. Some of them also invested heavily into research on optimizing enforcement tools, which seemed to be especially the case with Facebook and Twitter, although no company revealed any details about the scale of financial investment. Despite more extensive explanation, the information necessary for determining how the effectiveness of enforcement mechanisms was measured nonetheless remained largely undisclosed.

Lessons Learned from Facebook

Given that the e-safety experts I interviewed frequently characterized Facebook as the company leading the self-regulatory effort when it came to cyberbullying, I analyze Facebook's policies in more detail here, and use the company as an illustration how industry-wide policies in this area have evolved.

Facebook's relationship with regulators in the US and the EU seemed to be going rather smoothly while I was writing this book. But, as I briefly outlined in chapter 5, and as the following case of "panic button" illustrates, this may not have always been the case. Early in their development, companies have the potential to trigger fears in regulators and the public, especially if their user base outgrows the e-safety awareness of their leadership and consequently their companies' e-safety capacities.

Once they adopt a visible e-safety strategy (e.g., Safety Centers, NGO partnerships, or Community Guidelines), however, and start developing the language of advanced policies, they can successfully attenuate these fears and build a collaborative relationship with relevant stakeholders.

In May 2017, as this book was being completed, *The Guardian* leaked some of Facebook's previously undisclosed operational policies, including instructions the company gave to its moderators on how to handle some types of abuse. The content of these files caused significant criticism for the company and even calls on behalf of some policy makers in the UK for the company to become more transparent in how it handles its content moderation (Grierson, 2017). Citing these documents, *The Guardian* reported the company even allowed "the 'sharing of footage of physical bullying' of children under seven" as long as such sharing was done without a caption (Hopkins, 2017, para 7; see also Hopkins & Wong, 2017). These documents revealed that Facebook's operational policy for moderators defined bullying broadly as "an attack on private persons with the intent to upset or silence them," and one is a private person if they are not a public figure (Hopkins, 2017). It will be most interesting to see how the company will respond to the public reactions in terms of policy changes and whether this incident will affect the company's relationship with regulators internationally.

"The Panic Button"

The introduction of the reporting button ("flag") on this platform did not take place without a public debate that illustrates how e-safety design can be important for any platform's business model, and how little is publicly known about this dynamic. The ways in which a platform's business interests may be related to the choice and design of the preferred e-safety tools rarely finds its way into public discussions around e-safety.

The Child Exploitation and Online Protection Center (CEOP), a command within the UK's National Crime Agency, is a body that works primarily on protecting children from sex offenders and child pornography, but also engages in other e-safety issues.[5] In 2010, CEOP wanted to ensure that major social networks introduced a standardized "safety button," dubbed as "the panic button," which would be located on the profile page of every user who was under 19 (Facebook refuses to add safety buttons, 2010). By clicking on that button, the report would go directly to CEOP. Furthermore, the button allowed 10 different reporting options. For instance, if a child did not want to report to the police they could receive help via phone from counselors working at an NGO charity called Childline.

As the UK *Telegraph* reported, at the time Facebook was confronted with "mounting pressure" from parents and the UK government to improve its safety strategy ("Facebook refuses to add safety buttons," 2010). Facebook agreed on the point that allowing users to report cases to CEOP directly should be instituted on the platform. Yet they did not agree on the design of the button and the wording that should be used to report offensive content. According to the *Telegraph*, the company representatives said that in their experience users disliked big buttons and that such graphics "intimidate and confuse people," thus lowering the likelihood of reporting. Instead, Facebook preferred to include its own "report abuse" link and allow users the option to report to CEOP directly as well as to company moderators.

Bebo, a social networking site that was popular with young people at the time but whose user base had been rapidly declining, had adopted the CEOP report button (Barnett, 2009). CEOP criticized Facebook for refusing to do the same. How increasingly stringent safety measures may have influenced Bebo's popularity is a debate I will revisit in chapter 8, adding Ask.fm and Formspring to the list of examples. Microsoft's MSN chat and a number of websites also introduced the button.

At the time, the *Telegraph* reported, CEOP was receiving as many as 10,000 clicks per month, which resulted in 5,000 criminal investigations (the article did not specify how many were in reference to bullying vs. other e-safety issues). It also reported that the number of complaints to the police in reference to Facebook had "almost quadrupled" at that time in comparison to the previous year, which was why CEOP deemed it was especially important to have Facebook adopt the procedure ("Facebook refuses to add safety buttons," 2010).

Facebook delivered its rationale to the public for not adopting the button's design, saying that its own testing showed such action would decrease the likelihood of reporting; the *Times* newspaper, on the other hand, reported that according to the CEOP director, Facebook's reason for not adopting the button may have been the possible impact of such an action on the company's advertising revenue (Monaghan, 2011, cf. Fresco, 2009). Whether there would be any tangible impact on advertising is not a topic that frequently finds its way into public discussions, and the company to my knowledge does not disclose such information.

Other Options for Addressing Abuse

In addition to reporting abusive posts to Facebook, if some content bothered users but did not violate Community Standards, Facebook recommended that users block or unfriend people, hide them from their Newsfeed (updates users received from their friends), or send them a message and try to resolve issues on their own. Most companies provided a variation of at least some of these options (typically significantly more modest, unless the company was established), which had been adapted to the technological affordances of their particular platforms.

A detailed diagram explaining how the reporting worked was available on Facebook (Facebook Reporting Guide, n.d.), which stated Facebook had "hundreds of team members" working in 24 languages located in Menlo Park, and Austin in the US, and in Dublin, Ireland, and Hyderabad, India (Facebook Reporting Guide, n.d.). Moderators were then divided across four teams: the Safety Team, the Hate and Harassment Team, the Abusive

Content Team, and the Access Team. The majority of reports were handled within 72 hours, according to the diagram.

Difficulties Determining the Details

Similarly to other companies surveyed here, at the time of my research Facebook did not disclose information about the exact number of staff and moderators working on each team across its four offices; such information was classified, as was all documentation regarding the number of reports that were processed as "bullying" by the company's moderators in a given period of time and evidence that all or the majority of reports were indeed handled in 72 hours.

Companies with a longer history typically emphasize in their discourse that their users' safety is paramount to them, assuring that a robust e-safety effort is in place:

At Facebook, nothing is more important than the safety and security of the people who use our service. With a community of over 901 million people, Facebook maintains a robust reporting infrastructure made up of dedicated teams all over the world and innovative technology systems. (Facebook Reporting Guide, n.d.)

Nevertheless, specific criteria of effectiveness, evidence of effectiveness, or the details behind how the effectiveness of this effort is measured remain difficult to determine in the case of established and new companies alike.

Support Dashboard

Some of the e-safety experts I interviewed characterized Facebook's "Support Dashboard" as an important move made by the company to address complaints that it was taking too long to respond to reports about inappropriate content (e.g., Donoso, 2011; Bazelon, 2013b), and to introduce more transparency about its handling of these reported cases.

Having reported the content in question, the user would receive a link to what in 2014 was called Support Dashboard and in 2016 the Support Inbox. The dashboard/inbox explained whether the reported post was being reviewed, and, once it had been, notified the user about the moderators' decision (Facebook, 2016e). In 2014, the time span in which Facebook made its decisions was not specified; in 2016, it stipulated in a section titled "What to expect now" that the reported content would be assessed against Community Standards the same day.

Some e-safety experts, who believed the dashboard to be an important move on Facebook's part toward fostering transparency, said that from their purely anecdotal experience, its introduction appeared to coincide with fewer complaints about Facebook's flagging tools. Statistics as to whether or how the introduction of this tool has improved the effectiveness of the company's reporting system, however—either provided by the company or from any other source of evaluation or publicly available document—were not readily available at the conclusion of my research. Neither was such information provided by NGOs that I had the opportunity to interview and that were members of Facebook's Advisory Board at the time of my research.[6]

Moderation 2.0: Toward Advanced Policies

As social media platforms began to introduce flagging or reporting options for users, part of the responsibility for moderation was transferred to users— and hence the discourse on safety as a joint effort evolved, as summed up in this quote from an NGO representative:

Because in this world of web version 2.0 it is in fact the users who are moderators— their reports first alert service providers of content that breaks the rules and when people start losing confidence in that (reporting tools), then there is a problem. (Anonymous, personal communication with the author, June 30, 2014)

The difficulties of moderating vast amounts of reported content while avoiding the loss of user confidence—for instance, in cases where the effectiveness of the moderation was not to their liking—led companies to move toward more "advanced policies" that attempted to empower users by further deferring moderation to them. Such a move might also allow some companies to hire or subcontract fewer moderators. Consider an explanation given by one company representative:

But we have a lot of users and the ratio we have with the number of moderators is very good because we make sure the community polices itself. So as these communities get bigger you'll see them "moderating" each other quicker. (Anonymous, personal communication with the author, November 12, 2014)[7]

Social Reporting and Community Empowerment

Social reporting is an example of a policy that relies on the logic of community moderation. It seeks to empower users by providing them with tools designed to help them resolve conflicts among themselves, thereby delegating part of the responsibility for conflict resolution onto users. After extensive research, Facebook introduced the social reporting tool in an effort to better address the needs of its users; the company had noticed that moderators kept receiving a large number of reports they could not act upon because they could not establish that a case constituted bullying and had thus violated company policy.

For instance, the company may not necessarily be able to act if it receives a report of a photo of two girls smiling at each other, with no mean comments underneath. Even after looking into the context behind the post, the information provided might not be sufficient for moderators to determine that a case constitutes bullying. By taking such a photo down, the perceived peril for the company is that it would be curbing users' freedom of expression.

Facebook introduced "social reporting" in 2011 (Facebook, 2016d). It allows users to send a message to the person whose content they think is bullying or abusive in an effort to try to resolve the issue without reporting it to the company's moderators. In other words, when social reporting takes place, it happens without any notice being provided to the company's moderators. It is primarily intended as a remedy for the content that users mind or think constitutes abuse or bullying, but that may not qualify as such according to corporate policy.

Social reporting also allows users to reach out to a third party (e.g., parent/caregiver, teacher, friend) in order to seek help when one feels bullied. As part of social reporting, Facebook also provided "premade" (prewritten) messages (see examples in the next section) that a user could send when reaching out to another user who may have bullied them, or to a third party.

Social reporting was perceived as a more advanced enforcement tool than the simple content takedown because it could help address conflicts that could persist or originate offline. Facebook provided pages called "Details on Social Reporting" and "What is Social Reporting," which outlined the entire process (Facebook Safety, 2011; Facebook, 2016d) and provided step-by-step explanations on how to report (Facebook Help Center, 2016b).

Infrastructure for Community Autonomy

Facebook didn't provide a separate "social reporting" button. Rather, when users wanted to report (e.g. by clicking on "report" option), they were led through a series of prompts ("flows") which asked them to specify why they were reporting. At the time of this book's writing, not all of these flows would lead to the option of reporting the post to the company's moderators (i.e. "regular reporting"). Depending on which options the user decided to choose in these flows to explain to the company why they were reporting, at the end of the flow they would be given one or more of the following options: report to the company (i.e., "regular reporting," by which the content is supposed to go to the company's moderation system for inspection); engage in social reporting (i.e., reach out to the person who posted the abusive content, in an attempt to resolve the issue, or to a trusted person, in a plea for help or advice); or they would be given both options: to report to the company and engage in social reporting (then they could choose which one they prefer). At the end of the flow, users were also typically advised they could block, unfollow, or unfriend the person whose content they dislike.

For example, when I clicked on a post to report it, a dialog box opened with the following prompt (referred to by the company as "a flow"): "Help us understand what's happening."[8] I could then choose: (a) "It's annoying or not interesting," (b) "I think it shouldn't be on Facebook," (c) "It's about me and I don't like it" (provided as an option in 2014 and 2015 but not in 2016), and (d) "It's spam."

Consider the next level of choices: If I clicked on "It [the content] shouldn't be on Facebook," the following dialog box opened: "What's wrong with this post?" and I could then choose: (a) "It's rude, vulgar or uses bad language," (b) "It's hurtful, threatening or suicidal," (c) "It's private information like my phone number or address," (d) "It goes against my beliefs," and (e) "Something else."

If I chose "(a)" I would then be able to send a message to the person who posted the content, unfollow them, or submit the post to Facebook for review. If I chose "(b)" I would see a different dialog box, which said, "Help us understand the problem: how is it harmful?" I could then choose one of the following options: "It's mean," or "It offends gender, race, sexual orientation or ability," or "It's threatening or violent," or "I think they might hurt themselves." If I chose "It is mean," (the option perhaps very likely to correspond to bullying content), I would not be offered the choice to report the content to Facebook. I could only message the person, unfriend her, or reach out to a friend to resolve the issue. Hence, not all options in dialog boxes that the user might choose would necessarily result in the option to report the content to Facebook. This is why, perhaps, some of the content that could constitute bullying might not have the opportunity to be reported to the company.

The exact wording of these flows was said to vary based on the user's age (e.g., teens see different texts in these flows than adults do) and it was said to be tweaked regularly (sometimes every few weeks) based on extensive research, in an attempt to optimize the flows in a way that would match the language users employ to describe bullying behavior. In August 2016, a flow that a 14-year-old user might see, which is very different from the flow I described above, looked like the illustration in figure 6.1)

As seen in figure 6.1., the word "bullying" may not come up in the flows. This reflects the finding that teens tend *not* to identify with either the word "bullying" or with "bully–victim" roles (see chapter 2).

Interplay of Effectiveness and Efficiency

Facebook's organization of the reporting flows is designed to minimize the number of reports that users would file regarding content that does not violate the company's Community Guidelines, and about which Facebook could potentially do nothing about. It is an attempt to increase reporting *efficiency*.

The increase in efficiency is considered to be effective because users tend to understand the context of the conflict and are therefore perceived as best positioned to solve the cases for which the company cannot establish to have violated the company policy (Milosevic, 2015a). Community autonomy, then, implies that users participate in keeping the platform safe. Safety is portrayed as a coordinated effort between the users and the platform. The process of creating the community implies taking responsibility for one's actions and helping others; the entire e-safety onus does not fall entirely on the company:

We believe safety requires a coordinated effort from everyone—whether by reporting inappropriate behavior or making sure your account and passwords are secure. Let's work together to create an environment where we can all *share* comfortably. (Facebook, 2015e, emphasis added)

"Sharing comfortably" ensures "frictionless sharing" and seamless functioning of the company's business model—not just for Facebook, but also for social media companies in general (van Dijck, 2013)—and can be seen as another connotation behind such wording.

Scale of Effort

The wording used in social reporting flows is by no means arbitrary. Facebook partnered with psychologists and neuroscientists at the Yale Center for Emotional Intelligence, as well as with the Greater Good Science Center at the University of California, Berkeley, to develop the language for social reporting as well as for Facebook's cyberbullying prevention initiative, the "Bullying Prevention Hub" (Yale Center for Emotional Intelligence, 2013). In the view of some e-safety experts, such extensive effort was affordable primarily to large companies such as Facebook.

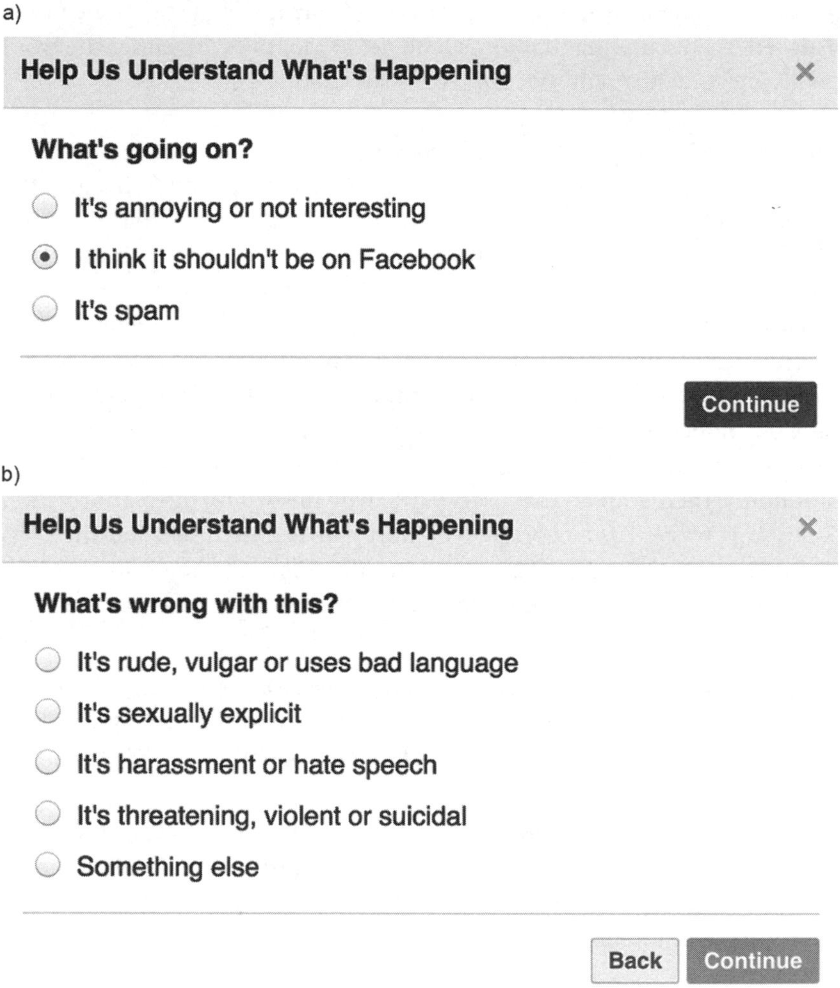

a)

Help Us Understand What's Happening	✕

What's going on?

- ◯ It's annoying or not interesting
- ⦿ I think it shouldn't be on Facebook
- ◯ It's spam

[Continue]

b)

Help Us Understand What's Happening	✕

What's wrong with this?

- ◯ It's rude, vulgar or uses bad language
- ◯ It's sexually explicit
- ◯ It's harassment or hate speech
- ◯ It's threatening, violent or suicidal
- ◯ Something else

[Back] [Continue]

Figure 6.1
Reporting Flow

c)

Help Us Understand What's Happening

This is hateful towards

○ A race or ethnicity

○ A religious group

○ A gender or orientation

○ People with disability or disease

○ An individual

Back Continue

d)

What You Can Do ✕

Here are some things you can do to handle this.

 Submit to Facebook for Review
Report this post if it goes against our Community Standards.

 Block Tijana
You won't be able to see or contact each other.

 Unfollow Tijana
You won't see her posts in News Feed, but you'll remain friends.

 Unfriend Tijana
You'll no longer be friends on Facebook.

Back Cancel

Compassion Research Day

In 2013 a team headed by an engineering director at Facebook organized an annual event called Compassion Research Day as a way to present, on a regular basis, the results of Facebook's research and collaboration with Yale, Berkeley and other academic institutions; Facebook also organized an in-house "compassion team" in order to help sociologists, psychologists, and neuroscientists, among other researchers, "conduct experiments" and "implement (their) findings on the network," all "funded in part via stipends from Facebook" (Tsui, 2014).

There seems to be an understanding among companies that users will not return to their sites if the platforms are infested with bullying or harassment. In line with this thinking, Bonnie Tsui summed up her report about Facebook's efforts to facilitate the ongoing Compassion Research Days: "If people enjoy their experience more, Facebook will do better as a business" (Tsui, 2014). But as the controversy over the "panic button" perhaps illustrates, a legitimate question (for any company) to ask might be: How does a company's business model benefit from its preference for using certain moderation tools rather than those methods characterized as ineffective, or as threatening to freedom of speech?

A researcher who consulted with teams at Facebook on social reporting, explained that one of the difficulties in providing statistics on effectiveness was that this research did not have a "typical before and after."

We say, "hey let's tweak this little thing," [referring to wording in social reporting flows]. We don't always tweak only that one thing and have the opportunity to evaluate just the change that that one little thing was able to impart upon people's completion rates. (Anonymous, personal communication with the author, December 3, 2014)

For example, a question in one of the platform's flows would ask the person who reported disliking the photo, "How does this photo make you feel?" The prefilled messages would read: "embarrassed," "sad," and so forth, with each option naming a particular emotion. The Facebook team found that a subtle change in the wording from "embarrassed" to "it's embarrassing," resulted in a lot more people completing the flow.

The data collected over 30 days of research revealed that of all the teens entering this flow, 76% were reporting photos and 24% were reporting posts (textual content). (The sample was collected in the US and consisted of "all 13–16 year olds who entered [the] resolution tool within a thirty-day period" see Compassion Research Day, 2013.) Within this sample, 15% selected the option "it's bullying" while 66% selected the option "it's annoying" (suggesting that perhaps teens might not find the word "bully-ing" to be helpful or to accurately reflect what they were trying to report).[9]

Out of the 25% of teens who used the flows, 90% messaged the per-son who posted the content they had a problem with, and 10% messaged a trusted adult or a friend. As many as 75% used prewritten messages as opposed to tailoring them themselves—which suggests that these were use-ful to teens.

Once the content creators were contacted, 75% of them were reported to respond back. Statistics relating to the type of response provided—whether it was favorable to the person who felt bullied or not—were not readily avail-able. However, 37% of them deleted the problematic content upon request.

Community Autonomy Efforts by Twitter, YouTube, Google+, and Tumblr

Twitter, another more established company, has also developed a reporting system that was explained in detail on the company's website (Twitter, 2016a, 2016c). The company created a Trust and Safety Council, a partnership with advocacy groups, e-safety experts, and researchers working to prevent abuse (Twitter, 2016b), similar to Facebook's Safety Advisory Board (see chapter 7).

Using the word "targeted abuse" in its policy rather than "bullying" allowed the company to intervene in those cases that met the conditions for targeted abuse rather than develop guidelines for specifically cyber-bullying tweets. The company's focus on freedom of speech permeates its abuse policy discourse:

At Twitter we look at abuse from a holistic perspective. Other tech companies fol-low a different approach and break down their policies very granularly. You may see hate speech, cyberbullying, etc. called out on their policies. When we outlined our Twitter Rules, which are our content boundaries, we emphasize behavior; we look at the intent of accounts. It's important to bear in mind that [they were] built *on the principle of freedom of speech*. We want the tweets to flow. (Patricia Cartes, head of Global Trust and Safety Outreach, Public Policy at Twitter, personal communication with the author, June 17, 2014, emphasis added)

As of the summer of 2016, the closest options to bullying in the report-ing queues (comparable to Facebook's flows) were "abusive or harmful" content, which then prompted users to choose among a number of sub-options, such as "targeted harassment" and "disrespectful or offensive con-tent." Just like Facebook, Twitter provided users who wanted to report a tweet with means to explain why they were reporting it.

This approach, whereby Twitter prefers to warn users rather than to take down specific cyberbullying tweets, is also conceptualized as effective, placing trust in the community's ability to autonomously regulate itself when provided with the right tools by the platform. But if the case is not one of a temporary fall-out between people, and when an account's sole purpose is judged to be abusive, the platform prefers to shut down such an account.

When we contact the person and give them a warning or even permanently suspend them we see in the very vast majority of cases—people will remove the tweets that they deem abusive. We see that people react to warnings and educational messages: in the great majority of cases there is no bad intent. You have two friends who fall out and one starts tweeting in a way that is not constructive. That type of user reacts very well to our educational messaging and our warnings and rectifies their behavior. (Patricia Cartes, Twitter, June 17, 2014, personal communication with the author)

Similarly, Google-owned YouTube provides for reporting abusive videos, and it relies on the logic of user autonomy and the user's ability to self-regulate:

You may not like everything you see. Some of the content here may offend you—if you find that it violates our Terms of Use, then click the button that says "Flag" under the video you're watching to submit it to YouTube staff. If it doesn't, then consider just clicking on something else—why waste time watching videos you don't like? (YouTube, n.d.a)

A "how to" video explains how to flag content, emphasizing that YouTube depends on its community to make sure that the Guidelines are respected. The rationale behind this shared responsibility for preventing abuse relies on the volume of user posts: with so much content being uploaded to YouTube, the company could not possibly be expected to monitor all the content on its own.

Users are warned again that "mildly annoying" content should be ignored rather than reported. Yet, *specific guidelines* on what YouTube will consider as "mildly annoying" *were not publicly explained.*

Google+ provided for similar procedures. User Content and Conduct Policy contained links explaining how to report content. Much like on the other social networks I've examined here, when clicking on the post to report it, you were asked to choose one option to explain why you were reporting the post, and led to subsequent options thereafter. Finally, you could choose to ask the owner of the post to remove it; remove the user from your circles (block the user); or report the post for review to Google. While Google+ did not label the procedure of asking the other person to remove the post as "social reporting," the idea behind this process appears to have been the same as with Facebook's social reporting tool.

Google+ also emphasized, similar to other companies, that while users may not like some content, or they may think it is mean or negative, Google+ would only remove it if it violated its "Content and Conduct Policy" (Google, 2016b, cf. Google, n.d.). A link to a webpage with more information on how to protect oneself from online bullying was provided (Google, 2016b). The webpage contained standard recommendations on what to do if one was involved in a bullying case, including channels for reporting, and an admonition to not retaliate.

At the time of this research, Tumblr was an older company that exhibited surprisingly little of the standard evolutionary trajectory in terms of cyberbullying policies and little of the discursive turn toward community autonomy I discuss in this chapter.[10] Because of its age, one might have expected it to have had a more elaborate Safety Center (Tumblr, n.d.a); in 2014 nothing resembling a report button was apparent next to posts on the platform itself. The Guidelines only specified that one should not harass or try to circumvent the "ignore feature"; they did not seem to explain what "ignore feature" meant and what it allowed users to do, or give examples of circumventions that it had referred to (the term was later changed to "block" [Tumblr 2015]) The Guidelines also specified that users could report any violation thereof to Tumblr, but no further explanation was given, outside of a link that was supposed to specify what the reporting options were, but the link only provided an email address to which users could report abuse.

By 2016, after updates to the platform, the Community Guidelines specified that "bullying" was not allowed, but much like on other platforms, the company provided no explanation for what "bullying" was specifically considered to be (Tumblr, 2016). "Targeted abuse" and "harassment" were defined as "sending you unwanted messages or reblogging your posts in an abusive way" (Tumblr, 2016). In the reporting flow, harassment was specified in a playfully vague manner (as "being a jerk") and as "circumventing the ignore feature in order to send someone mean or hateful messages" (Tumblr, n.d.c). When I clicked "report harm to minors" there appeared a follow-up notice that further defined such harm as "sexually suggestive or violent depictions of minors, or bullying *even* by another minor" (Tumblr, n.d.d, emphasis added)—which is an interesting distinction given that bullying is a term more often used to refer to conflict that happens *precisely* between minors. Elsewhere on the website, the company provided links to counseling services with helplines through which users could seek professional help (Tumblr, n.d.a.). The company never responded to interview requests.

Interventions on the Anonymous Platform Ask.fm

After Tinder owner InteractiveCorp (IAC) bought Ask.fm in 2014, and into early 2015, the platform's abuse policy specified that enforcement included blocking, reporting, and filtering. The words that were to be filtered, however, or any guidelines as to what determined whether the content would be filtered, were not apparent. Swear words typed in the search box, in an attempt to define them as filterable, yielded zero results. Suggestive terms, such as "hang yourself," also yielded zero results.[11]

Responding to public pressure, the company had been forced to adopt the discourse of a more established company early on, when the new owners pledged they would cut down on bullying. In 2016, the Ask.fm Community Guidelines specified: "Respect is the foundation of our community" (Ask.fm, 2016a). The company had already been partnering with well-known experts in the field of e-safety, with NGOs, and with other organizations (Ask.fm, 2016c, 2016f).

The focus that Ask.fm places on the shared responsibility for e-safety makes the platform particularly interesting. The company uses terms broader than "community" to reinforce that a complex phenomenon such as bullying is a wide-ranging social problem:

Rather than searching in vain for a safety silver bullet, ASK.fm leadership is committed to doing the hard work of *digging deep into the potential causes* behind the complex issues that online platforms like ours face with respect to safety. *Where does bullying start?* How is it defined? Where are we successful as a society at combatting this issue in the offline world, and how can we best apply a holistic lens to addressing this issue to our digital platform? These aren't just technical or product design questions, they are societal ones. *Only by working together* across communities, educators, government, law enforcement and industry can we find the most effective answers. (Ask.fm, 2016b, emphasis added throughout)

It is notable that information about how effectiveness of enforcement was defined and measured was not explained on this platform either. Although it provided detailed screenshots and instructions about reporting tools (Ask.fm, 2016d), along with links to e-safety expert organizations and individuals (e.g., Ask.fm, 2016c), it was difficult to tell how this "digging deep" took place, at least based on publicly available information.

Secret, Whisper, and Other Anonymous Apps

Other platforms that allowed anonymity, especially those early in their existence, provided even less information about policy enforcement and what the company did to handle reports of abuse.

Despite media reports about the company's moderation process, the anonymous app Whisper nonetheless disclosed very little information about how it regulated cyberbullying cases. In 2014 and 2016, the only reference to enforcement was that a violation of TOS and Community Guidelines could result in a termination of one's account or blocking of future access to the service.

Secret, an app that closed down in 2015, similarly did not provide an explanation in its corporate documents about how it enforced its policy and how it made sure that cyberbullying did not take place. Its Community Guidelines mentioned the option to report bullying content but did not explain how the reporting system worked or how the company handled such posts. Although it was not published or explained in detail to the public, an elaborate system for handling such posts did exist, as I discovered in an interview with Secret. A legitimate question to ask, therefore, is to what extent do other young companies employ elaborate enforcement mechanisms that they are under no obligation to discuss publicly, and whether additional disclosure or full transparency should be a requirement.

Secret's Proactive Moderation Procedures

As part of its bullying prevention initiative, Secret employed "advance screening" or "sentiment analysis" which was "automatic." Since the platform was strictly anonymous, no personal names were allowed on the platform. When someone wanted to post a name or a bad word, the system automatically checked the post against a pre-made database of first and last names and curse words. If the system detected a name or a bad word, it prompted the user with questions such as: "Are you sure you want to post this," or "say something kind?" Or it warned: "This is not a place where you should post negative things." Such prompts were meant to act as deterrents to posts that could violate Community Guidelines. The system also screened the post for its "severity level," and if it was determined to be "high" or "significant," the post was not published but instead withheld and sent to a human moderator for further review. The guidelines and standards for determining the severity level were not available to the public.

Once a post was published, a button could be used to report inappropriate content, a process called "community flagging." If a post was reported by numerous accounts, it was taken down automatically—a procedure that the companies focusing on freedom of speech would find invasive. According to Secret, every time a case was reported, it was reviewed by a human moderator. The moderators had a checklist to determine if a case constituted bullying. The details of the checklist were not available to the public but every case was said to be heavily dependent on context.

Typically, if a post contained a personal name, once it was reported, it would be taken down. If a user's post was taken down, that account was temporarily suspended. Suspension meant that the user was not able to post and comment on things but could be present on the platform and could "like" other posts. If a person's posts were reported two to three times, the person was permanently blocked from the platform.

These decisions were described to me as contextual, decided on a case-by-case basis, as there were no clear-cut rules. The blocked person could appeal the decision and file a complaint. Because each user was registered on the platform with either a phone number or a Facebook account, or both, the user could only open another account with a new phone number or a new Facebook account. According to Secret, such a situation would rarely occur, as it constituted too high of a barrier.

Yik Yak's Trajectory

Similarly, Yik Yak did not publicize the details of its policy enforcement procedures at the time I spoke with company representatives in late 2014. But my interview revealed an elaborate system that was otherwise not explained publicly, and the representative asked that I not publish it in this book because it had become outdated.

In 2016, however, some of the mechanisms that existed at the time of my interview were explained by company policy documents; the platform moved, to an extent, away from anonymity, adopting the discourse of a more established company with a Safety Center and partnerships with e-safety expert organizations. Much like the other companies, Yik Yak's definition of bullying remained undisclosed to the public except for the following command: "Do not bully or specifically target others. This includes but is not limited to, defaming, abusing, harassing, stalking and threatening others" (Yik Yak, 2016b).

An automatized tool that could also be considered a form of advanced policy—as it allows users to solve conflicts among themselves by providing them with the infrastructure adapted to particular technological affordances of the given platform—was the ability to "upvote" and "downvote," similar to the option to "like" and idea behind "dislike"). Five downvotes on Yik Yak

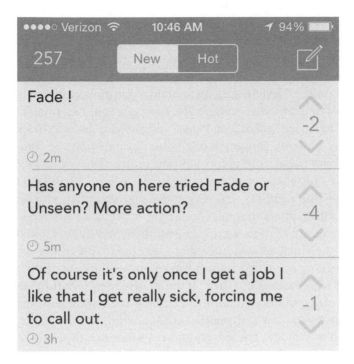

Figure 6.2
Downvoting

brought the content down automatically. "Downvoting" and "upvoting" is illustrated in figure 6.2, whereby downward arrows indicate "downvotes" and upward arrows "upvotes."

In February 2015, *TechCrunch* ran a story alleging that Yik Yak was "systematically" downvoting "mentions of competitors" on its platform (Constine, 2015). Yik Yak responded that this happened with a lot of other sites and games and not just competitor apps because "when we see repeated posts that say 'Go get this (app)' or 'go download this' we consider it spam" (DeAmicis, 2015). Whatever the case may be (see ThirdParent, 2015), it illustrates the potential interplay between e-safety policies and companies' business models, which is less understood in the absence of transparency.

Digital Messengers: Affordances Informing Enforcement

Apps that were primarily messengers or that did not perceive themselves as social media also provided little explanation as to how their bullying policies were enforced. Furthermore, they did not necessarily have flag/report buttons the way that previously analyzed companies did.

In the case of Voxer, in 2014, I could not locate a report button that, when strategically placed next to a message for instance, would have allowed users to report abusive content. Nevertheless, users could report abusive messages to Voxer by contacting customer service. The company had two primary ways in which it addressed bullying and abuse: by allowing users to block other users and by enabling "privacy mode," also illustrated on the company's website (Voxer n.d.a). Any user could turn on the "privacy mode," which meant that only those people who had that person's email could find the person on the platform. The user could sign up either with an email address or with a phone number. According to the company representative, a vast majority of users signed up with their emails. They could therefore change the email address in case of harassment and enable the privacy mode. Blocking prevented abusive users from sending any further messages to a user who had blocked them. If the abusive user went through the trouble of creating another account to continue the harassment, the victim could create an account with another email unknown to the abuser, and enable the privacy mode. The company considered such measures to be effective, given that it did not perceive itself as social media and hence not as a platform that was particularly conducive to harassment or bullying.

An option to report abusive messages to WhatsApp was not apparent at the time of this research; users could, however, block each other, and an account could be temporarily banned from the service. This could happen, among other reasons, if a user was blocked by "too many people in a short period of time" (WhatsApp, 2016a). A permanent ban could result from "being annoying to other users." At one point, its TOS even playfully stated that "an annoying person is anyone who is (capriciously or not) determined to be annoying by authorized WhatsApp employees, agents, subagents, superagents or superheros" (WhatsApp, 2016b). WhatsApp was a rare company that between 2014 and mid-2016 seemed to make no move toward establishing the e-safety discourse discussed above or explaining e-safety mechanisms in its corporate documents. Its TOS mentioned harassment, but did not reference bullying.

Kik's policy in 2014 only seemed to provide options to block an abusive user or report someone's message "as spam." Any reporting provisions specific to cyberbullying were not apparent. However, in 2016, there was an option to report a user based on "being abusive" (see Kik Interactive, 2016a, 2016b).

In an August 2016 email to me, Kik reported that it was "still in the early stages of formalizing policies" and requested that I contact the company in October 2016. When I initiated the follow-up communication, Kik declined to provide an interview at that time as well. It is particularly interesting to observe how a company whose e-safety issues were the repeated subject of mainstream media coverage since 2013 would not feel more pressured to have developed a policy several years later.

Snapchat in late 2014 did not provide a detailed explanation on how its enforcement mechanisms worked, but it did allow a user to report abusive content or the user who posted it, and to submit a written explanation about the incident to the company directly. Over time, the company developed a Safety Center, partnered with e-safety NGOs that created e-safety guides for the platform and started to employ the discourse of a more established company with an emphasis on community (Snapchat, n.d.a, n.d.b; ConnectSafely, n.d.). Bullying was mentioned in its 2016 TOS: "you may not upload, post, send or store content that: bullies, harasses or intimidates" (Snapchat, 2016); however, the TOS did not specify the behaviors that defined these terms, and neither did the Community Guidelines, which under the section "harassment, bullying or spamming" said: "This one should be simple: Do not bother or make other people feel bad on purpose. If someone blocks you, it's not okay to contact them from another account" (Snapchat, n.d.a).

There was no explanation as to how the company decided a user was bothering someone and making them feel bad, apart from circumventing the blocks. A cyberbullying guide detailing how children can stay safe on Snapchat, developed by ConnectSafely.org, a well-known NGO in the US e-safety community, said that the platform was "not the most likely 'place' for cyberbullying to occur because a lot of what is shared in the app isn't public, doesn't stick around long, and is usually shared only among friends, or—in the case of Stories — fans or people who care about what you're sharing" (ConnectSafely, n.d., para 2). While these features may limit public humiliation, bullying can also happen among one-time friends, as discussed earlier in the book (and as some company representatives pointed out). On the "Snapchat Support" website, one could "Report a Safety Concern" (Snapchat, n.d.c) using options to report various types of content on Snapchat such as Stories, Snaps, or Chats. Similar options were provided inside the app itself.

Degrees of Content Moderation

One significant factor that cannot be ignored in the consideration of e-safety policies is that the amount of content uploaded on these platforms is vast. Perhaps YouTube is an excellent illustration, with 300 hours of uploaded video *per minute* (Dormehl, 2015). At one point, 20,000 questions were asked on Ask.fm platform *per minute* (Ask.fm Safety Guide for Schools and Educators, 2017). Although no company revealed how many bullying-related reports it received in a particular timeframe (given the volume of sharing on each platform), one can assume that moderating the services can be extremely difficult and costly, especially if humans do the moderating.

Many companies I surveyed for this book tended to emphasize that the reported content was, to a large extent, reviewed by humans and not by automated means. Typically, though, they could not guarantee that a human reviewed every piece of reported content—not even the companies with substantial resources could make that claim. Companies emphasized that because bullying cases are so context-specific, they need to be reviewed by humans. Most companies do not disclose the numbers of in-house and outsourced moderators they employ, who they outsource their moderation to, and the amount of financial resources they invest in moderation and e-safety in general.

No company provided a breakdown of its moderator base according to language expertise. When users speak a variety of languages, it can become increasingly difficult to moderate bullying cases, which require moderators to understand the subtleties of context. For example, with a global user base, more than 80% of Facebook's daily active users were from outside the US and Canada (Facebook, 2015a). Having such expertise for every language where a company operates can become quite costly.

Some companies reported that even if they were to publish how many moderators they employed, there would always be those to whom these numbers would appear insufficient when compared against millions of users. Therefore, revealing these numbers was not deemed to be conducive to a constructive public debate (Milosevic, 2015a).

Outsourcing Moderation

Although the companies I researched tended to use some degree of in-house moderation, the vastness of this effort often required them to out-source their moderation services, and this was overwhelmingly done in developing countries, resulting in a number of media reports about moderation, which accused the companies of poor outsourcing practices.

In 2012, the UK newspaper the *Telegraph* wrote that Facebook outsourced its moderation to companies abroad where moderators were paid $1 per hour, and that there were no security measures in place to prevent moderators from uploading and sharing this content further or from accessing user data (Barnett & Hollingshead, 2012). According to the *Telegraph* reporters, Facebook had previously disclosed: "No user information beyond the content in question and the source of the report is shared."

The *Telegraph* claimed, however, that the names of those tagged in the reviewed posts (as well as the users who uploaded the posts) had been clearly visible; as per the article, Facebook explained that such user data was necessary to provide context for the moderators' decisions. Citing an interview with a moderator conducted by Gawker, and previous Facebook policy statements as well, the *Telegraph* reported that when moderators in places like Africa or Asia review the content, they can ignore it, delete it, or escalate it to employees in California (Barnett & Hollingshead, 2012). The article stated that such moderation was widespread across the Silicon Valley.

Twitter told the *Telegraph* that it had in-house moderation but would not answer the question on outsourcing for the article. An anonymous Facebook moderator also alleged in a blog post that outsourced moderators were paid $1 per hour unless they were American, in which case they were paid $30 (TheInternetOffendsMe, 2013; see also Solon, 2017). This moderator further suggested that Facebook received about 250,000 reportable issues (those that *actually* violated Community Standards) *per hour* and that the company relied on automation in the moderation process, so a number of reports were *not* handled by human moderators.

Facebook reported having very strict rules regarding its outsourced moderation. Its contractors were subject to rigorous quality controls and the company had implemented several layers of safeguards to protect the data of those using their service. Outsourced moderators addressed only simple, clear issues or false reports and forwarded any potentially contentious ones to in-house moderators. No exact numbers of either in-house or outsourced moderators were provided (Milosevic, 2015a). YouTube did not disclose such details and neither did Ask.fm. I asked some of the companies if I could witness the moderation process, but I was not allowed to, and my understanding based on this research is that the companies rarely allow non-employees to observe the moderation process (see Bazelon, 2013b; the author had the opportunity to witness Facebook's moderation process and describe it in her book).

It would seem that the less established companies that allowed for anonymity would be even less likely to discuss their moderation practices. Yet one such company, Whisper, was a rare example of a company willing to speak publicly about the exact numbers of moderators it had employed and its moderation process in general. Whisper told *Mercury News* in 2014 that it employed 120 human moderators to sift through posts in real time (Ortutay, 2014). Articles on the website *Gigaom* and in the *Guardian* alleged that Whisper was using TaskUs, an international outsourcing company with a team in the Philippines (DeAmicis, 2014; Lewis & Rushe, 2014 respectively), and the San Francisco-based Metaverse Mod Squad to outsource its cyberbullying moderation (DeAmicis, 2014). As the *Gigaom* reporter disclosed, "Moderators delete the bad stuff, shuffle cyberbullies into 'posts-must-be-approved-before-publishing' category and stamp suicide Whispers with a 'watermark,' the Number for the National Suicide hotline" (DeAmicis, 2014).

According to a *Wired* article from October 2014, Whisper allowed the reporter to view the moderation process and was one of the few companies that practiced "active moderation, an especially labor-intensive process in which every single post is screened in real time" (Chen, 2014). The article did not specify if all real-time screening was conducted by humans. If it was automated, then Whisper was not the only company providing such moderation; Secret did something similar, as I discussed above (at the time of that interview, all of Secret's moderation was outsourced to companies in Guatemala and the Philippines). According to Secret, the moderators received a few days of training until they learned the workflow and were never shown images, just text; according to the company representative, that diminished the peril of their transgression (e.g., taking someone's personal photo and sharing it on another platform).

Another start-up revealed that it had employed six in-house moderators for its then couple of million users, the exact number of which the company preferred not to reveal. In addition to employing in-house moderators, the process was also outsourced to a company in the Philippines whose name could not be revealed.

Proactive Moderation, Machine Learning, and AI

The type of moderation that occurs if users must first report content, and then wait for moderators to examine it and determine whether it constitutes bullying, can be described as "reactive moderation." On the other hand, "proactive moderation" implies the screening of content—even when it is not reported— as a means of cyberbullying prevention.

In September 2016, *Wired* magazine introduced Google's project Jigsaw, which had been developing a set of open-source tools called Conversation AI (artificial intelligence) to end harassment through algorithmic learning. *Wired* wrote that if Jigsaw were to find a way through "free speech paradox . . . it will have pulled off an unlikely coup: applying artificial intelligence to solve the very human problem of being nicer on the internet" (Greenberg, 2016). Informants representing the more established companies that invoked free speech protections would not necessarily see these proactive approaches as effective tools when childhood bullying is concerned (I discuss the particulars in the following paragraphs). Nonetheless, it will be interesting to observe how Jigsaw's strategy with respect to AI pans out, now that Google has seemingly embraced this approach and made it open source. Many interested parties wonder whether Google, a multinational for-profit company with a hand in digital public sphere, will gain financially from these apparently altruistic Jigsaw tools, as Google eventually hopes to do. Julian Assange, the founder of WikiLeaks, raised similar concerns about the fact that Jigsaw is run by Jared Cohen, a former State Department employee, implying that Cohen is extending govern ment interests via Google (Greenberg, 2016). The downsides of supervised machine learning that the informants lay out below are said to hold for Google's Conversation AI as well (see Greenberg, 2016).

Supervised machine learning in the context of bullying is a form of proactive content moderation: automatic crawling (monitoring) of the network that would allow for detection of cyberbullying cases as they happen (Dinakar, Jones, Havasi, Lieberman, & Picard, 2012; Xu, Jun, Zhu, & Bellmore, 2012). Hence, the content could be flagged for moderators' attention as "potentially cyberbullying" even if a user does not report it to the company. This approach can involve the development of an algorithm, a form of automated system to search the content on a given platform for bullying indicators (Dinakar et al., 2012).

Companies that prefer not to use such proactive moderation, may adopt a common rationale to defend their choice. Bullying is context-dependent and varies from case to case, which is why supervised machine learning may result in many false positives (cases misidentified as "bullying"), thus infringing on users' free speech. Consider, for instance, that young people sometimes use the word "bitch" to mean "friend or mate" which can result in the following problem:

When we were looking at the amount of tweets we were seeing where the word "bitch" was used in an abusive way, the percentage was tiny. It was surprisingly small. . . . It's just hard to determine the factors [behind bullying], because, as I said before you can have subtweeting, you can have abuse through images not just the key words. . . . So I don't think we would be satisfied at this time that there's an automated way to deal with cyberbullying. . . . I think if that technology was extremely accurate so if you could flag an extremely tiny percentage of false positives then perhaps we would consider it. (Patricia Cartes, Twitter, personal communication with the author, June 17, 2014)

But in August 2016 the *Verge* ran a story about Twitter's use of an algorithm to filter out abuse from responses to a question-and-answer session with the then US president Barack Obama, "and potentially" from another session with Caitlyn Jenner, a former Olympic gold medalist who underwent a sex change. Some tweets were said to have been moderated manually as well (Robertson, 2016). Twitter's erstwhile CEO, Dick Costolo, denied such accusations in a tweet as "sensationalist nonsense" (Robertson, 2016). In November 2016, in a follow-up conversation with the author, Twitter representative Patricia Cartes reported that Twitter did analyze patterns of behavior and at times would decrease visibility of certain tweets (however, primarily in connection to violent and extremist behavior). She reported Twitter had used "propriety spam tools to see if we (Twitter) could prevent abuse before it even happens." This tool, however, was not based on "specific words" but rather on "patterns of behavior" *and it was distinct from* "supervised machine learning" or "algorithmic learning." She said Twitter had never done any *"manual* manipulation of results."

The company was also accused of banning conservative voices on Twitter after a rightwing blogger, who the *Guardian* described as a "notorious troll," was permanently banned from the platform on grounds of abusive tweets (Hunt, 2016). The blogger responded by claiming that the platform was engaging in editorializing its content (Yiannoppoulos, 2016).

Bullying does not have to involve swear words; it can be subtle and involve ironic comments or hidden mockery—all cited as another reason why designing an accurate supervised machine learning system would be difficult. I conducted an interview with an academic who researched extensively the use of machine learning for preventing bullying, and who noted that the sophistication of this particular technique was not yet at the level where it could catch such subtle forms of bullying. However, as the informant explained, waiting for a perfect tool is not the right approach on behalf of the companies: "I think what should happen is you go fight with the army you have, not the army you wish [to have]."

Companies report that privacy concerns are another reason why they pre-fer not to apply these proactive approaches; they are wary of giving users the idea that they monitor content on the platform, especially the content that is not shared by users publicly but only among their friends. This point was reinforced in interviews with NGO representatives and e-safety consultants as well.

Efficiency is also cited as a problem when trying to apply proactive tools: given the large volume of content shared on these platforms, screening it in advance, especially using human moderators, would be almost impos-sible, as YouTube and Twitter acknowledged.

We don't do any proactive monitoring on the platform. You know—300 hundred hours of uploaded videos per minute—it's nearly impossible to do this sort of large crawling that is automatic. (YouTube representative, personal communication with the author, November 12, 2014)

When it comes to digital messengers, because of the private nature of such communication, employing proactive content moderation was regarded by some companies as not only undesirable, but also as unethical, in the words of one company representative:

This is private communication. We're not Facebook; we're not Twitter. Because these are not public forums . . . not only is there not a responsibility for us to monitor but we think it would be unethical for us to monitor what's going on. These are private conversations. (Anonymous, personal communication with the author, November 6, 2014)

Toward Transparency and Evaluation of Effectiveness

A number of important details that emerge behind the scenes in online intermediation by private companies can have significant implications for resolving the cyberbullying incidents that occur on their platforms and affect as well their efforts to create a more dignified paradigm of social rela-tions among youth.

The more established companies realize the value of e-safety for the suc-cess of their business models and tend to invest significant research-based efforts into policy enforcement. This value of e-safety is reflected in the ability of the company to assure its users that the platform is a safe one, but also in the ability to cite these efforts in front of the public and the regula-tors as evidence that the company is doing its best to address cyberbullying.

Company documents sometimes single out transparency as an impor-tant aspect of the policy and its enforcement. But even the more established companies provide little or no palpable evidence for the effectiveness of their enforcement tools. Even the results of in-house evaluation efforts tend to be sporadic and not readily available to users.

The promised transparency also belies what the companies do not reveal: the guidelines that their moderators use when deciding whether a case constitutes bullying (or harassment and abuse), for instance, or how many reports are received and processed per unit in time, or what percentage of reports are handled by humans (a point especially relevant for addressing subtle bullying), or any details about the amount the companies invest in e-safety measures. Many companies do not even stipulate what they mean by "bullying," such as the specific behaviors that their understanding or definitions of bullying, harassment, or abuse entail, which makes it difficult to understand how they approach and practice enforcement.

Particularly important is the move toward "advanced policies," those that allow the community of users to moderate itself. The language adopted for such policies tends to represent the user as an empowered actor and emphasize the shared nature of responsibility in addressing cyberbullying between users and platforms. The discourse of shared responsibility also signals that part of enforcement responsibility is delegated to users, caregivers, educators, law enforcement (if necessary), and NGOs (see chapter 7). These policies are described as *effective* because the companies themselves are not always able to determine that a reported case constitutes bullying and hence whether to act on it; a takedown may not solve the offline problem; and users are said to be best positioned to handle such conflicts because they understand the context behind the incident.

A policy that is defined as *effective* in this way, however, also tends to be *efficient* for the companies not only because it can cut down on the amount of non-actionable reports, but also because of the responsibilities and amount of work delegated to users. In the absence of an independent evaluation, or even in-house evaluation in the majority of the cases, the public, however, cannot know against which standards of effectiveness these policies and enforcement mechanisms are evaluated, and—in the light of such standards— how effective they are, especially from users' perspective.

What such discourse elides, despite the promise of transparency, is how the various enforcement mechanisms could affect the companies' business models and how such considerations may influence the decisions as to the preferred enforcement mechanism or the one described as "effective." For example, consider the case of the companies that invoke freedom of speech: Might active content mediation (takedowns, filtering, and proactive content moderation such as in the application of supervised machine learning) negatively affect their business models (user satisfaction but also data collection)? And how might these considerations play a role in deciding which policy will be adopted and characterized as effective?

Such use of advanced policies also seems to secure less independent scrutiny for the companies who adopt it. The more established a company is, the greater the likelihood that it will have adopted the logic of advanced policies (by using a greater degree of what companies describe as empowerment, and by providing tools for delegation). Some of the newer companies that garnered negative media attention in the context of e-safety may liaise with the more established companies in order to acquire this expertise, or they may partner with e-safety NGOs or hire professionals who are aware of the value of e-safety for the company's business model.

Because the user base of the new companies can grow very quickly, and faster than the necessary e-safety policies they attempt to put in place, these companies tend to be perceived by experts and sometimes regulators as in need of a greater scrutiny. While this may be the case, the more established companies that tend to have a greater skill at ensuring the perception of e-safety are *not* independently evaluated either.

This is not to say that the policies in place at more established companies are necessarily ineffective; there is evidence based on some of these companies' in-house research that specific measures, such as social reporting, could be helping some young users solve their conflicts. Nonetheless, until the industry considers the potential for independently established standards of effectiveness and evaluation—and those standards may indeed be different for each company if they aim to take into account of diverse technological affordances—it will remain difficult to even discuss this concept.

7   The Roles of NGOs in Search of Transparency and Effectiveness

The cooperation of non-governmental organizations (NGOs) is frequently visible in companies' Safety or Help Centers and in digital citizenship education—all of these being a part of advanced policies that exhibit the logic of user empowerment by providing tools for users to help themselves. In this chapter I examine various ways in which NGOs work with social media companies in an effort to address cyberbullying as part of self-regulatory and self-organizational structures. I use examples from US and Europe-based NGOs (some of which may, nonetheless, work internationally).

When discussing the role of NGOs in "global governance processes," the international politics scholar Daniel Drezner writes that they can provide "the activities that aid the monitoring and enforcement of existing sets of global standards" (Drezner, 2007, p. 69, cf. Mitchell, 1998). I analyze in this chapter whether and to what extent NGOs are in a position to provide critical monitoring and evaluation of efforts that social media companies make toward effective enforcement of policies against cyberbullying. I also examine how company discourse about effective monitoring and enforcement portrays and acknowledges the involvement of NGOs. While NGOs play a substantial role in helping companies to better their enforcement mechanisms, I argue that they can also assist them *in being seen* as making an effort (in the public and before the regulators). This is especially the case with more established companies, and is well illustrated by Facebook's anti-bullying event, which I discussed in chapter 1 (Facebook London Showcase, 2014).

In order to understand current NGO and companies' efforts toward preventing cyberbullying via digital citizenship, it is useful to examine what could be considered its predecessor—e-safety education—as briefly foreshadowed in the reference to the *Washington Post* article "They Call it Bunny Hunting" (Gibson, 2016). The article, which I discuss at the beginning of chapter 2, hints at some of the downsides of using scare tactics in e-safety- and consequently digital-citizenship education.

The European Commission organizes its projects on child safety in digital environments around a program that was originally called Safer Internet and is currently called Better Internet for Kids (BIK), in which NGOs play an active role. For instance, "27% of all participating entities" within Safer Internet were NGOs (Taraszow, 2013, p. 181). NGO assistance with respect to goals of "awareness raising" and providing third-party input for the social media industry (Staksrud, 2013a, p. 127; Taraszow, 2013) are particularly important for anti-bullying efforts and are both illustrated in the companies' Safety/Help Centers or Bullying Hubs.

In the US, e-safety NGOs have provided expertise or third-party advice in self-regulatory initiatives such as the Internet Safety Technical Task Force, or in the Online Safety and Technology Working Group at the Department of Commerce (see chapter 5).[1] NGOs served similarly in congressional committee hearings in connection to e-safety, as in the case of Megan Meier Cyberbullying Prevention Act (chapter 4).

In the field of e-safety, an increasing number of NGOs emerged in the US against the backdrop of fear-driven discourse around children's Internet use (see e.g., Collier, 2008, 2013; Marwick, 2008). Some e-safety experts observed that the coverage of youth and technology, especially at the time of the Communications Decency Act of 1996 (CDA) and the Deleting Online Predators Act of 2006 (DOPA), was frequently inaccurate in its exaggeration of risks, which threatened to make caregivers increasingly fearful (ConnectSafely, 2012; Marwick, 2008).

Some NGOs have attempted to counterbalance this protectionist discourse and e-safety education, emphasizing that research-based evidence for such risk estimates had largely been missing (ConnectSafely, 2012; see Finkelhor, Mitchell, & Wolak [2000], for one of the early e-safety studies, funded by the US Congress and published in 2000). They also took the position that children have rights to participation and provision, which can enable them to capitalize on digital opportunities (Collier, 2014a). This debate will become increasingly relevant in the context of digital citizenship discussed later in this chapter and in chapters 8 and 9.

When delivered to children by various law enforcement officers, e-safety education in the US overwhelmingly focused on dangers of the Internet, leveraging scare tactics and dramatic statements (see Jones, Mitchell, & Walsh, 2013; Gibson, 2016).[2] As independent evaluation and interviews confirmed, such messages may not resonate well with children and could even have an off-putting effect (Jones et al., 2013; Jones, Mitchell, & Walsh, 2014).

In 2009 the US Department of Justice commissioned one important effort at evaluating such e-safety education, which was executed by the Crimes against Children Research Center (CCRC) at the University of New Hampshire (Jones et al., 2013). This evaluation assessed the materials that the law enforcement officers had been using when delivering e-safety education, including cyberbullying, to children in US schools. The report was based on a content analysis of the youth Internet safety curricula characterized as the most developed and long-standing available at the time and examined the extent to which such e-safety education was based on academic research.

It brought forth a number of critiques, the first being that e-safety education conflated disparate topics—from cyberbullying and grooming to illegal downloading, spam, and sexting—even though the knowledge and skills that youth need to develop in order to address each of these are very different. Developing a capacity to address cyberbullying may require social-emotional learning, which is quite distinct from fairly straightforward instructions necessary to avoid spam (Jones et al., 2013). Bullying prevention, the report concluded, is a lot more complex than delivering a list of "dos and don'ts."

While children typically know that they should not be "nasty" and that they should report to parents or educators when they or others are bullied, they would nonetheless *choose not to follow this advice* (Jones et al., 2013). This means that teaching anger management or pointing out ways to resist the social pressure to "join in" nasty behavior might be a more effective tool (Jones et al., 2013, p. xiv). Addressing some of the risk or causal factors behind bullying, which also differ across age groups, and then tailoring interventions to address those factors, might have been a more effective strategy. I discuss this evidence in greater detail in the context of digital citizenship education later in this chapter.

NGOs as Third-Party Advisers

NGOs can play a number of roles when a social media company sets out to design or implement its cyberbullying policy. They can become the test pilots for a platform's new features, such as the tools for reporting cyberbullying or the user guides that explain e-safety measures.

Other NGOs play an advisory role based on their e-safety expertise and their work with children, thus providing feedback to a company about which tools are considered to be effective from the children's perspective, or which tools are supported by academic research. NGOs can also act as industry organizers, convening international conferences to discuss e-safety or provide companies with advice on the changing regulatory climate. Some NGOs work with users directly and offer information about reporting tools and cyberbullying policies to children, caregivers, and professionals working with children, such as educators or counselors. Running helplines that assist people when they need help in reference to e-safety, bullying, and cyberbullying problems on social media platforms is one example of such assistance.

NGOs can develop relationships with companies which allow them to "escalate" a case to the companies' attention or ask the companies to pay particular attention to a piece of content that may breach Community Guidelines and should be taken down. Such NGOs can have special communication channels with the companies—either contact forms designated for the NGOs or direct phone lines. The term "escalate" is also used in the name of the Educator Escalation Channel, a project of the Maryland attorney general's office (see chapter 5).

Despite this special status, NGOs have a limited power in the sense that they cannot ask the companies to take down content that does not violate TOS or Community Guidelines. An NGO might bring a case to a company's attention, however, and if a company takes too long to handle the report, the NGO may request the company to accelerate action, if it considers it to be necessary.

In spite of the language of partnerships exhibited in the policies, the companies are the ultimate arbiters on whether the content violates TOS and Community Guidelines. For the most part the NGOs that conduct this type of work neither spoke about individual cyberbullying cases (lest they infringe on the privacy of these individuals) nor provided data on the rate of resolution of such cases, which would constitute concrete evidence about the effectiveness of such tools of enforcement.[3]

NGOs and the Facebook Safety Advisory Board

The more established a company is, the more likely it is to foster partnerships with NGOs. Companies that face negative media attention in the aftermath of high-profile cyberbullying incidents (or a series of smaller ones) can also adopt the partnership strategy. Companies respond to pressure from the public to improve their e-safety efforts and, importantly, to demonstrate to the public and relevant stakeholders (shareholders, parents, educators, and policy makers) that they have done so by establishing partnerships with NGOs.

In my interviews with social media company representatives, they referred to their NGO collaboration as evidence of their companies' continuous work toward achieving effectiveness in the area of cyberbullying. These companies recognized that they could not be considered experts in the field of e-safety or psychology; they cited their NGO collaboration as evidence that they valued independent advice and assessment concerning the effectiveness of their policies and tools of enforcement.

Facebook, the company that many interviewees perceived as the leader in the industry's e-safety efforts, formalized its NGO cooperation in December 2009 by creating a body called the Facebook Safety Advisory Board (Facebook Newsroom, 2009). The company may have been under public pressure before the board had been created, which might have been a factor when deciding to establish it. This took place right before media reports alleging that Facebook had refused to implement "the panic button" designed by CEOP and opted to adopt its own reporting design instead (see chapter 6). The congressional testimony in reference to the Megan Meier Cyberbullying Prevention Act had also taken place several months before the announcement of the establishment of the board, which also drew public attention to cyberbullying. Although it is not clear whether and to what extent these developments may have influenced the creation of the board, this context is important to acknowledge nonetheless.

At the time when some of my research was conducted in 2014 and 2015, the Facebook Safety Advisory Board comprised five (non-governmental) organizations: Childnet International, ConnectSafely, WiredSafety, the Family Online Safety Institute, and the National Network to End Domestic Violence (Facebook, 2015g). In 2017, when this book was going to print, WiredSafety was no longer listed but two other NGOs had been added—Centre for Social Research (CSR) and Telefono Azzurro (Facebook, 2017).

Very little specific detail or evidence about how these NGOs helped Facebook measure the effectiveness of its mechanisms was forthcoming from either the company or the NGOs on the board that I had the opportunity to interview. Several e-safety experts observed that internal policies of many companies in the industry are rarely shared even with the companies' own trust and safety advisers, and given the omnipresence of non-disclosure agreements in the industry (see Carr, 2013b), non-governmental organizations and e-safety experts are often not allowed to say much. I briefly profile below three NGOs on the Facebook Advisory Board that have been on the Board since its foundation, and in each one address a different aspect of how an NGO fulfills its role as a board member.

Childnet International
Founded in 1995, Childnet International, a UK-based NGO, provided advice to Facebook by gathering feedback from children and school professionals where the NGO operated. The NGO was also appointed by the European Commission to coordinate the UK Safer Internet Center.[4]

Being a member of the Board gives us the opportunity to feed that [feedback] into the heart of Facebook if you'd like, to share that experience. And for us, that's in the mission of our organization to make the internet a great and safe place for our children. If we can help influence environments which are so popular with children, then we are. . . . That's exactly what we need to be doing. (Will Gardner, Childnet representative, personal communication with the author, June 30, 2017)

Family Online Safety Institute (FOSI)

Founded in 2007, the Family Online Safety Institute (FOSI) is a major international e-safety nonprofit with activities around the world that "convenes leaders in industry, government and the nonprofit sectors to collaborate and innovate new solutions and policies in the field of online safety" (Family Online Safety Institute, 2017). FOSI provided international, policy-related advice for Facebook as part of its service to the Facebook Safety Advisory Board. FOSI organizes a large annual conference that brings together stakeholders interested in e-safety (companies, researchers, policy makers, educators, etc.). I reference the conference throughout the book as a place where social media companies can acquire e-safety advice and network with NGOs. FOSI's organizational origins go back to 2007 and it evolved from the Internet Content and Rating Association (ICRA) (Staksrud, 2013a).[5]

ConnectSafely

In 2005, two long-standing and reputable participants in the e-safety community of NGOs, Anne Collier and Larry Magid, founded the California-based NGO called ConnectSafely.org (2015).[6]

According to Collier[7], representing ConnectSafely.org on the Facebook Safety Advisory Board involved providing feedback "on products and features and to talk about and hear about new developments." The NGO also provided similar services (advising on new products before and after their release) to other companies—for example, Google and Snapchat, mobile carriers, and app developers. Advising can also be informal—an individual working for one of these companies and knowing Collier might personally reach out to her for comments. The work broadly described as "product advice" varied from company to company and from request to request. According to Collier, the NGO could receive funding from a platform for project-specific work but ConnectSafely.org was not financially compensated specifically for being on the Facebook Safety Advisory Board.

Blogging at NetFamilyNews.org, which she founded in 1999, Collier called for an attempt to balance an alarmist and protection-oriented discourse—one that veered toward a preference for restrictive practices—with the need to understand technology in the context of children's rights to provision and participation (Collier, 2014a, 2014b, 2016).

Independent Advisers/Monitors or Consultants?

The question of NGOs' independence from companies is a complex one. Tatjana Taraszow, who researched NGO work in the context of child safety in the EU, writes that a "crucial challenge lies in the fact that NGOs often seek financial support from industry stakeholders with implications for the essential values of transparency and accountability that legitimize NGOs" (Taraszow, 2013, p. 189). Contractual details of relationships between companies and NGOs that specified any financial benefits were not forthcoming, and these tend not to be disclosed publicly. Some informants recognized that NGOs might also find their reputations boosted by their association with the established companies, especially if the market was saturated with NGOs providing similar services.

All the NGOs are keen to be referenced on Facebook, on the [Bullying] Hub, so that's the trade off for us—it gives us more visibility. (Representative of an NGO featured on the Hub, personal communication with the author, July 2014)

In a 2010 testimony to the US House of Representatives Committee on the Judiciary hearing on the subject of "online privacy, social networking, and crime victimization," Joe Sullivan, Facebook Chief Security Officer at the time, characterized the body as a "global" board of "outside experts who advise us, and on occasion, our community, about how to keep teens safe online"; the members of the board were described as "leading online safety organizations" that provide "independent advice" on online teen safety (US House of Representatives Committee on the Judiciary, 2010, p. 12). The establishment of the board was cited as evidence of the company's effort to drive collaboration among key stakeholders in the online safety community.

John Carr, an internationally recognized e-safety expert and a member of the UK Council for Child Internet Safety (UKCCIS), noted in a blog post from 2013 that the board could not be characterized as "global" since it only included NGOs from the US and the UK and that it could not be classified as providing "independent" advice without disclosing the details of the partnership.[8] In that same post he wrote: "I do not know if all of the organizations on the Safety Advisory Board receive money or other types of material assistance from Facebook but at least two out of the five do" (Carr,

2013a). In Carr's view, instead of framing the board as an independent advisory body, Facebook should label the NGOs as "consultants."

You know they used to refer to the existence of that Independent Advisory Board as if its existence validates anything and everything that they're doing as a company. So, they are using the fact that those five organizations sit on their Board as evidence that they must be doing the right thing, because, 'hey look, we're working with these child safety organizations.' (John Carr, personal communication with the author, July 3, 2014)

Carr further observed that he could not cite any examples where the board's existence impacted Facebook policy. There were no guarantees as to whether the NGOs on the board were "involved at a high enough level" during the company's decision-making process, or whether the company presented their decisions to the NGOs as a fait accompli (Carr, 2013b).

Childnet, however, reported that Facebook would make decisions in response to NGOs' feedback, but explained why it would nonetheless be difficult for the NGO to provide examples of how it influenced the policy:

Citing you a particular example where we have influenced policy would be impossible, because in order to discuss the new and upcoming ideas/services, we sign an NDA with Facebook, but also it would be impossible because there are a number of people on the [Advisory] Board and we discuss particular issues and Facebook has to make a decision as a result of what they hear. (Will Gardner, Childnet, personal communication with the author, June 30, 2014)

Transparency Concerns

Originally, there was another NGO on the Facebook Safety Advisory Board: Common Sense Media. According to an article in the *New York Times Magazine*, Common Sense Media left the board because it disagreed with Facebook on privacy issues; the *Times* quotes the CEO of Common Sense Media as saying: "'When we disagreed with them [Facebook] on privacy, they wanted us to keep quiet'" (Bazelon, 2011). The NGO insisted that they talked publicly about what they perceived as a deteriorating state of teenager privacy on the platform. This article by Emily Bazelon, a well-known legal scholar who also wrote a book about cyberbullying (Bazelon, 2013b), drew attention to the possible conflict stemming from any material benefits that may be provided to the NGOs. There was no evidence of any formal contracts between companies and NGOs available to the public and NGOs overall preferred not to discuss such specifics. The few NGOs that discussed funding details openly reported that the industry would not fund their overhead expenses. Rather, if there was any funding involved, the companies would fund specific projects for the NGOs.

Delegating the Work for Effectiveness and Efficiency

Some NGO informants saw themselves as actors with the potential to lighten the industry workload by handling problems that users may be having on the platform and fulfilling requests for information about the companies' cyberbullying policies. Consider the example of an NGO that provided helpline services for educators and counselors working with children. When professionals working with children had a problem with an incident on a platform, they could call the helpline for advice. The helpline staff had a thorough knowledge of the relevant companies' policies and they could then look into a case to investigate. Only if the helpline felt that a case breached corporate policy would they instruct the callers to report the case to the company, and if the company did not react in time, the helpline could escalate the case to the company's attention, as an NGO representative explained:

The first thing is—the relationship we have [with companies] is built on trust. Very much so. And the secret of our success is that the companies trust that we have fully investigated and exhausted all opportunities before we go back to them for help. So we never inundate them. So to give you a flavor: about half of our reports are about Facebook but in only 10 percent of them do we actually go back to them [Facebook] to deal with [the reports]. So we're doing a lot of work on their behalf. (Anonymous NGO representative, personal communication with the author, July 11, 2014)

This type of NGO support could contribute to more efficient handling of the reporting process for the companies, and it links to the argument previously discussed on the interplay of effectiveness and efficiency. While NGO partnerships are considered a token of both a social media company's policy effectiveness and its public visibility efforts, they also contribute to efficiency.

Perhaps a legitimate question to ask reflects the perception of some informants I interviewed, and it goes back to the debate about whether the NGOs serve as independent advisors or consultants: Is it, to some extent at least, the responsibility of the industry to provide some compensation for the work that the NGOs do? One e-safety expert observed that the companies might be reluctant to pay the NGOs since such action would imply consulting rather than the provision of independent advice and assistance, thus tipping the balance of the relationship.

Companies and NGOs may develop mutually beneficial partnerships whose inner workings may not be entirely disclosed to the public, or whose entire range of benefits for each party may not be clear. Reputation building, both for companies and NGOs, appears to be important here too, even if no financial compensation is involved, and even if work is delegated to some extent from companies to NGOs, as in the following example.

Facebook offered training to another NGO that provided helpline services, part of which was intended for the helpline managers to learn about Facebook's reporting tools. Details behind the financial aspects of the relationship, if there were any, were not forthcoming from the NGO, other than that there was no "written agreement," that "the partnership developed organically" as the two organizations "share the common vision," and that the company was "a natural partner" of not just this, but any helpline. Although according to the NGO, Facebook had offered the training, the NGO representative wrote to me, in response to my email query about its collaboration with the company, with the following assessment: "There was a joint decision that child helplines would find it useful to receive training on the tools offered by the company," given that they may not always know how to assist children on the platform.

Such examples, in practice, support the proposition that companies provide training for NGOs in order to benefit from the NGOs' enhanced potential to handle the cases that raise questions on company platforms, thus delegating part of the workload onto NGOs.

Summing Up the Company/NGO Relationship

NGOs play a number of important roles in helping companies address cyberbullying. Caveats regarding transparency are important to acknowledge in a system that operates in a relatively tight circle of players exhibiting close-knit relationships with interdependent actors. It might be difficult to characterize NGO advice as independent given a paucity of publicly available evidence on the nature of the relationships. Nonetheless, the companies that rely on such relationships appear to derive from them a degree of visible legitimacy for their policies and tools of enforcement in front of users, government regulators, and the wider public. Based on available information, it remains difficult to understand to what extent the NGOs can influence the decision making of these companies regarding cyberbullying and e-safety *in practice*, especially in respect to adopting those policies that may clash with the companies' business interests.

The process of delegation that occurs via advanced policies (such as partnerships with NGOs) could also allow the companies to handle their work more efficiently, as illustrated with helplines. The existence of these NGOs depends (to some extent) on social media companies because the

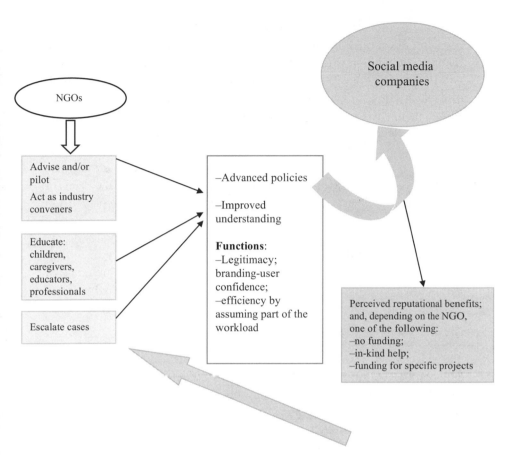

Figure 7.1
E-safety NGO functions

cyberbullying cases that take place on social networks constitute a rationale for their work. While e-safety NGOs may not always be remunerated for the number of important roles they play, the possible reputational benefits from their association with social media platforms can be an important currency as well (see figure 7.1).

Safety Centers as Hubs for Digital Citizenship?

Bullying prevention can also take place through social media companies' educational initiatives, which established companies tend to feature clustered around Safety Centers or Bullying Hubs, the sections of companies' websites devoted to information about e-safety.

Safety Centers tend to be developed with the help of NGOs and may contain educational articles about bullying prevention, typically written by or in cooperation with the NGOs that the company partners with. They can also contain educational videos, instructions on how to report content, and explanations of what the company does to resolve bullying, as well as links to the NGOs' websites. It is in these Safety Centers that the concept of "digital citizenship" or "digital citizens" comes up frequently.

Whereas the rationale for the companies' partnerships with NGOs is to solicit their expertise, the companies that describe users as their partners in ensuring safety on their platforms ask them to be good digital citizens or community members, giving them a sense of ownership in the prevention or regulation of cyberbullying.

Digital citizenship is also perceived as an advanced form of policy, sometimes described as the ability to teach or lead the community to moderate itself on its own. Getting the community of users to self-moderate or self-police also tends to be efficient for the company, which is why digital citizenship also follows the pattern of effectiveness as efficiency.

Facebook and Digital Citizenship

The video titled "Facebook Stories: We Are All Daniel Cui" once opened the Bullying Prevention Hub. This section of the company's site provides educational advice along with instructions on how to report bullying; it refers young users to expert organizations, primarily NGOs, more than 30 of those as of August 2016, where they could seek further help. The video narrative depicted Daniel Cui, a freshman soccer goalkeeper from California, who, after a streak of his team's losses, failed to keep the opponent's ball out of his net at a decisive moment (Facebook, 2015c). Soon after, a photo assembly of his failures tagged as "the worst goalie ever" emerged on Facebook, generating attention at the school. After the situation got worse and Daniel, being bullied and feeling depressed, started skipping classes. His soccer teammates made a key turn by posting a photo of Daniel where he made a save, along with a message in support of him, as their profile pictures. This created a ripple effect across the school, taking Daniel from the position of a bullied teen to a hero—an exemplary event for promoting digital citizenship.

Conveying the message that Facebook can be used for bullying but also for empowerment, the Hub asks young users to be good digital citizens while informing parents, caregivers and educators that the platform can be leveraged for good. When it was created in 2013, the Bullying Prevention Hub drew from the Compassion Research Day–related research (Compassion Research Day, 2013, see chapter 6).

Another important message on these pages explained that the platform could not take down content unless such content had violated Community Guidelines. Therefore, the focus of the Hub was on helping users build social and emotional learning skills, conflict resolution skills, and the ability to discern in which cases it is necessary to report bullying to Facebook, as well on providing instructions for how to do it.

A non-governmental organization listed on Facebook's Bullying Prevention Hub, as one of the company's Partners in Action, was the Education Development Center (EDC). The EDC had received Facebook's Digital Citizenship Research Grant and produced a study whose goal was to evaluate the role of social media platforms in addressing bullying (Schneider, Smith, & O'Donnell, 2013b). The study revealed that most students had not been aware of social media companies' efforts to address cyberbullying, such as standard reporting mechanisms. Those who had been aware doubted that these mechanisms would be effective, and some even feared retaliation if other users were to learn of their reporting.

In light of these findings, the study called for social media companies to develop guides for schools on how to incorporate a more positive use of social media in the classroom (Schneider, Smith, & O'Donnell, 2013b, p. 25). It also concluded that a successful cyberbullying prevention approach requires a "trifold" action from parents, schools, and social media, whereby the sites should ensure they were raising the visibility of their reporting efforts and enhancing bullying education initiatives that promote digital citizenship.

While the findings appear to support the actions already illustrated in the Hub—tools for users to solve their conflicts (e.g., social reporting), leveraging digital citizenship, and ensuring that the reporting mechanisms were well explained—these company efforts are yet to undergo independent evaluation of effectiveness. Furthermore, given that the EDC research had apparently been funded through the company's grant, it would be helpful if the company provided more information on its relationship with this third party.

Twitter, Google, and the YouTube Digital Citizenship Curriculum
In a manner similar to Facebook, Twitter partnered with a number of selected NGOs in different countries within its program titled "Twitter for Good" (Twitter, 2017), which the representative characterized as the company's main program for corporate social responsibility (CSR). Despite labeling this strategy as CSR, the representative, similarly to other companies, did not perceive it as an obligation but rather as part of the daily work the company

did. The partnering NGOs could receive grants from Twitter and the company could promote these NGOs' projects.

Twitter's NGO partners engaged in a number of activities—from running a helpline for children on a variety of e-safety issues and escalating these to the company, to providing Twitter with feedback on the wording in its "reporting queues," or in the articles that the company publishes on its Safety Center page.

Empowering NGOs by training them and then delegating part of the work and responsibility, appears to take place here as well:

As part of my role I travel around the world and I train these safety partners in our policies and procedures, since a lot of them run helplines and face reports from the public on a regular basis. That means that over time they develop a strong expertise on the Twitter policies, and in most situations they can find a resolution to the cases themselves. When they can't, they have a dedicated reporting mechanism and get specialized support from our safety partner support team (Patricia Cartes, Twitter, personal communication with the author, June 17, 2014).

Just like Facebook's and Twitter's Safety Centers, the jointly developed Google/YouTube Safety Center, bearing the logos of e-safety NGOs Common Sense Media and ConnectSafely.org, relied to a great extent on the concept of digital citizenship. The tips for educators included in the YouTube Digital Citizenship Curriculum explained, in a visually engaging way, how to report and flag content and provided specific lesson plans that covered the use of "Google products" in the classroom (Curriculum: Understanding YouTube . . . Lesson 4., n.d.; YouTubeCurriculum, 2012; Google, 2015b).[9]

Toward Developing Standards of Effectiveness

When providing either cyberbullying and harassment-related tips or digital citizenship education, some Safety Centers nonetheless included prescriptive messages such as "think before you post," and "tell a parent or trusted adult (report cyberbullying when you see it)." Cyberbullying was also sometimes covered together in one lesson with other e-safety issues, which, according to the previously cited evaluation, required distinct educational measures (Google, 2015a). Some Centers warned that cyberbullying had reached "epidemic proportions" and reminded parents of high-profile cyberbullying incidents that contributed to suicides. These could be classified as scare tactics, as I discussed earlier in this chapter, which the independent evaluation warned against (Jones et al., 2013). One NGO reported that when it pilot-tested some of the online documents in such centers with children, the children did not always have the patience to read through them.

While widely acknowledged in the e-safety community as important and commendable, Safety Centers may nonetheless benefit from an established and specific set of effectiveness standards, against which they could be evaluated on a regular basis by an independent body.

Digital Citizenship: Empowerment Tool or Branding Strategy?

The process described as *empowerment through digital citizenship education* can hardly be understood outside of social media companies' struggle, as one e-safety expert observed, to not only do their best but also *to be seen as doing their best*. Some company representatives would refer to digital citizenship using the term "e-safety product," contributing to the wider debate on the commercialization of citizenship. Digital citizenship, while arguably a commendable effort, is part of the companies' branding strategy, too, as instilling confidence in their users that the platform is safe becomes increasingly important for its commercial success.

Empowerment conferred via digital citizenship education also implies a delegation of responsibility for e-safety to young users who are asked by the platforms to be good digital citizens and to refrain from bullying, while being given educational and sometimes advanced reporting tools to do so.

Underlying digital citizenship education (see chapter 2) is the idea that restricting technology use and punishing students are approaches that merely attend to the symptoms behind the problem of cyberbullying and not the root causes (Ohler, 2011; Family Online Safety Institute Annual Conference, 2013; Schneider, Smith, O'Donnel, 2013b). Rather, educators in the broader community should focus on character-building education, which includes honest talks about technology and—of immediate relevance to cyberbullying—leveraging empathy (Ohler, 2011).

Perhaps most importantly, digital citizenship—at least conceptually— should ensure that not only children's right to protection, but also to participation and provision, are ensured (see Livingstone, 2016, and chapter 2). Ideally, by being good digital citizens, children can participate in online environments, and have access to digital opportunities, while being safe.

Several e-safety NGO informants from both the US and EU expressed their concerns that the term "digital citizenship" ran the danger of being used by various stakeholders merely as a rebranded or more appealing phrase for "e-safety," or as "a tool for classroom management" (see also Collier, 2014a)—that is, as a term reflecting the plethora of ineffective and scare tactics that have developed a negative reputation. Such tactics had also been traditionally applied to a wide range of e-safety issues that each required distinct educational methods. In the words of two informants:

All of us who work in this field, we are all very well-meaning, we think we know what's best for young people. The minute you talk to a young person about what's best for being a digital citizen, you have lost them. It's so uncool, they do not want to think about that. . . . We can teach them but we need to do it in a way that they do not know that we are teaching them. So this [digital citizenship] is just [the] sort of stuff you teach in the class, and they say "yes miss, yes miss" and then they go, and go and do the opposite. It's not relevant to them. (NGO representative, personal communication with the author, July 11, 2014)

It's about not providing lists of rules—often people are not doing something wrong because they don't know what the right steps are—there's a whole range of other reasons. . . . It has to be about exploring, I suppose, skills rather than just knowledge. Let's say: "I shouldn't talk to strangers." When might that be a problem and how do I recognize when I'm in a situation where actually this is fine? Because there are plenty of forums where you can go online and talk to strangers, and 99% of the time it's going to be absolutely fine. (E-safety expert, personal communication with the author, June 30, 2014)

While no single agreed-upon definition of digital citizenship emerged from interviews with NGOs and e-safety experts, and there is an acknowledgment that digital citizenship may be construed differently in various cultures, respondents nonetheless tended to agree that it centers on the idea that users should behave online as they would offline—the same rules of respect and civility apply in both spaces.

Some interviewees described digital citizenship as "a powerful tool in the preventative language." Or, in the context of cyberbullying, they define it as teaching children to stand up for the bullied ones. But evidence as to how the concept of digital citizenship worked in practice, and why it was considered an effective way to address cyberbullying, was not readily available.

One evaluation of digital citizenship proposed putting digital citizenship education into practice by focusing on the ability of youth to exercise respectful behavior and civic engagement online (Jones & Mitchell, 2015); its authors proposed that should educators indeed embrace digital citizenship as the way forward, the concept needs to be well defined and "target specific educational goals and outcomes" (p. 2074).

Company Responsibility and Self-Regulatory Effectiveness

Bearing in mind the vast number of incidents that take place on social media platforms—which may or may not amount to bullying, and many of which originate offline—it can become difficult to imagine an effective way for companies to assist in every case where two children have a falling out and send mean comments to each other one day, only to become friends again the following day.

However, some informants explained that these pervasive conflicts, which might seem mundane and perhaps even trivial from an adult perspective, are also very important in children's lives. In the following chapters I discuss why reframing the problem as one of culture and dignity rather than focusing narrowly on e-safety might shed light on innovative solutions. Furthermore, if the companies and policy makers respond to these conflicts of "falling out just to be friends again" by providing users, caregivers, and educators with tools and the necessary help to handle them on their own, then the tools and the help should be evaluated against agreed-upon standards of effectiveness from young users' perspective.

From their experience of working with children, several NGOs noticed another obstacle standing in the way of the companies' efforts at developing effective reporting tools: no matter how easy the companies make it for users to report, the most vulnerable children, those that are at the greatest risk of self-harm when cyberbullying happens, tend not to report bullying incidents or even reach out to trusted adults or peers.[10] This is precisely why it may be important to think about ways in which these children could be assisted proactively, and not merely by providing them with generic helpline contacts. I make some pertinent suggestions in the following chapters.

No Perceived Alternative to Self-Regulation
Most NGO representatives I interviewed worked with companies in some capacity and had a constructive relationship with the industry. Among those informants who expressed their attitude on industry self-regulation, no one could see an alternative to self-regulation when it comes to cyberbullying. They did not think that government laws could keep up with fast-paced technology developments, and they saw cyberbullying problems as originating offline, which is why taking content down would not get to the heart of them. Negative implications behind criminalizing children's behavior (see chapters 3 and 4 in particular) were another expressed concern. Due to such misgivings of Command and Control regulation, the NGOs I interviewed would not call for government laws as part of their activism.

Several informants observed that some NGOs that did call for government regulation of the industry did so in a way that did not necessarily help further the debate or the policy:

Some anti-bullying NGOs . . . make it their business to be critical of social networks whether they're right or not. Because they want somebody to be the bad guy and it's nice and easy to blame the industry for things, rather than trying to work with industry to improve. And we see that a lot. (NGO representative, personal communication with the author, July 11, 2014)

My attempts to secure an interview with BeatBullying, a UK-based NGO (charity) that called for legislation and criticized social media companies for their handling of bullying, met with little success. The issue of ineffectiveness when criminalizing children's behavior was occasionally raised in media coverage of BeatBullying's calls for legislation (Wilkinson, 2009; Whitworth, 2010). Another voiced a concern that although the UK law at the time did not define cyberbullying, a number of other laws could apply to cyberbullying cases; and that not having a law to address cyberbullying specifically did not necessarily leave users without possible remedies (see my discussion of these issues in chapter 3). Enforcement could be a factor as well: the police may be reluctant to intervene in cyberbullying cases unless an incident had reached a certain level of severity.

This NGO eventually closed down when the UK Charity Commission, a governmental body that registers and regulates charities in England and Wales (Charity Commission, n.d.) reported that the NGO did not comply with its reserves policy (Hillier, 2014). The *Independent* observed that the demise of the "award winning charity," which provided various types of bullying-related counseling to children, left UK children who relied on its services "in despair" (Dearden, 2014).

Is Self-Regulatory Effectiveness a Process or an Outcome?

Julian Coles is a long-standing e-safety consultant formerly with the BBC and a working member of the UK Council for Child Internet Safety, which is often characterized as a "multi-stakeholder" body that brings together government representatives, industry, NGOs, and other e-safety experts to address child safety online.[11] Coles has participated in several self-regulatory initiatives in the UK and at the EC level, including the UK-led project in which US social networking companies with global reach (including Yahoo, My Space, Facebook, YouTube, and Bebo, as well as AOL and MSN) collaborated on the Good Practice Guide for Social Networking Services in 2008.

In discussing the self-regulatory dialogue around moderation, Coles proposed re-focusing the discussion about self-regulatory effectiveness on the value of the process itself, rather than merely focusing on the document at the end of it (outcome effectiveness). According to Coles, NGOs had come into the meetings about moderation with key moderation points on their agenda. For example, they wanted industry to show what form of moderation (e.g., technical vs. human, pro-active or reactive) was being used in specific spaces; industry was resisting because they thought this would be "a hostage to fortune – the lawyers weren't at all keen." After what was described as robust negotiations[12] with NGOs and other stakeholders, Coles explained the industry recognized that some measure of transparency about the form of moderation being used would be of great value to parents. At the same time, the NGOs realized why some of their other demands may have been difficult to operationalize: for example, why (from the industry's perspective) it wasn't feasible to publish a standard maximum response time to user reports when, for instance, third-party moderation might need to be involved. It is this educational process, whereby every stakeholder is able to see the situation from the perspective of another, arriving at a level of middle ground, which might be considered as one key part of an effective self-regulatory process—in his view at least:

You did find that sometimes you changed your view about what was possible or desirable as you were doing this . . . the experience of going through it was almost as important as the outcome (Julian Coles).

Furthermore, in this view, there is sometimes a risk that legislators may try to pass laws that go further than they may themselves have intended and may even reduce the incentives for active self-regulation. For example, the UK government wanted to create a legislative requirement for moderators (where the moderation was being done in the UK) to undergo a criminal background check (e.g., to prevent child sex offenders from engaging in moderation). Coles reports there was a danger that some companies might decide that moderation itself was so risky (what if one of their moderators did "groom" a child from a position of trust?) that they would give up on moderation altogether or outsource their moderation services to other countries where standards were lower—the process previously referred to as "the international forum shopping" (see chapter 5). In the end, the legislation was more narrowly drafted than many people had feared and what Coles characterized as "the perverse incentive not to moderate at all" was significantly reduced.

E-safety experts and NGOs realized it was better to have some moderation than none at all and to trust that the companies involved would see that it was done properly, with the Good Practice Guidance on moderation becoming the recognized benchmark (UK Council for Child Internet Safety, 2010). Specific measures for what effective moderation is (and evidence thereof) are still not deployed, as Coles recognizes, but having some moderation with the good practice guidance as a standard setter was seen as better than none at all. Bearing in mind that the companies seemed to have been facing even less pressure in the US to establish benchmarks, the middle ground achieved by the guidance on moderation and social networking was considered as part of a successful educational (self-regulatory) process for the relevant stakeholders.

While Command and Control regulation was not perceived as a recommendable solution, at least among the NGOs that cooperated with the industry, an independent evaluation of social media companies' cyberbullying policies was perceived by some informants as an important self-regulatory tool, not only for assessing whether government regulation was needed, but also for the sake of sustaining the companies' business models. Furthermore, a widely reported attitude was that if bullying was present on the platform, it would likely turn users away from it—a proposition I question in the following chapter.

Tracking the Effectiveness of the NGO/Company Collaboration

NGO partnerships, predominantly a factor among the more established companies or those that suffered in the face of high-profile incidents, serve an important set of functions in assisting the design and enforcement of social media companies' cyberbullying policies. Such partnerships with NGOs can also provide the companies' policies and enforcement mechanisms with legitimacy in front of government regulators, users, and the wider public by acting as an assurance that the platform is safe.

Companies can cite their collaboration with NGOs that have an e-safety expertise or a track record of working with children as evidence in front of relevant stakeholders that they are doing their best, thus implying that the policies are effective even when they are not being continuously and independently evaluated. To what extent such NGO advice can be considered independent might be questionable, given the paucity of publicly available evidence on the details behind the partnerships.

Digital citizenship, often a key component in companies' Safety Centers and a widely commendable effort in what it professes to achieve, was also critiqued from the standpoint of effectiveness and commercialization.

Concerns were raised that it should not be used merely as "a rebranded term for e-safety," a signal of increasing delegation of responsibility away from the companies and onto young users (or caregivers and educators), or solely as a branding strategy for companies struggling to be seen as doing their best. An independent evaluation of effectiveness of digital citizenship messages that companies put into practice is advisable (see the policy solutions section, chapters 8 and 9).

III Policy Solutions

Cyberbullying policies of social media companies have not been a frequent object of academic study. My goal in researching and writing this book was to uncover the logic behind policy-making efforts. Now, I would like to explain what can be known about the strengths and limitations of the current self-regulatory environment as well as the self-organizational efforts of individual platforms. As such, this book should complement the current body of knowledge about online intermediation processes by private companies.

Advocating for Policy Effectiveness

Social media companies have come up against various pressures that contributed to the current design of cyberbullying policies and enforcement mechanisms. To explain these challenges I provide examples of what could be characterized as "misguided" pieces of government regulation (Marwick, 2008) that do not necessarily help youth solve their conflicts, but they do have serious implications for freedom of speech and the privacy of adults.

Advanced policies can position these platforms strategically in front of the public and policy makers, resulting in less independent scrutiny. Not only do the texts of these policies help elide a significant lack of transparency in how companies enforce their policies, but they also obscure the companies' profit-pursuing interests in specific policy design (Gillespie, 2010, 2015; van Dijck, 2013; Crawford & Gillespie, 2016).

However, the status quo—where standards of effectiveness are vague and not fully articulated and operationalized, nor regularly measured and evaluated—allows all multi-stakeholder actors in this space—the industry, various regulators in the US and EU, and NGOs—to participate in a system that appears to be working without necessarily taking responsibility when it is not.

With these findings in mind, this book should signal the importance of conducting independent evaluation of social media companies' enforcement mechanisms. The current self-regulatory framework provides guidelines for the minimum measures that social media companies should have in place in order to address bullying on their platforms. Establishing specific effectiveness criteria, however, in terms of what standards of effectiveness mean in the context of technological affordances of every platform, and then evaluating every platform's enforcement mechanisms against these standards, has yet to be undertaken.

The research I cite in this book should also make a strong case against criminalization of youth behavior or regulation that under the guise of protecting minors affects adult civil liberties, or indeed privacy and free speech of children themselves, without actually serving its intended purpose of addressing cyberbullying.

A constructive, nuanced, and collaborative effort toward solutions that work for children is a lot more complex than blaming the industry for not being able to solve users' behavioral or psychological problems. Yet, the industry should not use this rationale to avoid taking responsibility for bullying that occurs on its platforms. The industry's proposition—that in a large number of cases, or at least when behavior cannot be established to violate company policy, bullying can be well addressed through infrastructure that requires young users and their caregivers to handle bullying on their own—should be examined via independent evaluation.

While advanced policies involve delegating the ways in which incidents are handled to users, caregivers, and NGOs, the more important point here is their connotation, which delineates the responsibility of the industry: there is only so much the industry can do, and providing the infrastructure is said to be an effective and efficient way for the industry to fulfill its duties and take its portion of responsibility. Despite some companies' emphasis on the fact that they do take down content that needs to be taken down, the lack of transparency as to how this is done and evidence of effectiveness makes it difficult (if not impossible) to verify such claims.

How Restrictive Policies Might Affect Platform Popularity

Social media companies operate in a competitive environment: e-safety and cyberbullying policies play a particularly important role in it, by gaining and sustaining user confidence and ensuring the perception of their platform's brand as a safe one. Cyberbullying-free environments are conceptualized as part of pleasant, positive user experiences, which are vital for the commercial success of the platform.

The logic behind this claim is that cyberbullying, harassment, or abuse-infested spaces will repel users, especially young ones, and frighten their parents and caregivers—a logic confirmed by various stakeholders (companies, NGOs, independent e-safety advisers, and policy experts). The most recent speculations about the demise of Twitter and the case of Ask.fm, both discussed in this book, may support this point. The implication is that the platforms that are successful are probably also doing something right in terms of e-safety.

But a different possibility might be worth entertaining as well. A piece of evidence that is only anecdotal, yet germane to this point, emerged in my discussion with Justin Patchin, a professor of Criminal Justice at the University of Wisconsin-Eau Claire, and the co-director of the Cyberbullying Research Center who, at the time, served as an e-safety adviser to Ask.fm. Although bound by a nondisclosure agreement (NDA) as to how much he could reveal, he observed that the company had introduced strict enforcement mechanisms. And among those, filtering, which appeared to be effective in banning wording that was associated with bullying from the platform (the specific guidelines for such filtering had not been made available by the company to him either). Coincidentally, however, with this tightening of restrictive e-safety enforcement mechanisms—based on the purchase of Ask.fm by IAC, and its reported significant investment into e safety the company's popularity began to decline. Formspring, a site that used to provide similar affordances to Ask.fm, and had shut down in 2013, was speculated to have seen its demise coming due to enhanced restrictive safety measures (Taylor, 2014).

This demise, of course, can be due to numerous factors, and any possible relationship here entirely spurious. Yet the following proposition may be worth entertaining: restrictive policies (such as filtering and content removal) can significantly and negatively impact platform popularity and may be a reason for some companies' reluctance to use or strengthen such mechanisms. The argument here is not that these mechanisms would necessarily be effective (as I explain later in the chapter), but merely that such factors should be taken into consideration. While corporate policy documents characterize safety of young users as a paramount value for the company, ensuring platforms' commercial success is the less discussed and understood side of the policy coin. Patchin proposes a related question for future research: whether there is an inverse correlation between safety protections and youth participation on these platforms.

Another possibility worth entertaining is that Ask.fm was more popular when it had few policies and enforcement mechanisms in place precisely because it was an unregulated Wild West of sorts, where young users could escape the watchful eye of adults and exercise their right to be transgressive, even if that meant being hurtful and mean to others. This point may help introduce the discussion around bullying being a wider cultural and social problem: a problem of humiliation vs. dignity.

Some companies and e-safety experts may be inclined to say that there always has been and there always will be bullying, and that platforms can do little about it. Yet this observation reduces platforms' responsibility for providing venues (if not facilitating) such behavior (and monetizing it). Others say that Ask.fm, Yik Yak, or Secret spin-offs will surface in the future.

This is precisely why there should be a discussion about which minimum standards need to be in place when it comes to future start-ups. But the burden of evidence should also be placed on the more established companies to demonstrate concrete evidence for the effectiveness of the mechanisms they consider as advanced. Further, raising questions about social and cultural factors contributing to digital bullying can pave the way to avoiding techno or media panics.

Toward a Collaborative Relationship with Regulators

Investing significant resources and e-safety expertise to address cyberbullying is important not only for keeping users satisfied, but also for citing the existence of such policies in front of regulators as evidence that company self-organization is working. Advanced policies appear to ensure less government scrutiny for the companies that adopt them. Although most e-safety experts would agree on the need to establish minimum e-safety standards for start-ups, which are seen as more problematic, few perceive the need for greater supervision and evaluation of the more established companies.

A frequently observed pattern seems to be the following: start-ups that quickly develop large numbers of young users, garner negative media attention, and subsequent public anxieties over cyberbullying can then trigger an investigation by a government entity. But as the companies become more established and continue to adopt advanced policies, they tend to develop more collaborative relationships with regulators and are less frequently subjected to independent scrutiny.

Politics and Policy Makers
Perhaps it is fair to observe that policy makers, too, who are constrained by limited time and funding, are forced to prioritize. If the established companies stay out of media coverage for high-profile cyberbullying incidents

and are able "to be seen [by regulators and the public] as doing something," as one e-safety expert phrased it, then there may not be too much effort on behalf of regulators to scrutinize the effectiveness of that "something."[1]

The two self-regulatory environments in the US and the EU are very different (see chapter 5), and the European Commission can be said to play a proactive role of an industry convener, but they both exhibit a relative scarcity of independent evaluations. Investigations into Ask.fm or Snapchat in the US on behalf of the Attorneys General can better be characterized as examples of legalistic self-regulatory tradition in the US (Newman & Bach, 2004, p. 388) than efforts to establish a continuous examination of the industry's mechanisms.

Contradictions in Regulatory Environment

There is nonetheless a strong commitment to self-regulation in both the US and EU, and most informants do not see an alternative to self-regulation given that laws are seen as too slow for the fast-paced technological developments. Effective alternative regulatory measures, as some of the policy makers I interviewed observed, allow the companies to create adequate measures faster than traditional regulation would. The dangers of criminalizing youth behavior, problems around separating bullying and cyberbullying, and around defining cyberbullying, were other cited reasons as to why creating regulation can be problematic. Perhaps, as one e-safety expert observed, the ideological commitment to self-regulation, at least in the EU, may be a consequence of fearing to drive away technology investment by instituting demanding regulation, and of an inaccurate perception by governments that they do not necessarily have the expertise to create effective regulation.

Interestingly, this preference for self-regulation in the policy-making community stands in conspicuous opposition to tendencies for the "knee-jerk regulation" (Staksrud, 2013b) I discussed in chapter 4, which emerged from high-profile cyberbullying incidents. The self-regulatory framework with respect to cyberbullying allows (to an extent, at least) for a largely unregulated but nonetheless, (to an extent, at least), user-responsive industry, combined with periodic calls for laws that focus on punishment of so-called bullies (even criminalizing youth behavior) or for restrictions on youth access to technology. Research and educators caution against such approaches (see Ohler, 2011; Bulger, Burton, O'Neill, & Staksrud, 2017). Laws that focus on punishments and restrictions may do little to support dignified relationships among youth but they tend to be the preferred solutions, perhaps because they can be politically popular for those who sponsor them. Policy makers should be particularly wary of such efforts and focus their involvement on supporting a prevention-oriented, educational, infrastructure. Furthermore, government authorities should be responsible for ensuring regular independent evaluations of industry self-regulatory efforts and work toward the laws that provide funding for educational initiatives.

Establishing the Case for More Transparency

While companies see the need to handle incidents in a timely manner, for example by removing the content that violates TOS/Guidelines, they would not provide specific evidence of such effectiveness, nor would they publish the guidelines that they use for evaluating effectiveness of their own mechanisms. Some companies may say that on average all incidents are handled in 24 to 72 hours, but the evidence of such effectiveness is not provided. Most companies would also not disclose if all the cases of reported content are handled by humans, and if not, which percentage of these are automated. This is especially relevant for bullying, whereby incidents may be subtle, and relying on expertise of a human being might be crucial for determining the context behind the case and hence whether it violates TOS/Guidelines or not.

Facebook, the company often cited as leading the self-regulatory effort, does provide some statistics regarding its more advanced policy—social reporting—based on its in-house or contracted research. Such statistics show the percentage of teens who, after using social reporting to reach out to the person who bullied them, received a response from that person; as well as the percentage of teens who took such allegedly bullying content down when being told that it was hurtful.

These statistics were, however, based on a sample of US teens, while Facebook operates globally, and were not cited in the company's corporate documents, but were provided in video presentations that may not be readily available to end users. It might be beneficial for the company and other companies that conduct similar efforts to have such data readily available. Such statistics are not a result of an independent evaluation but of research conducted in-house or by the experts who consult for the company.

At the time I was writing this book there was no standing, independent, government-initiated or third party effort (either in the US or EU) to evaluate social media companies' cyberbullying policies according to a set of pre-established principles. The limited number of government-initiated, independent evaluation efforts of social media companies' tools to address abuse were dated, even at the time of my research, given that the social media landscape keeps changing significantly (Staksrud & Lobe, 2010; Donoso, 2011; O'Neill,

2014b). Most importantly, there has not been an effort to continuously evaluate these mechanisms across the industry *from the perspective of children.*

Other aspects of companies' activities that might provide such evidence of effectiveness are far from fully transparent either. The companies would typically not disclose the numbers of moderators they employ, the numbers of bullying-related reports they receive per unit in time, or the amount of financial investment they make into their e-safety and bullying-related efforts specifically.

While some companies explain that these numbers may be difficult to provide for logistical reasons, there is also the perception acknowledged by some companies that providing these numbers may not be helpful in furthering the public debate; upon seeing the numbers, the media and the public could always dismiss them as being too meager an effort in addressing issues that involve millions of users.

Perhaps most importantly, by not revealing how many moderators the companies employ with the expertise in specific languages, it becomes difficult to conceptualize how the companies handle reports of bullying in a wide variety of languages. These companies being global entities, their user base is often, to a large extent, located outside of the Anglo-Saxon speaking area and cultural domain. Bullying is a context-dependent occurrence; having not only language but also cultural expertise may be crucial for effective moderation. Moderation is often outsourced to companies in developing countries, which has been a subject of controversy in media coverage, putting the reliability of the outsourced moderators handling user data in question.

Sharing best practices in terms of policy enforcement can sometimes be subject to intercompany competition. While some companies willingly share their expertise with other, especially newer, companies, other platforms that may not be as established, and that may provide similar technological affordances, may not necessarily be willing to do so.

It may be therefore advisable for policy makers to consider requiring the companies to disclose data on *how* they exercise enforcement.

What the Language of Free Speech and Privacy Elides

The companies that place particular value on freedom of speech in their policies would not consider systems such as notice and takedown or supervised machine learning (advance crawling of the platform for bullying content ahead of it being reported) as effective tools in addressing cyberbullying on their platforms. They see notice and takedown as possibly leading to false reports and thus resulting in free-speech infringements. Likewise, algorithmic learning was characterized as largely ineffective by such companies because of the vastness of shared content on platforms and because the technology currently available cannot detect subtle forms of bullying.

This situation is one of those instances where the business motives for preferring some policies over others may not be clear and where an independent evaluation of effectiveness may be particularly relevant. Some of the bullying that happens on social media platforms such as Facebook or Twitter is described as more subtle than blatant. Supervised machine learning tools available at the time of this book's writing, were said not to be able to identify such forms of subtle bullying and could pick up on a lot of false positives. This is why some companies would not consider these tools to be effective as their application may result in false warnings and wrongful takedowns.

It is questionable, however, whether companies should wait for a "perfect tool." Rather, they may consider using the existing tools nonetheless as a way to flag potentially harmful content, which could then be further examined by human moderators. It will be most interesting to observe how other social media companies will position themselves with respect to using various forms of AI for bullying and harassment in light of Google's recent announcement that it is pursuing such options with its project Jigsaw's open-source tools called Conversation AI (Greenberg, 2016).

Another reason cited for not using proactive forms of content monitoring were fears over end users' privacy. Users are perceived as not wanting to have the content they share on these platforms among their friends (the content that is not necessarily shared with the settings set to "public") crawled by the company and potentially its moderators, a concern said to be particularly germane in the post-Snowden era.

Language that focuses on the protections of civil liberties such as freedom of speech and privacy elides not only the discussion of how such proactive forms of moderation may negatively impact users' "frictionless sharing," but also the ability of companies to profit from users' sharing practices (van Dijck, 2013).

Taking content down, flagging, or perceived surveillance might lead to users' dissatisfaction with the platforms, and thus negatively impact the companies' business models. Perhaps more importantly, such efforts may disrupt frictionless data collection. Users understand little about how companies "utilize their data to influence traffic and monetize engineered streams of information" (van Dijck, 2013, p.12).

The platforms on which bullying is less subtle and more blatant, or the newer companies that found themselves in the midst of abuse-related controversies, tend not to invoke concerns about civil liberties as much in their discourse and report providing proactive, often automatic screening and filtering tools (although the degree of "automatic" is not specified). The scale of their efforts, however, is typically not elaborated on in their policies or on their websites; but it should be noted that especially the new companies tend to conduct more operational effort than they formally specify in public.

Such evidence should provide further grounds for policy makers to consider creating a requirement for the companies to publish their operational tools of enforcement.

Transparency and Privatization of the Digital Public Sphere

A particularly problematic point is that no company (not even an established one, perceived by policy makers as well-behaving) releases to the public the guidelines that its moderators use to investigate whether a case constitutes bullying (see the discussion in chapter 6 on the leaking of Facebook's operational policies). The companies that had a rationale for the decision not to disclose the guidelines reported that, given the extensive nature of their moderators' training, such information can hardly be summarized into a piece that can be easily shared in such manner. Other concerns include the fact that bullying is so context-specific that such decisions are determined on a case-by-case basis and could not be easily generalized.

This is where the process of privatization of the digital public sphere and the tension between the need to protect from cyberbullying while also ensuring free speech is most evident. If the content cannot be taken down following a cyberbullying or a harassment-related law that may apply to cyberbullying cases, the final arbiter on the case is the particular private company in question.

The company's decisions work both ways—as much as it can leave users without remedies, the company can also wrongly decide that a case constitutes cyberbullying and infringe upon other user's freedom of speech. In the absence of sufficiently transparent information on how most companies make decisions in such cases, there is little that the public can do but trust that the companies are doing their best. This lack of complete transparency is particularly relevant for those cases where abuse or bullying reports may be used to take some valid content down that has little to do with bullying, and where such abuse of reporting tools may constitute an attack on politically unpopular speech (MacKinnon, 2012).

Creating a requirement for the companies to publish details on their moderation systems could provide another avenue for policy makers to take toward evaluating a policy's effectiveness.

Can NGOs Serve as Independent Advisers?

I was able to find little evidence to suggest that NGOs that collaborate with companies are providing independent assessment of effectiveness of companies' anti-bullying enforcement mechanisms. The NGOs that work with social media companies on developing these policies sometimes conduct pilot testing of the companies' cyberbullying intervention and prevention tools, but the results of these are not apparently published. They could also be difficult to classify as independent evaluation since the relationships between the companies and the NGOs may involve economic, in-kind, or reputational benefits, the details behind which are typically not disclosed publicly. The NGOs that collaborate with social media companies on the development of their cyberbullying policies play a number of significant roles in this process, but they also convey a sense of legitimacy to the companies' cyberbullying policies—they serve to instill confidence in their users and validate the companies' e-safety efforts in front of regulators. At the same time, the very existence of these companies provides some work for NGOs (and possibly other benefits). Although this tight-knit ecosystem can secure important services to children, parents, and educators, independent evaluation would help ensure that the mechanisms are effective from the perspective of children.

On the other hand, concerns were raised that NGOs calling for government regulation, and those critical of the companies in a negative rather than a constructive way, can have a fraught relationship with the industry and even a vested interest in being critical. A requirement for a heightened level of transparency on what NGO-industry partnerships actually entail in terms of benefits and obligations of every stakeholder could help understand the position of independence of NGO as a stakeholder.

Ensuring transparent funding for NGOs from the industry along with monitoring and evaluation of industry and NGO efforts should be a preferred policy solution to any efforts to criminalize youth behavior (Christensen, 2009; Sacco, Silbaugh, Corredor, Casey, & Doherty, 2012; Tang, 2013; Suski, 2016, cf. Bradshaw, 2013; Bulger et al., 2017).

Partnering with academic institutions in conducting independent evaluations of companies' enforcement mechanisms could also constitute an option for the future. Such institutions could bring their own funding for evaluation purposes when regulators are unable to do so. Alternatively, if the industry is to fund its own evaluation, a self-regulatory or governmental body should ensure the independence (i.e., the impartial nature of the results) of the third party conducting such evaluation. Provided that transparency and sound research design are ensured, such efforts could be executed in partnerships with NGOs as well. NSPCC, a UK charity, conducts surveys with children and parent panels to ask if they are aware of blocking and reporting mechanisms on the most popular platforms, and in some cases whether children find these tools to be helpful. NSPCC then rates the companies accordingly in a simple way for parental and children's information (NetAware, 2017).

Researchers could consider creating fictitious profiles of child users on various platforms in an attempt to test enforcement mechanisms (Staksrud & Lobe, 2010).[2] Surveys, focus groups, in-depth interviews, participant observation, or more innovative methods (Barbovschi, Green, & Vandoninck, 2013), with the goal of understanding how children use these enforcement mechanisms and think about effectiveness, could also inspire a proactive solution.

The Digital Citizenship Debate

Digital citizenship education, often a key component of companies' Safety Centers, was characterized as an advanced policy and referred to as "the way forward." Yet a number of respondents, among them internationally recognized e-safety experts, voiced their concerns about the perceived effectiveness of this approach, noting that it should do more than rebrand the term "e-safety," which has a negative reputation (in the US at least) precisely because of its instructional tone and educational tactics that were not always found to resonate with youth (see Jones et al., 2013; Collier, 2014a).

A factor that appears to influence social media companies to adopt digital citizenship is yet again that they are under a lot of pressure to make an effort regarding e-safety but also *to be seen as making an effort*. With such implications, corporate social responsibility may be a more suitable term for digital citizenship, even when companies report that they do not perceive it as CSR.

Perhaps most importantly, this policy also signals delegation of responsibility away from companies and onto young users, educators, parents, and NGOs. It is up to young users to be good digital citizens, and if companies provide the tools (such as Safety Centers) for young users to learn how to be good digital citizens (together with tools that allow the community of users to self-moderate or self-police), then bullying will become less of a problem—or at least become the users' problem. After all, in companies' corporate policy discourse, the problem of bullying is sometimes described as one of "few mean users," not as behavior that is pervasive on their platforms. Referring young users, parents, caregivers, and educators to NGOs for digital citizenship and bullying advice in general constitutes another aspect of delegating both the actual work and responsibility.

To further compound this point, digital citizenship was sometimes described by company representatives as "e-safety *product.*" This apparent consumerization of the concept of citizenship is worth exploring further and mirrors the debate on users as citizens versus consumers. As consumers, children are afforded a more circumscribed set of rights than as citizens (Staksrud, 2013a, pp. 151–155; see also Drotner & Livingstone, 2008). Elisabeth Staksrud writes, "As a consumer, our participatory rights are not secured. Our rights are not linked to us as subjects but to the product in question and our relationship with it, given that we are able to, and choose to, procure it" (Staksrud, 2013a, p. 154). But when applied to social media platforms, which, despite their scale, remain private companies and not public utilities, such conflation becomes problematic. This debate links to the question of protection versus participation rights (see chapter 9) and is important lest digital citizenship becomes a term that is largely commodified and stripped of meaning—used merely for companies to be seen as doing something in front of the public and the regulators.[3] It is, further, especially important in the context of underage users and the General Data Protection Regulation (GDPR) discussed in chapter 9.

Perhaps in contrast with a fairly decisive embrace of digital citizenship as a way forward, there have been surprisingly few studies to examine its effectiveness when applied in the context of e-safety education (Jones & Mitchell, 2015). Developing effective strategies to address the complex psychological and developmental phenomena such as bullying and cyberbullying requires more than a brief set of instructional messages; rather, at the very least, it demands a sustained effort at social-emotional learning.

Industry as "Judge and Jury"

A valid question to ask is whether users and governments would want the industry to be the "judge and jury," as one informant phrased it, of cyberbullying cases on the platforms. This is why providing users with tools to resolve bullying incidents among themselves, rather than having the companies decide on the incidents, was described as an effective way of dealing with the problem. But as it stands now, even with the advanced policies, the companies are still the final arbiters, on what constitutes cyberbullying on their platforms and thus violates their corporate policy, while the details of how this decision-making is done are largely kept away from the public.

Private Platforms versus the Public Sphere

Some government regulators may not fully recognize that social media platforms are indeed venues where the digital public sphere unfolds, and that they have taken on the nature of public utilities. Instead, regulators see platforms primarily as businesses that the government is legally prohibited from interfering with, unless they are of course in violation of the law, which may further contribute to regulators' preference for little or no involvement. Such a situation seems further compounded by regulators' fear that by becoming involved in the companies' work, they could be perceived as interfering in the free-speech arena. Hence, they may not see it as problematic that the details behind private companies' decision-making processes on what is taken down and what stays on the platform are not transparent.

A relevant illustration or test case as to what can happen when legislation places decision-making responsibilities concerning takedown requests made to a private company is the aftermath of the "Right to be Forgotten" ruling by the European Court of Justice. It gave individuals the right to ask the Google Search Engine to consider delisting content that may poorly reflect on these individuals from its search results. Google then has to weigh the public interest in knowing such information against the damage made to a particular person if it were to publicize such information.

While Google has thus far complied with a number of delisting requests, "this has been done without disclosing its internal processes, removal criteria or how it is prioritizing cases" (Powles & Chaparro, 2015). The decision-making process has been characterized as "idiosyncratic," and Google was said to have shaped the interpretation to its own corporate ends.

Google tried to legitimize this process by creating an advisory council comprising reputable experts on the issue (an idea remarkably similar to Facebook's Safety Advisory Board or Twitter's Safety Council), which according to the *Guardian* was an attempt to "insulate the process with a veneer or authenticity" (Powles & Chaparro, 2015).

If legislation were to institute similar demands on social networking systems for cyberbullying, the result may be a deluge of complex situations from a legal standpoint. The law may also miss its initial purpose of helping children in resolving their bullying-related issues. A content takedown model could be useful for specific types of bullying (see the mention in this chapter regarding the Digital Millennium Copyright Act [DMCA], as well as discussions in chapters 1 and 3), but it should take into account an understanding of the complexity around creating a privatized bureaucracy for these purposes.

Another content takedown model illustrated in this book is the Australian bill "Enhancing Online Safety for Children Act," which created an Office of the Children's e-Safety Commissioner designed to help users complain if a social media company did not take down the content reported as bullying within 48 hours after a user had reported it. If the commissioner then issued a takedown request, the social media company would be obliged to respond or pay a fine of AU$17,000 for every day that the content remained on the site (Sharwood, 2014, 2015; Office of the Children's eSafety Commissioner, n.d.). The law arguably limits negative implications for the freedom of speech for adults as it only applies to cyberbullying content affecting "an Australian child." Nonetheless, cyberbullying material is broadly defined in a way that is very much subject to interpretation as "the material [that] would be likely to have the effect on the Australian child of seriously threatening, seriously intimidating, seriously harassing or seriously humiliating the Australian child" (Parliament of Australia, n.d., please see page 7 in this document for the complete definition). The boundaries of "serious" are presumably left at the discretion of the commissioner and the extent to which such a solution actually helps children is yet to be the subject of research.

What impact this law might have on the process of "frictionless sharing" and companies' business models through advertising and data collection is a question rarely raised in the public discourse concerning such actions. Perhaps there is little doubt that calls to action about cyberbullying in the aftermath of high-profile incidents will continue to be met with public approval (and hence be politically popular). But ensuring regular evaluations of effectiveness of these takedown provisions from the perspective of children is crucial for understanding the value of such actions, especially if some of the most vulnerable and self-harm-prone children are not likely to report abusive content, as some informants observed. On the other hand, government regulation that would leverage public funding for educational purposes may hold more promise of effectiveness, yet it seems far less politically popular among politicians and policy makers.

Addressing the Anonymity Issue

Another element in some sites' cyberbullying policies and practices is anonymity. Although it can be a valuable asset in protecting controversial opinions, in light of the findings that in many cases victims of cyberbullying or harassment know the so-called perpetrators (Mishna, 2012; Kowalski, Giumetti, Schroeder, & Lattanner, 2014), anonymity is not necessarily the key component of the problem. Rather than thinking that platforms allowing anonymous users are *inherently* more conducive to bullying, it may be more helpful to think of them as venues where different types of bullying take place.

While incidents on platforms such as Facebook, Twitter, and YouTube may be more subtle, using fewer swear words and more ironic videos, allusive references or "subtweets," the bullying on Ask.fm, Secret, Whisper, Yik Yak, or other (largely) anonymous platforms may be more blatant and sometimes, perhaps, easier to identify and take action on. What we choose to think of and label as cyberbullying can become a tool in framing certain platforms as conducive to bullying versus not conducive to bullying, leading to further simplification in an understanding of the phenomenon's nuances. Consider that some digital messaging apps see themselves as providers of "private communication." As such, they do not think of themselves as platforms likely to witness bullying—which can absolve them, and future platforms providing similar services, from duty to develop specific children- and bullying-oriented policies and enforcement mechanisms. Cyberbullying can take various forms, and if content is not shared publicly but only among friends, or even if it does not "stick around long" (ConnectSafely, n.d.) that may not necessarily mean that cyberbullying is less likely to occur. Rather, when cyberbullying happens, it will, perhaps, take different forms.

Consider also the research indicating that it may be easier for bystanders to express support when they perceive themselves to be anonymous (Macháčková, Dedkova, Ševčíková, & Cerna, 2013). Until there has been an independent audit on whether and how exactly "the real name culture" contributes to diminished bullying on various platforms, calls to ban anonymity should be regarded with caution. No platform publishes any statistics on rates of incidents of bullying, and it is hard to assess how pervasive various types of bullying are on each of them.

Policy Recommendations

Based on these findings, several recommendations emerge that might be useful for guiding the policy, granted that the subsequent passages may reflect the following difficulty:

Policy makers may be sceptical about recommendations from researchers who fail to grasp the political necessity of forging consensus among rival constituencies, whereas researchers may see policymakers as too quick to compromise on issues where such tactics are not supported by empirical findings. (Lunt & Livingstone, 2012, p. 156 citing Kunkel, 1990, p. 116)

When Publishing Policy Guidelines, Define and Disclose

In an effort to ensure more transparency, companies should publish their policies and provide more information about what they consider to be cyberbullying, specifically in the context of their platforms' technological affordances: how they define it, for example, meaning the specific behaviors their moderators would consider to be cyberbullying; what counts on their platforms as "repetition"; what contextual factors they take into consideration; and how they proceed with deciding whether a case constitutes cyberbullying.

Given that platforms tend to outsource their moderation, they may leave these criteria at the discretion of the outsourced companies or consider it proprietary information and therefore feel no obligation to make it public. Such circumstances illustrate the complexity of leaving the governance of the public sphere and the provision of children's rights—as a matter of protection, but also participation—primarily in the hands of private companies.

Similarly, companies should consider publishing how many bullying reports they receive per unit in time and how quickly they handle them in practice, and what percentage of these reports is handled by humans versus automated learning. Furthermore, publishing which specific enforcement mechanisms they use and whether they use proactive algorithmic crawling on their platforms (e.g. some application of methods similar to supervised machine learning), and how they execute it, could be another step toward a more transparent framework that may not have to hurt companies' business models and could actually instill greater confidence in users.

The less established companies should provide explanations as to which enforcement mechanisms they have in place and how these work, and they should also provide clear and specific guidelines for caregivers and adults working with children to help them understand how the given platform attends to e-safety. Ensuring that venture capital firms that fund social media start-ups understand some of the minimum e-safety requirements in connection to children and cyberbullying, and making these minimum standards a prerequisite for providing funding, could be a step in this direction.

In the case of established companies: provide evidence of effectiveness of the companies' enforcement mechanisms in ways that are more readily available to users. For instance, the companies that already conduct in-house research on effectiveness of their tools of enforcement could display this evidence in a clear and prominent manner. Such efforts could also be favorable to the companies' business models, of which e-safety is an important component.

As long as companies do not disclose specific evidence of effectiveness of their policies (in accordance with how they define this effectiveness for their specific platform), and as long as various regulators do not conduct continuous monitoring and evaluation of this effectiveness, it will be difficult to assess the success of the self-regulatory and self-organizational work.

Make "Safety by Design" a Requirement for Start-Ups

Some informants voiced the perception that every company in the industry affects not only the strength of self-regulation but also the industry's reputation. If smaller companies and start-ups are not doing enough, their behavior affects the perception of the entire industry, even the more established companies. A concern with the smaller companies is that their popularity and user base grow quickly while their e-safety expertise may be lagging behind.

In an attempt to address this issue, the UK Council for Child Internet Safety (UKCCIS) created "A Practical Guide for Providers of Social Media and Interactive Services" (Gov.uk, 2016). According to Julian Coles, a working member of UKCCIS and a long-standing e-safety consultant formerly with the BBC, the idea behind it is to encourage businesses, including start-ups, to think about "safety by design" to help make their platforms safer for children and young people under 18. One way to spread the message is to see that the guide is distributed to venture capital (VC) firms interested in funding social media start-ups, with the aim that some of these good practices in the guide could in effect become preconditions for funding the newer, smaller social media platforms and services in the future—helping to protect the VC investment and the young social media brand's reputation.

It is worth noting, however, that these guidelines are based on input and best practices of established social media companies with Safety and Help Centers that had, nonetheless, *not* been independently tested for five years at the time of this book's writing (since Donoso, 2011; see also O'Neill, 2014b with the caveat that this evaluation did not include specific testing of the sites, as I elaborated in chapter 5).

Establishing Specific Criteria of Effectiveness

Currently, any discussion of the effectiveness of cyberbullying policies takes place in the absence of specific criteria of what is considered an effective tool of enforcement. Following self-regulatory guidelines, social media companies should have "simple and robust reporting tools for users" (Staksrud & Lobe, 2010; Donoso, 2011; Lievens, 2016). What is considered to be "robust" and "simple," however, is not specified *in relation to the particular technological affordances of specific platforms*, especially bearing in mind the swiftness with which new platforms gain popularity among youth. Given the great variability in technological affordances of these companies, establishing a one-size-fits-all definition may not be advisable. This is why having an independent evaluation agency develop specific criteria for each platform (in cooperation with the platform itself and with the help of various stakeholders such as the NGOs) could be helpful.

Options for Establishing a Standing Body as an Independent Evaluator

Policy makers could consider establishing a standing body (agency) whose purpose would be to conduct independent oversight and evaluation of the companies' policies and tools of enforcement. An independent evaluation would not be commissioned by, paid for, or executed by the companies themselves or by any related bodies that might have financial, in-kind, or reputational benefits from the companies. Alternatively, if commissioned and paid by a company, this body (agency) or a government regulator should assert the ability of the third party conducting the evaluation to provide impartial evidence and advice. Given that evaluations were described as costly and that it may be difficult for policy makers to find funding even for standard regulatory instruments, let alone alternative ones, then encouraging independent researchers and academic institutions to engage in such research could be an avenue to consider.

Consider Independent Evaluation of Digital Citizenship Advice

Conducting an independent evaluation of the content of social media companies' Safety Centers might be a useful next step in further driving this aspect of advanced policies. If education and digital citizenship advice provided in the centers is indeed a way forward, there should be evidence to support this claim.

Caution with Regulatory Requirements

This book calls for a more nuanced understanding of what responsibility means when it comes to platforms and against introducing government regulation that is not supported by research. Establishing traditional forms of regulation (which should be research-based) that actually work for children and teens when it comes to bullying can be very difficult. I suggest focusing on several factors that are infrequently considered when contemplating regulation.

Platforms significantly differ in terms of their technological affordances and definitions of online behaviors; the term "cyberbullying," for instance, is frequently conflated with harassment and cyberstalking, or indiscriminately applied to children and adults. Cyberbullying is used to denote everything from violent threats and trolling, to the cases of relational bullying or drama.

And while all can be equally harmful, companies can consider relational bullying as too pervasive, ineffective, and inefficient for them to police; rather they deem it best handled by parents, educators and children themselves. Any regulatory effort would need to begin with a thorough understanding of what the companies consider to be bullying (or harassment or abuse) on their platforms, an examination of what this means in practice when it comes to children and teens, and, consequently, the scale at which each type is present on each platform. Such an understanding can be achieved by asking for a greater degree of transparency on behalf of the companies.

Pros and Cons of Notice and Takedown
For those cases where cyberbullying is meant to signify blatant harassment (e.g., one or more users repeatedly targeting another, a whole page devoted to harming someone's reputation, or where violent threats are involved) rather than relational bullying, a DMCA-like notice and takedown could work for some children under such circumstances. Such a tool could be prone to abuse, but mishandled reporting could be addressed through additional human moderation. The downside of such an effort would be that, especially for start-ups with fewer resources and little means to invest in human moderation, it might inadvertently serve as an incentive to keep even non-bullying content down to shield from possible liability. Furthermore, such an effort may also present a peril to the companies' business models by affecting users' satisfaction with the platforms. This is why proposing any such solution should be handled with great caution and a robust research effort *ahead of* considering any legislation.

For instance, we need to be able to understand to what extent and under which circumstances taking content down actually helps young users (Van Royen, Poels, & Vandebosch, 2016). Such content takedowns may be effective for those online spaces that the legal scholar Brian Leiter called "cyber-cesspools," which are "devoted in whole or in part to demeaning, harassing, and humiliating individuals." Not surprisingly, Leiter sees them coupled with "implied threats of physical or sexual violence, "non-defamatory lies and half-truths about someone's behavior or personality," "demeaning and insulting language," "tortuous defamation," and "infliction of emotional distress" (Leiter, 2010, p. 155; see also Citron, 2014a).

I would argue, however, that bullying among children is a phenomenon that more often than not requires more layered solutions than merely content takedowns. Whereas repeated abuse of an individual could require content takedown to make a point that such action is not sanctioned and to stop the abuse, solving relational problems requires more complex solutions.

Further, based on the findings I present in this book, it is highly unlikely that the self-regulatory environment, either in the US or EU, would favor such an approach, especially given the availability of blocking and reporting mechanisms provided by the companies, which purport to do just that (yet whose evidence of effectiveness they nonetheless do *not* provide). And finally, it is questionable to what extent parents and caregivers (who could request such content takedowns) are in the position to make educated and constructive choices in such situations that place children's rights to protection and participation in conflict.

What about Filtering and Supervised Machine Learning?

Filtering may be more suitable for the platforms where bullying tends to be blatant and open, and this mechanism is particularly interesting given its above-discussed relationship with platforms' business models. As long as companies chose not to publish the details of how filtering is implemented, it will be difficult to assess its implications for free speech. If the companies were willing to measure and disclose the incidence of reported bullying incidents before and after the introduction of filtering, such statistics may improve public understanding as to the extent to which such tools could be considered as effective. Consider also some of the research findings suggesting that filtering specific words may fail to deliver due to users' ability to leverage "lexical variations" in order to circumvent restrictions (Chancellor et al., 2016). While Instagram may filter search results for hashtags typically associated with eating disorders, users who wanted to tag such content quickly found ways to bypass the restrictions by turning "anorexia" into "anorexiaa" and "thigh gap" into "thyghgapp" (see Chancellor et al., 2016).

Despite a number of companies' reluctance to employ supervised machine learning because the algorithms are described as unable to detect subtle bullying through irony, for instance, using these tools to crawl publicly shared information on the platforms (thus minimizing privacy infringements) could be effective enough at preventing these conflicts from escalating by flagging some content in advance for the moderators' review.

Ensuring Help for the Most Vulnerable Children

A number of laws I examine in this book, had been proposed or passed on the grounds of preventing future self-harming incidents in connection to suicides, implying they would ensure assistance for the most vulnerable children, those at the highest risk of self-harm. But as I discussed earlier, rather than necessarily providing such help by specifically targeting children at high risk of harm, they even threatened the personal freedoms of adults.

It will be crucial to evaluate the extent to which future legislation proposed in the name of preventing suicides would actually and specifically identify and target children at high risk of self-harm. In addition, other solutions may include the following: On behalf of the industry, ensuring that products are tested with vulnerable children is important, as reported by some NGOs. Joint public and industry funding for mental health professionals to engage with children who share self-harming content on social networks could be another proposed solution. Rather than merely providing a helpline number, they could engage in conversations with children.

Such public health monitoring can be ethically problematic in its privacy implications, and this point should be acknowledged, especially if it were to be applied to the communication that is shared with the settings set to "private" or "limited" or on messaging apps rather than publicly. It is precisely the regulation that would provide funding for education or user empowerment that is much needed, and was largely missing from various proposals for the regulation that I discussed earlier in this book.

Finally, ensuring that helplines receive some funding from the industry for their overhead expenses in a manner transparent to the public could reflect the process of work delegation in a more equitable manner.

Tax-Based Incentives?

Once there is an agreed-upon set of standards of effectiveness established via self-regulatory initiatives, the regulators could entice companies to comply by providing "tax rebates or grants [. . .] to shape firms' behavior in directions desired by governments or the public" (Lunt & Livingstone, 2012, p. 25, cf. Baldwin & Cave, 1999). Such actions could be used to motivate firms to comply with, for instance, providing evidence of effectiveness of their reporting tools, or funding educational measures previously evaluated as "effective" —not only for children but for parents and caregivers, too, especially in light of how much onus is placed on parental responsibility (consider COPPA and the GDPR). While the industry may argue that providing social media guides for parents is enough, such methods should be evaluated against previously agreed upon measurable standards of effectiveness.

The most recent debates over how much taxes social media companies should pay in countries where they physically operate are relevant here (Sandle & Humphries, 2013; Gibbs, 2016), and in light of this question, a more difficult one arises: Should the provision of educational measures (as long as these measures are research-based and regularly evaluated against established standards of effectiveness) be mandated rather than merely recommended or left to the companies' good will?

Social Reporting–Type Tools for Use among Peers

As for the cases where cyberbullying is a problem that takes place in the context of peer relationships and social positioning, social reporting tools or similar mechanisms could be well positioned to address this issue by facilitating proactive coping strategies and thus helping children build resilience (d'Haenens, Vandoninck, & Green, 2013). These tools may actually help children in the process of social positioning by addressing the origin of the problem, which could be offline. In any event, tools of this kind should be regularly and independently evaluated, and regulators and the public might wish to pay attention as to how advanced mechanisms can be discursively leveraged by platforms to delegate responsibility for cyberbullying away from their companies and onto young users, caregivers, educators, and NGOs.

9   Toward a Culture of Dignity

Against the context of the dignity framework I discussed in chapter 2, a number of punitive measures outlined in this book do not appear to address the heart of the bullying and cyberbullying problem: the relational dynamic among young people. Removing content, punishing individuals involved, criminalizing behavior, or having the companies pay fines without investing in education or psychological counseling seem merely to address the symptoms, rather than the root causes of the problem.

Toward Dignity-Based Solutions

Fostering conditions where dignity is more than part of a catchphrase (i.e., occasionally invoked in policy circles without concrete implications attached to it) requires a research-based effort to understand what is effective for youth. This is especially pertinent as they struggle to navigate the process of social positioning, which is part of their development but which persists into adulthood as well.

The normative framework of dignity can help elucidate how the struggle for popularity among a group of teens—where good looks, money, branded clothing, or any criterion of "coolness" are a measure of success—may not be much different from the world of adults where individuals are encouraged to derive their self-worth from high-ranking and well-paid jobs, or other insignia of social status (Fuller, 2003, 2006; Fuller & Gerloff, 2008; Hicks, 2011). The struggle for popularity among teens may result in exclusion of certain children from a group, or even in drama or cyberbullying, just like the more severe examples of adults striving and struggling for power can escalate into mobbing or workplace bullying. Or perhaps either may leave little trace or symptoms other than quiet suffering—which nonetheless, I would argue, warrants the question of what kind of a society we want to live in, and if this is the best we can do. Although such questions may be dismissed as utopian (the observation that "there always has been and there always will be bullying" cropped up during this research process time and again), it is also true that as long as we continue to perceive and treat them as utopian, they will continue to be so. Asking such normative questions can allow us to go beyond seeking faults or deviance within individuals, and merely stigmatizing "bullies" or "perpetrators" and casting them against "helpless victims," by noticing wider social and cultural patterns at play.[1]

Introducing these discussions into school curricula may be a good place to start, as well as asking the industry to convene workshops or other venues where young people could discuss how they see these problems or how their platforms could be used to facilitate such discussions. Introducing skill-based education to children on how to detect "warning signs of rankism" (Fuller & Gerloff, 2008) or imagining what it would look like in practice to think and live by the ten elements of dignity proposed by Donna Hicks (2011)— both of which I discuss in chapter 2—could constitute a way forward and become a component of digital citizenship education. What is important here is *not to impose any normative conclusions onto children* lest such efforts backfire in a way that prescriptive e-safety messages did—or as digital citizenship may, when used merely as a rebranded term for compliance as compromise (Collier, 2014a). Such skill-based education needs to be adapted to target children's respective age groups, and it can take place through play or fun exercises. Prior to their introduction into the curricula or incorporation into self-regulatory initiatives, these educational strategies should be tested through research for their ability to resonate with children.

Facebook could, perhaps, argue that the company is already moving in this direction: the Bullying Prevention Hub provides examples of how the platform can be used to combat bullying and promote prosocial behavior. They could also cite the Anti-bullying Ambassadors Program Showcase event, which I refer to in chapter 1, as a program that speaks the language children understand, thus succeeding at making it cool *not* to be a bully. But if efforts like these are to be adopted as models for successful multi-stakeholder interventions, they need to be continuously independently evaluated, and the companies must also be able to provide concrete evidence of effectiveness of their reporting and other anti-bullying enforcement mechanisms. Companies should use these multi-stakeholder initiatives as more than public image boosters: in other words, for more than the appearance of "doing something," while ensuring that their particular platform is perceived as both safe and cool among young users, their parents, caregivers, educators, and regulators.

This debate is closely connected to the issue of rights, and to what it means *in practice* to ensure that children have the rights to protection but also to provision and participation, and what platforms' responsibilities are in ensuring those rights. Despite the growing evidence that scare tactics in e-safety education tend to backfire, it still appears to be difficult, at least in the US, to move away from fear-infused rhetoric (Gibson, 2016). The question of how to ensure safety in the face of online risks while also enabling children to capitalize on digital opportunities is the challenge that lies ahead. Research findings from the EU Kids Online network indicate that restrictive practices may perhaps ensure less exposure to online risks from harms such as cyberbullying, but the more exposure to risks children face, the more they may also be likely to capitalize on opportunities in online environments, such as the acquisition of digital skills and access to learning that digital environments can afford (EU Kids Online, 2014; Livingstone, Mascheroni, & Staksrud, 2015; Livingstone, Mascheroni, & Staksrud, 2017). Furthermore, a certain amount of exposure to risk may be necessary for building resilience, which is also part of the learning process. Rather than vilifying certain apps, or advocating for their banishment, or introducing provisions that interfere with civil liberties, those who channel their energies on laws that purport to prevent future suicides should focus on identifying vulnerable children, especially those that are most likely to resort to self-harming practices, and on ensuring that they receive the right help before the problems escalate.

Rights versus Company Responsibility

Whatever a good balance of protection versus provision and participation looks like in theory, let alone in practice, is far from straightforward and is perhaps well illustrated in the most recent vehement debate around the EU's General Data Protection Regulation (GDPR), adopted in 2016 and coming into effect in 2018. GDPR introduces a provision like the much older COPPA regulation in the United States that prohibits social media companies from collecting personal information specifically from children under a certain age (Fernback & Papacharissi, 2007; Montgomery, 2015). After what was characterized as an opaque and behind-closed-doors GDPR negotiation process—lacking impact assessment (Carr, 2016; Collier, 2016) that did not seem to honor children's right to participation by soliciting their opinions on the subject—age 16 emerged as the minimum proposed age to use a social media platform (the equivalent was age 13 under COPPA), perhaps much to the irritation of the companies (boyd, 2015).[2]

Such a measure would effectively require social media companies to ban access to those under 16, as they would now to those under 13, or go through what could be a tedious process resulting in more data collection to ensure verifiable parental consent from those under 16. Eventually, the European Commission decided to leave it open to individual member states to settle on a specific age (between 13 and 16) within their jurisdiction—possibly making matters worse as the companies would now have to be mindful of the differences between the EU countries.

It is questionable how the GDPR could be more effective than COPPA when overwhelming evidence in both the US and EU shows that numerous tweens (10-to-12-year-olds) or even younger children are using social media (boyd et al., 2011; Livingstone, Olafsson, & Staksrud, 2011). One may also legitimately ask if the idea behind obtaining parental consent is justified if few parents understand the process of data collection, and giving them the power of consent may not make them more informed (boyd, 2015). This can also become problematic when LGBTQ children need access to some social media sites, they may not wish to let their parents know about their sexual orientation; let alone abused children who may turn to social media platforms to escape such abuse and seek help from peers (boyd, 2015; Hinduja, 2016).

Companies, of course, report to remove underage accounts when notified and, when asked how many underage children they have on their platforms, respond with "none that we are aware of," as the law absolves them from liability if there is no awareness.

Perhaps they do not know *how* many, but they are surely aware that there are many—at the very least there is research to support such observations (boyd et al., 2011; Livingstone, Olafsson, & Staksrud, 2011). An e-safety expert observed that anonymous platforms could do little in the way of knowing who the underage users were given the technological affordances of such platforms. Yet, I wonder to what extent this can be considered as an accurate observation, considering the current level of sophistication of data processing for advertising purposes.

When the European Commission proposed 16 as the minimum age, the companies, as well as some members of the e-safety community, raised the issue of participation and provision rights, emphasizing that teens should not be banned from social media platforms in the name of protection without even being consulted—which is, indeed, a legitimate concern. There's another question that could be asked here: If social media companies care about children's rights in practice, should they not be equally worried about their underage users who, given that they are using platforms in violation of the policy, are invisible to the platform (even as consumers let alone as citizens)? This is what Elisabeth Staksrud aptly calls "illegal digital aliens" (see Staksrud [2013a, pp. 156–163]). Or, put differently, what kind of a regulatory mechanism do we need in order to encourage the companies to innovate for children under 13 if COPPA prompted them to stop doing so (boyd, 2015)? As it stands now, cyberbullying policies and enforcement mechanisms are not even designed with illegal digital aliens in mind, and social media companies have no responsibility for ensuring their right even to protection from cyberbullying.

Here are other pertinent questions to ask, perhaps: What does a commitment to digital citizenship, provision, and participation rights on behalf of the platforms entail, beyond merely discursively deploying these terms when doing so favors companies' interests? What are *the practical* implications behind companies' commitment to digital citizenship? In the case of GDPR and COPPA, this might mean ensuring *in practice* that data is not collected from those under 13. Would platforms have an incentive to formally allow those under 13 on their platforms if it had to be guaranteed that their personal information was not collected in order to honor their digital citizenship and full spectrum of rights—protection, provision, and participation? Perhaps not, because platforms are indeed private companies even when they acquire the scale and substance of public utilities

Using privacy policy as an illustration, ensuring the full spectrum of rights, therefore, is a shared responsibility of the social media industry and of regulators in designing a law that actually accomplishes its goal (if a ban on collecting personal information from those under 13 is indeed what regulators wish to achieve), rather than creating a law that provides only nominal safeguards. Honoring the full spectrum of rights and dignity in the context of digital bullying is to ensure that the mechanisms provided (be it reporting, or advanced *"products"* such as "digital citizenship") are actually effective from young people's perspective, and understanding what effectiveness means for young people may be a good place to begin.

Appendix A

Chapter 6 is an analysis of social media companies' Terms of Service (TOS) and Community Standards/Principles/Guidelines, as well as any other cyberbullying-related policies that the companies may have in their corporate documents; the companies' corporate statements and blogs; the media coverage these policies have received; the legislation that surfaced in relationship to the platforms; and the interviews with company and NGO representatives and e-safety experts.

My initial research and analysis was conducted, together with the majority of the interviews, as part of my doctoral dissertation research, in 2014 and 2015, and updated between May and October 2016 to reflect relevant changes, where applicable. Some of the most recent media-related developments from 2017 have been added in the meantime. Thus my account attempts to provide a longitudinal perspective as well. For my doctoral research, I interviewed representatives from the following companies: Facebook and Facebook-owned Instagram, Twitter, Ask.fm, YouTube, Voxer, Secret, and Yik Yak. I edited, or omitted from the manuscript altogether, some or all of the information from the interviews upon the request of certain companies or due to the inability to obtain a written release from a non-disclosure agreement for the purpose of this book. I do not disclose the names and specific titles of the representatives to protect their anonymity (unless they provided explicit written permission for use of their names); the representatives either held high-ranking positions at their respective companies' Safety or Policy teams or held high-ranking positions in their company leadership (such as CEO positions). Other companies either did not reply to repeated interview requests over the two-year period of time or replied but did not provide an interview.

The e-safety NGOs and organizations I interviewed as part of doctoral dissertation research or as part of the book writing process include: two members of the UK Council for Child Internet Safety (UKCCIS) who did not speak on behalf of the organization but in the capacity of independent e-safety experts and consultants; a representative of the Child Exploitation and Online Protection Center (CEOP), a National Crime Agency Command in the UK that works specifically on child protection online; the UK-based NGO Childnet; the NGO Family Online Safety Institute (FOSI), based in Washington, DC, and London; Two NGOs that provide helpline services and whose

Table A.1
User base

Company	User base
1. Facebook	1.39 billion monthly active users, October 2014 (Protalinski, 2014). 1.71 billion monthly active users, June 2016 (Newsroom.fb.com, 2016)
2. YouTube	More than 1 billion users, October 2016 (YouTube, n.d.b).
3. WhatsApp	700 million monthly active users, January 2015 (Statista, n.d.a.).
4. Google+	300 million monthly active users January 2015 (Smith, 2016). However, the status of this network's popularity is contested (e.g., Gallagher, 2015).
5. Tumblr	420 million users, not specified if it was active monthly, October 2014 (Dredge, 2014). 305 million blog accounts, July 2016 (Statista, n.d.b).
6. Instagram	More than 300 million, not specified if monthly active, December 2014 (Statista, n.d.c). 500 million monthly active users, June 2016 (Smith, 2016).
7. Twitter	284 million active monthly users, end of 2014 (Statista, n.d.d). 313 million monthly active users, September 2016 (Twitter, 2016g).
8. Kik	200 million monthly active users, January 2015 (Kik, 2015). 300 million registered users as of May 2016, (Statista, n.d.e).
9. Ask.fm	180 million active users per month (according to my interview with the company representative, November 2014). 150 million "monthly uniques," September 2016 (Ask.fm, 2016e).
10. Snapchat	100 million monthly active users, August 2014 (Shontell, 2015). 150 million *daily* active users, June 2016 (Ingram, 2016).
11. Whisper	20 million monthly users, December 2015 (Kosoff, 2015).
12. Yik Yak	Almost 2 million monthly active users, December 2014, allegedly dropped to under two million in 2016 (Constine, 2016).
13. Voxer	70 million users, according to some sources, in 2012 (Phaneuf, 2012).
14. Secret	Did not release numbers but was included in the study based on controversial reputation in the media regarding cyberbullying (see Woollaston, 2015).

names I omit here to protect quote anonymity; the Brussels-based NGO European Schoolnet, which through its coordination of the European Commission's InSafe program operates throughout Europe; a representative of the Attorney General of Maryland's office; the San Francisco–based NGO NoBully; the Washington, DC–based NGO iKeepSafe; the San Jose, California–based NGO ConnectSafely.org; the Greater Good Science Center at the University of California, Berkeley; and an e-safety consultancy organization Third Parent. Other e-safety experts interviewed were either academics or consultants working on cyberbullying and e-safety related issues, policy makers (e.g., the former Director General in the European Commission), or were not affiliated with organizations. I conducted 30 interviews in total.

Appendix B

Company Profiles

Facebook

Founded in 2004, Facebook is the oldest among the companies examined in this book, and one regarded by a number of interviewees (NGO representatives, e-safety experts, and some other companies) as the one with the most extensive cyberbullying policy, the details behind which I analyze in chapter 6. It is also sometimes described as an economically powerful company with an established reputation. As such, Facebook has set what many informants perceive as high standards in terms of self-regulatory effort for other companies. Users need to be 13 years old to access the platform and the platform asks for a user's age at the sign-up process.

Once users are "friends" they can (unless they set specific restrictions) see other users' content via a function called the "newsfeed," which provides for simultaneous sharing with a number of other users. Facebook algorithmically curates its users' newsfeeds, which means that based on the information that Facebook collects on users, some of a user's friends have a greater likelihood of appearing in her newsfeed than others (Facebook, 2014). Users can also live-chat privately or message each other privately.

Instagram

Instagram is an image- and video-sharing platform on which users can also post comments. It is primarily an app but also a website that is owned by Facebook, yet it has different features from Facebook. While Facebook requires its users to go by their real names on the platform, Instagram allows for pseudo-anonymity. Users can also follow each other so that relationships are asymmetrical—they do not need to be friends but one can follow without being followed back. The app has the reputation for being popular among teen and preteen users (i.e., "tweens," typically ages 10 to 13 but sometimes the term is used to include 8- and 9-year-olds) (Shamberg, 2013; Blaszczak-Boxe, 2014; Simmons, 2014). Instagram has been in the news for alleged bullying cases (see Boroff, 2014; "Watertown teens arrested . . .", 2014). Users needed to be 13 to access the platform but were not asked to provide their age during the sign-up process at the time of this research.

Twitter

Twitter is a social network, or a "microblogging platform," which allows users to post messages or "tweets" composed of 140 characters of less. Like Instagram, it allows for pseudo-anonymity as well as asymmetrical relationships (Larson, Nagler, Ronen, & Tucker, 2016). Users can favorite each others' tweets, retweet each other, or send direct messages. They can also use a function called "hashtag" (#) which assigns a topic to a tweet. Users can post a tweet, and by adding a hashtag (e.g., #WorldCup), all users who search for that hashtag can see these tweets (even if they are not following the users who posted them). Hashtags can be used on some other platforms as well, such as Instagram, Facebook, Google+, or Tumblr. Twitter does not appear to be as popular with teens and tweens as some other platforms featured here (e.g., see Elgersma, 2016; Gauthier, 2016) and it has been in the news a number of times for cyberbullying (see Dewey, 2015).

Leaked emails from Dick Costolo, the company's CEO at the time, cited him as admitting that he felt "ashamed and embarrassed" by how his company handled bullying and harassment on the platform (McGrath, 2015). Cyberbullying, harassment and trolling were cited as a reason that the company's user base and subsequent financial success were in decline. This was a rare occasion at the time, to have the discussion of effectiveness of a company's cyberbullying policies in the media tied to the implications for its business model (an issue I discuss in chapter 6).

In mid-2016, Twitter's ability to handle abuse and harassment came into the limelight again, so much so that rumors began to spread about the company's projected closing in early 2017, even prompting a trending hashtag, #SaveTwitter. BuzzFeed even ran a story on Twitter's failure to effectively handle abuse provocatively titled "A Honeypot for Assholes: Inside Twitter's 10-Year Failure to Stop Harassment" (Warzel, 2016). Twitter denied these allegations (Kapko, 2016).

Twitter used to have a provision in its TOS, which explicitly stated that users under 13 were not allowed on the platform. However, this provision was moved to its Privacy Policy at the time of this writing; the Privacy Policy only stipulated that the platform's service was "not directed to persons under 13," that the company does not knowingly collect personal information from children under 13, and that if one becomes aware of a child under 13 using the service, Twitter would take the steps to remove such information and terminate the child's account (Bennett, 2014a; Twitter, 2016f).

Ask.fm

Ask.fm is a platform that allows users to post anonymous questions to other users. Users could choose to reveal their identity when asking questions, and the system of "following" is asymmetrical—it works much like Twitter and Instagram. Users can choose to share the answers they give on Ask.fm on their Facebook or Twitter profiles, and such connectivity allows for spillover of potentially bullying content. In 2014 it was said to have 180 million active users per month, which in 2016 declined to 150 million (Ask.fm, 2016e). At one point, 20,000 questions were asked on the platform *per minute*.

Children under 13 are not allowed on the platform and users are asked to provide their age during the sign-up process. Should they provide a date of birth that is under the age of 13, they are informed that their registration cannot be processed. The network had generated substantial controversy over bullying incidents, as I detail in chapter 4.

The company has had as many as three owners. Two Latvian brothers, Ilja and Mark Terebin, were the first owners. An American internet company called IAC/Inter-ActiveCorp bought it in 2014; at the time IAC owned more than 50 brands including College Humor, Tinder, Ask.com, and Match.com (IAC, n.d.). IAC, according to one informant, allegedly bought Ask.fm because it had been generating negative press for its own platform, similarly called Ask.com. The new company owners believed that previous owners had mishandled e-safety and demanded that they leave the company as part of the acquisition. The price of the sale was not publicly disclosed.

At the time of my interview with the company's new Chief of Trust and Safety Officer, the company was undergoing significant e-safety changes. In an agreement struck with the Attorneys General of Maryland and New York in August 2014, Ask.fm agreed to revamp its e-safety policy, ensuring that children under 13 were not on the platform (Bodley, 2014). It was not clear whether the agreement forced the company to make any payments if it failed to make the required improvements within six months of the agreement (Perez, 2014).

According to the BBC, in July 2016, IAC sold the company to Noosphere, "an asset management firm that specializes in tech," ("Ask.fm changes hands again," 2016). One reason for the sale, as cited by the company, was that Noosphere was "a more strategic fit" ("Big news from Ask.fm today," 2016). While it was not clear whether or to what extent e-safety played a role in this second change of ownership, the UK child protection charity NSPCC reported in April 2016 that Ask.fm rated fourth among the top five sites where UK children and young people reported seeing inappropriate content, and Yik Yak rated fifth (News O2, 2016).[1]

YouTube

The Google-owned video sharing service allows users to share videos and follow each other by creating channels. Users can follow (subscribe to) each other's channels and thus receive updates about posted videos. Videos also contain a comments section, which is where mean comments or cyberbullying can appear. The platform has a reputation for being popular among teens and tweens (Ault, 2014; Bennett, 2014b; Brouwer, 2014; Smith, 2016e) and has also been in news accounts of bullying and harassment (Kiberd, 2016; Williams, 2016). In most countries, users need to be 13 to have a Google account, which allows one to sign into YouTube (Google, 2016a). The exact wording of the age requirements in YouTube's TOS varies by country and the terms tend to specify a version of the following warning: "You may not use the Service and may not accept the Terms if you are not of legal age to form a binding contract with YouTube" (YouTube.au, 2010; YouTube.gb, 2010). I address the most recent issues with the company's bullying and harassment policies in chapter 6.

Google+

Google+ is a social networking service provided by Google. It allows users with Gmail accounts to follow other users and label them as "friends," "family," "acquaintances," or simply "following." At the time I selected the sample of companies for this research, the platform's reported large number of users seemed to belie its reputation for being a less-popular social network (Grandoni, 2014; Cain Miller, 2014; Elgan, 2015). Google+ has been, nonetheless, frequently recognized as a dying platform since (Garcia-Martinez, 2016; Fiegerman, 2015; Morris, 2015).

Snapchat

Snapchat, released in 2011, is an app that allows users to capture photos and videos that "self-destruct" in 10 seconds once the recipient opens them (Magid, 2013). The company appeared in the news many times, frequently in connection to sexting (it had even acquired a reputation as a "sexting app") as well as bullying (Shontell, 2014; Barnes, 2016; Bell, 2016). Over time, it introduced a number of other features, such as "Stories"—"compilations of snaps (i.e. photos or videos) that create a narrative" (Snapchat, n.d.e) and which could be seen by anyone with whom the user shared them for up to 24 hours (Mercury News, 2016). The *New York Times* reported in 2016 that this affordance was so popular that Facebook-owned Instagram copied it (Isaac, 2016). Snapchat also added "Memories" the same year, a feature that allowed users to add photos or videos that had been taken outside of Snapchat, to Snapchat Stories (Read, 2016).

The platform has witnessed a growing popularity since the time it was introduced. In 2016 Forbes and Wired described it as "going mainstream" (Hempel, 2016), from its start as a niche "sexting app" to one that appealed to adults, too (Silver, 2016). The Pew Research Center reported in 2015 that Snapchat was the third most popular social media platform for US teens (Lenhart, 2015).

In June 2014, Snapchat entered a settlement with the Attorney General of Maryland who sued the company for "deceptive trade practices" because of Snapchat's claims that snaps "disappear forever" (Maryland Attorney General, 2014). Users could take screenshots of images and share them on other platforms. The company had also been allegedly in violation of COPPA and was collecting names and phone numbers from users' electronic contact lists, without disclosing such practices to consumers (Maryland Attorney General, 2014). As part of the settlement, Snapchat agreed to address these issues and pay a fine of $100,000. Snapchat now informs the sender if the recipient creates a screenshot of the sent image, although reportedly there are ways to circumvent screenshot detection.

WhatsApp

Founded in 2009, WhatsApp is a Facebook-owned mobile messaging app, which Facebook bought in 2014 for as much as $19 billion (Statista, n.d.a). WhatsApp is a mobile messaging app on which users can exchange text messages, photos, and videos. The platform was reported to be popular among teens and young people (Olson, 2013) and sometimes associated with alleged bullying (Bullying.uk, n.d.; Espinoza, 2016).

In a revision to its TOS in late August 2016, the minimum age was lowered to 13. Before this change, it did not seem to be clear whether users had to be 16 or if they could still use the service under the age of 16 as long as they had parental consent. On the one hand, the TOS stated that by signing up for the service the user affirmed that he or she was "at least 16 years of age as the WhatsApp Service is not intended for children under 16" (WhatsApp, 2016c). On the other hand, they also stated that the user was "either more than 16 years of age, or an emancipated minor, or possesses legal parental or guardian consent."[2]

Kik Messenger

Founded in 2009, Kik Messenger is the only non-US company profiled in this book. It was founded in Canada by a group of University of Waterloo students. As the *Guardian* reported in 2016, Kik claimed as many as 40% of US teens were using the app (Wong, 2016).[3]

Kik relies on usernames rather than telephone numbers for its Kik accounts, which, the company says, allows users to "always" be "in complete control of who they talk to on Kik" (Kik Interactive, 2016c). But this feature also allows users pseudo-anonymity if they choose to be registered with a name that is not their real name or one via which their contacts may not be able to associate with their real identity. Users can also connect to those they may not know in person (Kik Interactive, 2016b).

The app found itself at the center of controversy when Nicole Lovell, a 13-year-old girl from the US, chatted with an 18-year-old boy on the app who later allegedly killed her (Kobie, 2016). Kik had also appeared in the media as a platform where 12-year-old Rebecca Ann Sedwick had allegedly been bullied before she committed suicide (see chapters 1 and 4). The platform was mentioned in the news a number of times in reference to bullying, and its popularity among teens was widely acknowledged among the interviewees for this book.

Despite these cases, which date to as early as 2013, when I contacted the company in August of 2016 for an interview, a representative asked if the interview could be conducted later in October, as the company was still "in the early stages of formalizing its policies."

The company reports its pride in being backed by venture capital firms that had developed other well-known social media companies and gaming platforms such as Twitter, Foursquare, and Zynga (Kik Interactive, 2016e). Kik's TOS prohibit children under 13 from using the service and those who are "under the age of majority" at the location where they live can use the service only if a parent or guardian agrees to the terms on their behalf (Kik Interactive, 2016d). At the time of this book's writing, however, the age verification procedure for Kik was the same as for many other platforms—users needed to provide a birth date during the sign-up process, which, of course, allowed them to lie about their age (Hughes, 2016).

Voxer

Launched in 2007, Voxer is a digital messaging service that offers text, photo, and location sharing, live and recorded voice, one-on-one chats, and large group chats (Voxer, n.d.b). Voxer seems to be particularly used for voice messaging (Dale, 2015) and appears to be oriented toward adult users and businesses in particular. But this platform, too, was mentioned in the media in relation to 12-year-old Rebecca Ann Sedwick's alleged bullying and suicide (Bazelon, 2013a). The company reported that it thought Voxer was only an app on Rebecca Ann Sedwick's phone, and that it was probably not used for bullying that allegedly contributed to this incident. The app occasionally surfaced in news media and was described on some parenting online resources as popular among teens (Gaggle, n.d.; Birdsong, 2013; Young, 2014) and sometimes in relationship to bullying (Alvarez, 2013b), although the company does not disclose the numbers of its teen users. Its TOS stipulates that users must be 13 to use the service or have parental consent if under 18. I was not asked for age verification, however, when I signed up for the service.

Whisper

Released in 2012, the Whisper app allows users to post text laid over photos, which appear to be algorithmically suggested to users by the app. I once tried to create a message using the name "Michelle" and the suggested photo was that of Michelle Obama, even though "Obama" was not the last name used. Users can upload a photo of their own, however, so in theory, if users wanted to bully someone, they could write a harassing post and plaster it over that person's photo.

The app uses geolocation to generate users' newsfeeds. Users do not know if they are connected to other people posting content in terms of whether these are contacts from their phonebook or whether they are followers or friends on other networks (Ortutay, 2014). Users are also given the option to find their school on Whisper and communicate with their classmates who are using Whisper while on campus.

The company has been a subject of privacy and bullying-related controversy in media coverage (Giantasio, 2014). While the company alleged that it did not track its users, the *Guardian* revealed in October 2014 that the company did track the whereabouts of its users, despite the existence of an opt-out button, which was apparently not working (Lewis & Rushe, 2014; Rushe & Lewis, 2014). The *Register* website reported that Whisper worked closely with BuzzFeed to help the news service find breaking news from anonymous posts, which is why it was important to know the geolocation of its users (Thomson, 2014). The *Register* also reported that it could not obtain an interview with Whisper even when the reporters tweeted Whisper leadership team while they were standing in front of Whisper's office in Los Angeles (McCarthy, 2014).

A Change.org petition (REACH of Macon County, 2013) called for the company to introduce age verification by asking for the birth date before downloading the app. At the time of this research, the minimum age for downloading Whisper was 13, but if users were between 13 and 18, the TOS demanded they had consent from parents or guardians (Whisper, 2016a). As with many other apps described here, parental consent was not verified upon the sign-up process and neither were users asked to provide their age during sign-up. The app had the reputation of being popular among teens (Elgersma, 2016), although it was not clear how many teen users it had.

Secret

Secret was the youngest company among those I surveyed in this research, but it went out of business in 2015, before I had finished writing this book. The app had become available on Apple and Android in February 2014, and it also allowed users to post content without revealing their identity. According to its CEO, Secret was a place where people could talk freely without the burden of their identity leading to any potentially negative consequences. Secret's algorithm determined whom an anonymous post would be shown to. Anonymous posts were then shared with people in their phone books and/or with their Facebook friends, or with friends of friends, or with anyone else using Secret.

Users could log in via their Facebook accounts, which meant that Secret had access to their Facebook contacts, although sharing on Secret was nonetheless anonymous. In Brazil, a judge declared the Secret app to be "unconstitutional for its alleged promotion of bullying," stressing that freedom of expression provisions in the country do not cover anonymous speech (Bernocco, 2014). A court order then asked the Apple App Store and Google Play to remove the app, or to otherwise pay a fine for each day that the app stayed in their app stores. Google refused to take it down, but Apple complied (Russel, 2014). At the time of the interview, Secret was changing its TOS to allow only users who were 17 and older to be on the platform (previously 13 and older). The change had allegedly been made in response to the company's realization that the app was more suitable for adult communication.

Yik Yak

Yik Yak was founded in November 2013 and a year later, with app users on 1,500 college campuses in the US, it ranked among the top 10 social media apps in the Apple App Store (Medina, 2014; Rusli, 2014).

Accessing the app allowed users to view the feed—a live stream of anonymous messages shared by people in their geophysical vicinity—which is why the app was geared toward college campus communities, with students who live in close proximity and have common interests (Yik Yak, 2014). Users could also "upvote" and "downvote" content—messages that they liked and disliked. Anonymous messages, so-called Yaks, were organized around specific communities such as Stanford or NYU, or around selected topics such as "freshmen advice" or "sports." In the fall semester of 2014, Yik Yak was running a bus tour to promote the product to university campuses on the West Coast (Yik Yak, 2014). By that time, the app had already gathered significant media attention for alleged violent threats and bullying (O'Neil, 2014).

As of April 2016, the TOS stipulated that the minimum user age was 18 (Yik Yak, 2016), yet no age-verification was provided at sign-up. The company was also using geofencing, a method that uses GPS location data to ban students from accessing the app in specific places (e.g., high schools). Primary and high school students could access the app at home, but geofencing effectively kept them from communicating with their fellow students unless they were physically close to each other. Schools could request Yik Yak to set up geofencing around their campuses, and the app had been doing it proactively.

While the app's age limit and geofencing were meant to prevent students younger than college age from accessing the app, incidents involving high school students and the app, emerged in the media. These incidents primarily involved violent threats, but in media coverage they were sometimes portrayed as cyberbullying, which could further contribute to the public confusion about the term. For instance, in November 2014, threats were posted against students at Southeast Polk High School in Iowa, after which a shooting occurred nearby (Rusli & Elder, 2014). Yik Yak cooperated with the local police and turned over the data on three students who posted the threats, but the threats were unrelated to the shooting incident. According to the *Wall Street Journal*, one of the three students arrested in this case was only 13 years old (Rusli, 2013). At the same time, a report of a separate incident involving both threats and name calling at a high school in Hawaii disclosed that school officials canceled an already scheduled anti-bullying assembly and notified the police department of the threats ("Kaiser High School reports cyberbullying . . .," 2015). (Note that the companies I interviewed preferred not to discuss the cases where they revealed identities of users to the law enforcement but always emphasized that such provisions were made only after valid requests on behalf of law enforcement.)

In 2016, however, Yik Yak introduced usernames or handles to replace the type of anonymity described above and users were now also able to mute abusive account handles in addition to flagging abusive content that had already been available on the platform (Heath, 2016). In early 2016 there were reports that Yik Yak was losing popularity and had dropped from being the third most-downloaded app in late 2014 to number 63 among social networking apps (Kosoff, 2016). Yik Yak closed down in April 2017, when this book was going to print (Carson, 2017).

Tumblr

Tumblr is a microblogging platform that allows users to create profiles and share content with their followers as well as to follow other users. Yahoo! acquired Tumblr in May 2013 for $1 billion (Abbruzzese, 2014). The minimum age for users was 13.

Tumblr was mentioned in interviews with NGO representatives a number of times as relevant for children's and teens' experience, and it was widely perceived as a popular platform for teens (Bennett, 2013). It also appeared in the news in connection to abuse and bullying (Nguyen, 2015). Furthermore, the site was blamed in the media for hosting self-harming content. Tallulah Wilson, a 15-year-old girl from London who died by suicide was allegedly an avid user of Tumblr, where she posted material about self-harming (Rawlinson, 2014).

Notes

Chapter 1

1. Throughout the book, I use the terms "child" and "children" to refer to those under 18 years of age, in accordance with the UN Convention on the Rights of the Child (UNCRC); what constitutes "a legal minor" may differ in various legal frameworks. Hence when using the term "children" I refer to teens as well. I specify "teens" only when I want to emphasize that the relevant piece of information refers specifically to those who are 13 years of age and above.

2. This case did not involve only cyberbullying (see chapter 4 for more information).

3. See also Anti-bullying Showcase 2013 at Facebook HQ (2013).

4. Communications Decency Act of 1996, (CDA), Pub. L. No. 104–104 (Tit. V), 110 Stat. 133 (Feb. 8, 1996), codified at 47 USC 223, 230.

5. See also the work of NSPCC, a UK-based NGO that relies on a survey to ask children whether they are aware of reporting and blocking tools on the most popular platforms (NetAware, 2017).

6. For a discussion on connotations of multi-stakeholderism, see Raymond & DeNardis (2016).

7. See appendix A for more information on the interviews.

8. No platform discussed in this book allows for "true anonymity" but rather "pseudo-anonymity" (Kling, Lee, Teich, & Frankel, 1999). True anonymity would mean that one's actions online cannot be traced to the person who executed them, and true anonymity can be achieved using encryption services such as Tor or I2P. Otherwise, one's actions can be traced to their IP address; moreover, one typically needs to use either an email address or a phone number to sign up for a platform. Pseudo-anonymity would refer to cases where one can use a social network under a name that is not their real name (e.g., "Fancy Clouds"). Facebook, for instance, asks users to register with the names they hold in the "real life" (even though this provision can be violated), while allowing users to access its service via Tor in an attempt to ensure that users who may

be living under oppressive government regimes can avoid government tracking. Instagram allows for pseudo-anonymity. So-called anonymous services such as Whisper and Secret allow users to share content that is not associated with either a real name or a pseudo-name. Nonetheless, users still need to provide an email address or a mobile phone number to register or sign up, and hence, the company can trace their online activity. For a discussion on anonymity and regulation, see Levmore (2010).

9. For more on trolling, see Phillips (2015).

10. The Todd and Parsons cases included sextortion and child pornography. I discuss the problems that stem from describing them as "cyberbullying" cases in chapter 4.

Chapter 2

1. The concepts of "media panic" and "moral panic" are laden with some theoretical and epistemological issues. For more information on this point, see Buckingham & Strandgaard Jensen, 2012.

2. For a comprehensive discussion on online risk see Staksrud (2013a).

3. EU Kids Online is a network of more than 150 researchers in 33 countries in Europe. The network conducted a rigorously designed survey of internet and digital use habits of European internet-using children (ages 9–16, totaling 25,000 children) in 2010. The results were compared to the findings of its sister project, Net Children Go Mobile, in 2014. See Net Children Go Mobile (n.d.).

4. American Academy of Pediatrics (AAP) used to advise that children under two years of age should not be allowed screen time due to a lack of sufficient evidence about effects of such exposure/engagement. However, as of 2015, AAP is reconsidering these guidelines, too (Brown, Shifrin, & Hill, 2015).

5. I thank Dr. Patricia Aufderheide for this insight.

6. For a different interpretation of introduction of bullying laws in the US states, please see Bullying Symposium 2013 Keynote Speaker Nancy Willard. YouTube. Retrieved from https://www.youtube.com/watch?v=8ZlZwX4gqxU.

7. See more on this point in Patchin, 2014.

8. Some have found that this is the case for girls, ages 13–14; see Livingstone, Mascheroni, et al., (2014).

9. While definitions of what constitutes a minor vary from country to country, UNCRC defines a child as anyone under the age of 18. It is worthwhile noting that the US had signed but not ratified the convention and hence it is not bound by its provisions, see Humanium (n.d.).

10. "Private sector actors" includes social media companies.

11. See Staksrud (2013a), chapter 7, "From Authority to Advisory."

12. While online intermediaries are not content providers or creators, many social media companies provide educational materials (e.g., against bullying) or link to other content such as games on their platforms (e.g., Zynga's Farmville on Facebook).

Chapter 3

1. See the section later in this chapter titled "Children's Online Privacy Protection Act (COPPA)."

2. See chapter 5 for the historical context behind the DMCA.

3. Some authors observed that the companies would, in such situations, need to make decisions about torts that are "notoriously ambiguous such as negligence and intentional infliction of emotional distress (IIED)" (Chang, 2010, p. 522).

4. I revisit GDPR in chapter 9.

5. See also Bamberger & Mulligan (2015) for a discussion on this point.

Chapter 4

1. Reveal her breasts.

2. The abbreviation involves a swear word and signifies that she did not care.

3. See chapter 3 for further details on liability exemptions for social media companies and cases where harassment and defamation provisions or specific local laws may apply

4. For the latest version of the Enhancing Online Safety for Children Act, 2015, see https://www.legislation.gov.au/Details/C2016C00781.

Chapter 5

1. When referring to the corporate policies and enforcement mechanisms of the companies I analyze in chapter 6, I will use the terms "private regulation," "individualized self-regulation" or "self-organization." See Latzer et al. (2013).

2. For a comprehensive analysis of these documents, see Lievens (2010, pp. 88–142) and Staksrud (2013a, chapter 6, "Regulation as Legitimate Protection").

3. It is legitimate to ask is: How can parents/caregivers be expected to know everything (and should they) given the increasing number of issues that demand their attention in the context of contemporary life and ever-changing technology?

4. Command and Control regulation, in more formal terms, can be defined as: "state promulgation of legal rules prohibiting specified conduct underpinned by coercive sanctions (either civil or criminal in nature) if the prohibition is violated" (McLaughlin, 2013, p. 78, cf. Morgan and Yeung, 2007, p. 80).

5. The primary concern motivating this piece of legislation was children's exposure to pornographic material. The implementation of the law's filtering component led to overblocking of legitimate sites (for instance, sites with valuable health information that did not contain "obscene" material). The law was subsequently questioned in court on grounds of violating the First Amendment and strengthening the digital divide—affluent people could have access to any site, because they could afford the internet access from home; however, people with limited means who relied on internet access in public libraries could not (Menuey, 2009).

6. Consider, however, that this working group was convened "pursuant to the Protecting Children in the 21st Century Act," which is a piece of legislation that Alice Marwick described as a "2007 version of DOPA," the Deleting Online Predators Act of 2006, and therefore much criticized (see Marwick, 2008).

7. For more on "escalation" in the context of NGOs, see chapter 7.

8. Directive 2000/31/EC of the European Parliament and of the Council of 8 June 2000 on certain legal aspects of information society services, in particular electronic commerce, in the Internal Market ("Directive on electronic commerce"). Retrieved from http://eur-lex.europa.eu/legal-content/EN/ALL/?uri=CELEX:32000L0031.

9. For an elaborate classification of activities that self-regulation can encompass see Marsden (2012), cf. Black (1996, p. 55).

10. These are, by no means, the only classifications, see Latzer et al. (2013, p. 377), who explain that, accounting for different types of government involvement, some authors have identified the following, among others: "enforced self-regulation" (Braithwaite, 1982); "mandated self-regulation" (Gunningham & Rees, 1997); and "regulated self-regulation" (Schulz & Held, 2004).

11. Some authors summarize that co-regulation implies when "self-regulation is combined with statutory regulation" (De Haan et al., 2013, p. 111; Lievens, 2010, p. 169). Other authors suggest that independent evaluations could be taken as a token of co-regulation, and what the EU in its documents refers to as "self-regulation" overlaps with the concept of co-regulation precisely because of independent evaluations (McLaughlin, 2013). But as research strongly indicates, independent evaluations are nonetheless rare when it comes to cyberbullying specifically.

12. See also Marsden (2011). At the time of writing, referring to social networking sites, the author observed that there was "no cross-sectoral SRO (self-regulatory organization)" and that "the regulation of these systems takes place at corporate and user level, in the same way" (p. 74).

13. For more on "analytical categories for evaluation of self and co-regulation." see Latzer et al. (2007).

14. Ask.fm commissioned a law firm, Mishcon de Reya, to do such an evaluation after the Hannah Smith suicide, but I could not find the results of this evaluation in

the form of a publicly available report (Rudd, 2013b; Saul, 2013). Via its digital citizenship grant, Facebook funded research that prompted recommendations aimed at social media companies. To my best knowledge, however, such studies did not set out to provide an evaluation of the effectiveness of Facebook's anti-bullying mechanisms. See the report in Schneider, Smith, & O'Donnel (2013b).

15. Note also that this evaluation did not include any testing.

Chapter 6

1. "Roasting," a practice sometimes placed under the umbrella of "cyberbullying," is an event in which one individual is subjected to what can be either ill-intentioned or good-natured jokes at their expense, and is typically intended to amuse a wider audience (Espinoza, 2016).

2. Given that the oldest companies in the sample originated in the early to mid-2000s, arguably all social media companies are young. Yet, I refer to older companies in this sample that typically had a significant user base and that tended to be perceived in the community of e-safety experts as having significant financial resources to invest in e-safety (see Marsden, 2011, p. 81) as "the more established companies," e.g., Facebook, YouTube, or Twitter.

3. Patchin is a professor of Criminal Justice at the University of Wisconsin-Eau Claire, and the co-director of the Cyberbullying Research Center. The interview took place on Skype on August 31, 2016.

4. Instagram blocked tags that are frequently associated with promoting eating disorders ("pro-ED"), which meant that if one was to search for them on the platform, such searches would not return any results; but "banned tags can still be used in posts" (Chancellor et al., 2016, p. 1), which implied that filtering took place at the level of search results only and that the content itself was not filtered out. For an explanation of how such filtering on Instagram can fail to deliver due to users' ability to leverage "lexical variations" to circumvent restrictions, see Chancellor et al. (2016).

5. CEOP's counterpart in the US is the Center for Missing and Exploited Children (NCMEC), a non-profit organization established by the US Congress in 1984.

6. Facebook's Advisory Board, which I discuss in chapter 7, comprises experts from organizations providing e-safety advice for the company.

7. I edited this quote to conceal not only a personal identity but also the company in question.

8. Upon checking in 2016, I was not provided with an option to report a post on my timeline—I could only report a post in my newsfeed.

9. See also boyd (2014) and Marwick & boyd (2014) as I discussed in chapter 2.

10. Although older, it is questionable whether the company could be characterized as more established. "While Tumblr's users have increased at a steady pace since its acquisition by Yahoo," it "did not meet its $100 million revenue target for 2015" (Great Speculations, 2016).

11. In the summer of 2016, after the company was sold to its third owner, Noosphere, and the design of the platform appeared to have been altered, information about filtering was no longer available. At that time, the platform offered the option to report "bullying and harassment." After clicking on the appropriate button, the flow offered an option to further describe the post by choosing one of the following reasons: "this post is cruel or hurtful," or "this post is threatening or aggressive," or "this image is offensive." The confirmation of the report followed with a message that the company would do its best to review it in 24 hours.

Chapter 7

1. The latter was organized around the Department of Commerce's National Telecommunications & Information Administration (NTIA).

2. Members of The Internet Crimes Against Children Task Force for example, would organize such training.

3. See Matias et al., 2015 for the description of how one organization focusing on harassment of women worked with Twitter and p. 19 in this report for statistics on how many reports escalated by the NGO the company took action on.

4. Safer Internet Centers are part of a European Commission initiative that established a center in every participating European country. The centers contain helplines (to help with content harmful to children), hotlines (to help with illegal content in relation to child protection), and awareness centers (aimed at educational practices regarding online risks). See Digital Single Market (2015).

5. For a more detailed background on ICRA see Staksrud (2013): pp. 97–98, and ICRA's transformation into FOSI: pp.166–168.

6. The NGO is sometimes referred to as ConnectSafely and sometimes Connect-Safely.org.

7. Anne Collier no longer represented ConnectSafely.org at the time of this book's completion.

8. The blog post had been written before Facebook added an NGO from India and an NGO from Italy to the Board.

9. The content of the links has changed since (Google, 2015a; 2015b).

10. For a discussion on vulnerable children and the context around reporting and using helplines see Hunter, Boyle, & Warden (2004); Fukkink & Hermanns (2009); Andersson & Osvaldsson (2011); Livingstone, Ólafsson, O'Neill, & Donoso (2012).

11. For a discussion on connotations of multi-stakeholderism, see Raymond & DeNardis, 2016.

12. The transcripts of which are not publicly available—making them publicly available was seen as potentially inhibiting the ability of some stakeholders to discuss the issues frankly and freely.

Chapter 8

1. The cases that garner high-profile news coverage can force politicians to act, or perhaps they constitute too good of an opportunity not to act.

2. For a discussion on ethics regarding fictitious profiles see Staksrud (2015).

3. For a debate on commodification of youth culture (outside of the context of digital citizenship) see Wasko (2008).

Chapter 9

1. This is *not* to say that there are no cases where the term "helpless victim" accurately describes a situation or an individual—and such cases, of course, require taking a stand against the individuals engaging in bullying or harassment and ensure that it stops. The reference here is to point out that social positioning is often at play—and this might require a more nuanced approach in addressing the issue.

2. Inspired by COPPA, the EC proposed the age of 13 at first, but then changed it to 16, apparently inexplicably.

Appendix B

1. The results were based on a survey of 1,725 children, ages 11–18, from 12 schools across the UK. It is not clear if the sample was representative (NSPCC, 2016; News O2, 2016).

2. "You affirm that you are either more than 16 years of age, or an emancipated minor, or possess legal parental or guardian consent, and are fully able and competent to enter into the terms, conditions, obligations, affirmations, representations, and warranties set forth in these Terms of Service, and to abide by and comply with these Terms of Service. In any case, you affirm that you are at least 16 years old as the WhatsApp Service is not intended for children under 16. If you are under 16 years of age, you are not permitted to use the WhatsApp Service" (WhatsApp, 2016c).

3. Note that according to *USA Today*, 40% of Kik users are US teens, which is a different interpretation of numbers provided by the *Guardian* (Hughes, 2016).

References

Abbruzzese, J. (2014, August 22). Report: Tumblr is growing, but not helping Yahoo's Bottom Line. Mashable. Retrieved from http://mashable.com/2014/08/21/tumblr-not -helping-yahoo-numbers.

Adler, P. A., & Adler, P. (1998). *Peer Power: Preadolescent Culture and Identity*. New Brunswick, NJ: Rutgers University Press.

Ahmed, E., & Brathwaite, V. (2006). Forgiveness, reconciliation, and shame: Three key variables in reducing school bullying. *Journal of Social Issues, 62*(2), 347–370.

Albertson, A. K. (2014). Note, criminalizing bullying: why Indiana should hold the bully responsible, 48 IND. *L. REV., 243*, 256–261.

Almasy, S., Segal, K., & Couwels, J. (2013, October 16). Sheriff: Taunting post leads to arrests in Rebecca Sedwick bullying death. *CNN*. Retrieved from http://edition.cnn .com/2013/10/15/justice/rebecca-sedwick-bullying-death-arrests/index.html.

Alvarez, L. (2013a, October 15). Felony counts for 2 in suicide of bullied 12-year-old. *New York Times*. Retrieved from http://www.nytimes.com/2013/10/16/us/felony -charges-for-2-girls-in-suicide-of-bullied-12-year-old-rebecca-sedwick.html?_r=1.

Alvarez, L. (2013b, September 13). Girl's suicide points to rise in apps used by cyber-bullies. *New York Times*. Retrieved from http://www.nytimes.com/2013/09/14/us/sui cide-of-girl-after-bullying-raises-worries-on-web-sites.html?pagewanted=all.

Alvarez, L. (2013c, November 21). Charges dropped in cyberbullying death, but sheriff isn't backing down. *New York Times*. Retrieved from http://www.nytimes.com /2013/11/22/us/charges-dropped-against-florida-girls-accused-in-cyberbullying -death.html?pagewanted=all.

Amanda Todd: Police alerted to extortion suspect before her suicide. (2014, December 4). *CBC News*. Retrieved from http://www.cbc.ca/news/canada/british -columbia/amanda-todd-police-alerted-to-extortion-suspect-before-her-suicide-1 .2860418.

Amanda Todd suicide: RCMP repeatedly told of blackmailer's attempts. (2013, November 15). *CBC News*. Retrieved from http://www.cbc.ca/news/canada/amanda -todd-suicide-rcmp-repeatedly-told-of-blackmailer-s-attempts-1.2427097.

American Civil Liberties Union. (2009). Re: Subcommittee hearing on "Cyberbullying and other online safety issues for children." Retrieved from https://www.aclu .org/files/images/asset_upload_file92_41198.pdf.

Ames, B. (2013, April 11). Grace's Law, a cyberbullying bill, called 'landmark legislation. *Baltimore Sun*. Retrieved from http://www.baltimoresun.com/news/maryland /howard/ellicott-city/ph-ho-graces-law-passes-20130410-story.html.

Andersson, K., & Osvaldsson, K. (2011). *Evaluation of BRIS' Internet Based Support Contacts. Executive Summary*. Sweden: Linköping University. Retrieved from http:// www.bris.se/upload/Articles/BRIS_evaluation_of_webbased_se.

Angelopoulos, C. (2013). Beyond the safe harbours: harmonising substantive intermediary liability for copyright infringement in Europe. *Intellectual Property Quarterly* (3), 253–274. Retrieved from http://ssrn.com/abstract=2360997.

'Anonymous' won't release names of Rehtaeh Parsons suspects. (2013, April 12). *CBC News*. Retrieved from http://www.cbc.ca/news/canada/nova-scotia/anonymous -won-t-release-names-of-rehtaeh-parsons-suspects-1.1365232.

Anti-bullying Ambassador School's Showcase Facebook London 2016. (2016). *Diana Award*. Retrieved June 1, 2017 from: http://www.antibullyingpro.com/london-show case-2016.

Antibullyingpro.com. (n.d.). The Diana Award Anti-bullying Ambassador Training Programme. Retrieved from http://www.antibullyingpro.com/training.

Anti-bullying showcase 2013 at Facebook HQ. (2013, December 3). *Antibullying Pro*. Retrieved from https://www.youtube.com/watch?v=ONi3D6_pk-A.

Arce, N. (2014). Facebook now allows breastfeeding photos, #FreeTheNipple campaign a success. *Tech Times*. Retrieved from http://www.techtimes.com/articles/8506 /20140615/facebook-now-allows-breastfeeding-photos-freethenipple-campaign-a -success.htm.

Arseneault, L., Bowes, L., & Shakoor, S. (2010). Bullying victimization in youths and mental health problems: "Much ado about nothing"? *Psychological Medicine, 40*, 717–729.

Ask.fm. (2016a). Community Guidelines. Retrieved from http://safety.ask.fm/com munity-guidelines/.

Ask.fm. (2016b). Ask.fm: A View on Safety. Our philosophy: Safety equals collaboration. Retrieved from http://safety.ask.fm/our-philosophy/.

Ask.fm. (2016c). Contributors. Retrieved from http://safety.ask.fm/contributors/.

Ask.fm. (2016d). Safety Tools. Retrieved from http://safety.ask.fm/safety-tools/.

Ask.fm. (2016e). Ask.com acquires the largest Global Q&A Social Network Ask.fm. Retrieved from http://about.ask.fm/ask-com-acquires-largest-global-qa-social-network -ask-fm/.

Ask.fm. (2016f). Safety Center. Retrieved from http://safety.ask.fm/.

Ask.fm changes hands again (2016, July 4). Ask.fm changes hands once again. *BBC News*. Retrieved from http://www.bbc.com/news/technology-36702766.

Ask.fm Safety Guide for Schools and Educators. (2017). *Ask.fm*. Retrieved from http://safety.ask.fm/ask-fm-safety-guide-for-schools-educators/.

Aufderheide, P., & Jaszi, P. (2011). *Reclaiming Fair Use: How to Put Balance Back in Copyright*. Chicago, IL: University of Chicago Press.

Ault, S. (2014, August 5). Survey: YouTube stars more popular than Mainstream celebs. *Variety*. Retrieved from http://variety.com/2014/digital/news/survey-youtube-stars -more-popular-than-mainstream-celebs-among-u-s-teens-1201275245.

Austin, L. M., Stewart, H., & Clement, A. (2014). Bill C-13 has little to do with cyber-bullying. *The Star*. Retrieved from http://www.thestar.com/opinion/commentary /2014/11/22/bill_c13_has_little_to_do_with_cyberbullying.html#.

Balkin, J. M. (2004). Digital speech and democratic culture: A theory of freedom of expression for the information society. *New York University Law Review, 79*(1), 1–55.

Baldwin, R., and M. Cave. 1999. *Understanding Regulation: Theory, Strategy and Practice*. Oxford: Oxford University Press.

Bamberger, K. A., & Mulligan, D. K. (2015). *Privacy on the Ground. Guiding Corporate Behavior in the United States and in Europe*. Cambridge, MA: MIT Press.

Bangemann Report Europe and The Global Information Society: Recommendations to the European Council. (1994). Retrieved from http://www.cyber-rights.org/docu-ments/bangemann.htm.

Barbosa, A., B. O'Neill, C. Ponte, J. A. Simoes, and T. Jereissati. (2013). Risks and safety on the internet: Comparing Brazilian and European Results. Retrieved from http://www.lse.ac.uk/media@lse/research/Research-Projects/Researching-Childrens -Rights/pdf/Barbosa-et-al-(2013).-Risks-and-safety-on-the-internet.-Comparing-Bra zilian-and-European-children.pdf.

Barbovschi, M., Green, L., & Vandoninck, S. (2013) Innovative approaches for inves-tigating how young children understand risk in new media: Dealing with method-ological and ethical challenges. EU Kids Online Network, London. Retrieved from http://eprints.lse.ac.uk/53060.

Barnett, E. (2009, November 19). Can Bebo's Panic Button beat cyberbullying? *The Telegraph*. Retrieved from http://www.telegraph.co.uk/technology/social-media/6600 032/Can-Bebos-panic-button-beat-cyber-bullying.html.

Barnett, E. (2010). Bebo fights back: social media by numbers. *The Telegraph*. Retrieved from http://www.telegraph.co.uk/technology/social-media/8185101/Bebo -fights-back-social-media-by-numbers.html.

Barnett, E., & Hollingshead, I. (2012). The dark side of Facebook. *The Telegraph*. Retrieved from http://www.telegraph.co.uk/technology/facebook/9118778/The-dark -side-of-Facebook.html.

Barnes, M. (2016, June 10). Teen kills herself after vicious cyberbullying on Snapchat. Rollingout. Retrieved from http://rollingout.com/2016/06/10/teen-kills-vicious-cyber -bullying-snapchat.

Bauman, S., Toomey, R. B., & Walker, J. L. (2013). Associations among bullying, cyberbullying, and suicide in high school students. *Journal of Adolescence, 36*(2), 341–350. doi:10.1016/j.adolescence.2012.12.001.

Bazelon, E. (2011, October 12). Why Facebook is after your kids. *New York Times Magazine*. Retrieved from http://www.nytimes.com/2011/10/16/magazine/why -facebook-is-after-your-kids.html?_r=0.

Bazelon, E. (2013a). Bullies taunted Rebecca Ann Sedwick with texts like "Can u die please?" and then she did. *Slate*. Retrieved from http://www.slate.com/blogs/xx_factor /2013/09/18/rebecca_ann_sedwick_suicide_lessons_for_parents_in_the_scary_age_of _cyberbullying.html.

Bazelon, E. (2013b). *Sticks and Stones: Defeating the Culture of Bullying and Rediscovering the Power of Character and Empathy*. New York: Random House.

Bazelon, E. (2014). The Sheriff overstepped. *Slate*. Retrieved from http://www.slate .com/articles/news_and_politics/doublex/2014/04/rebecca_sedwick_suicide_sheriff _grady_judd_never_should_have_arrested_katelyn.html.

Beck, U., & Beck-Gernsheim, E. (2001). *Individualization: Institutionalized Individualism and its Social and Political Consequences*. London: SAGE.

Bell, L. (2016, July 7). Snapchat acknowledges sexting as it reveals biggest feature update so far. *Mirror*. Retrieved from http://www.mirror.co.uk/tech/snapchat-acknow ledges-sexting-reveals-biggest-8369395.

Bennett, S. (2013, October 8). Instagram & Snapchat: How teens use social media. http://www.adweek.com/socialtimes/teens-social-media/492148.

Bennett, S. (2014a, September 29). Minimum Age Requirements: Twitter, Facebook, Instagram, Snapchat, WhatsApp, Secret. *WebWise*. Retrieved from http://www.web wise.ie/parents/ask-fm-a-guide-for-parents-and-teachers-2.

Bennett, S. (2014b, February, 24). Teens, Millennials prefer YouTube to Facebook, Instagram to Twitter. *Adweek*. Retrieved from http://www.adweek.com/socialtimes /teens-millennials-twitter-facebook-youtube/496770.

Bennett, W. L., Wells, C., & Freelon, D. (2011). Communicating civic engagement: Contrasting models of citizenship in the youth web sphere. *Journal of Communication, 61*, 835–856.

Berkman Center for Internet & Society. (2008). Enhancing Child Safety & Online Technologies: Final Report of the Internet Safety Technical Task Force. Retrieved from http://cyber.law.harvard.edu/sites/cyber.law.harvard.edu/files/ISTTF_Final_Report .pdf.

Berkman Center for Internet & Society. (2010). Internet safety technical taskforce. Retrieved from http://cyber.law.harvard.edu/research/isttf.

Berlin, I. (1958). *Two concepts of liberty: An inaugural lecture delivered before the University of Oxford on 31 October 1958*. Oxford: Clarendon Press.

Bernocco, A. (2014, August 21). Brazil bans Secret app as unconstitutional. *HNGN*. Retrieved from http://www.hngn.com/articles/39823/20140821/brazil-bans-secret -app-as-unconstitutional.htm.

Bernstein, J. Y., & Watson, M. W. (1997). Children who are targets of bullying: A victim pattern. *Journal of Interpersonal Violence, 12*(4), 483–498.

Best, J. (2013). Hannah Smith suicide: Ask.fm announces new safety measures in wake of tragic teen's suicide. *Mirror*. Retrieved from http://www.mirror.co.uk/news /world-news/hannah-smith-suicide-askfm-announces-2185445.

Big news from Ask.fm today. (2016, July 4). *Medium*. Retrieved from https://medium .com/@askfm/changes-at-askfm-big-news-from-the-askfm-team-today-askfm-has -joined-the-noosphere-family-and-is-60eeecc18398#.lbyxc9bdk.

Bill 61: An Act to Address and Prevent Cyberbullying. (2013). 61st General Assembly, 5th Session. Retrieved from http://nslegislature.ca/legc/PDFs/annual%20statutes /2013%20Spring/c002.pdf.

Birdsong, T. (2013, November, 19). 7 things parents need to know about Voxer voice app. Retrieved from https://blogs.mcafee.com/consumer/7-things-parents-need-to -know-about-the-voxer-voice-app.

Black, J. (1996). Constitutionalizing self-regulation. *Modern Law Review, 59*(1), 24–59.

Blaszczak-Boxe, A. (2014, October 8). Teens ditch Facebook for new social media favorite. *CBS News*. Retrieved from http://www.cbsnews.com/news/kids-social-media -survey-instagram-twitter-facebook.

Bodley, M. (2014, August 14). Ask.fm, Attorney General reach agreement to keep children safer online. *Baltimore Sun*. Retrieved from http://articles.baltimoresun.com

/2014-08-14/business/bs-bz-ask-fm-20140814_1_ask-fm-gansler-maryland-attorney -general.

Boroff, D. (2014, January 27). Texas parents to sue 6 cyberbullies for allegedly harassing their teen daughter on Instagram. *New York Daily News*. Retrieved from http:// www.nydailynews.com/news/national/texas-parents-sue-cyberbullies-instagram -post-article-1.1592841.

Bostad, I. (2008, June). *What are the values that will guide the development of children in our schools?* Paper presented at Conference of European Ministers of Education, Ljubljana, Slovenia.

Boutilier, A. (2014, May 13). Amanda Todd's mother raises concerns about cyberbullying bill. *The Star*. Retrieved from http://www.thestar.com/news/canada/2014/05 /13/amanda_todds_mother_raises_concerns_about_cyberbullying_bill.html.

boyd, d. (2014). *It's Complicated: The Social Lives of Networked Teens*. New Haven, CT: Yale University Press.

boyd, d. (2015, December 18). What if social media becomes 16-plus? New battles concerning age of consent emerge in Europe. *The Medium*. Retrieved from https:// medium.com/bright/what-if-social-media-becomes-16-plus-866557878f7#.skvnifxhd.

boyd, d., Hargittai, E., Schultz, J., & Palfrey, J. (2011). Why parents help their children lie to Facebook: Unintended consequences of Children's Online Privacy Protection Act (COPPA). *First Monday 16*(11). Retrieved from http://firstmonday.org/ojs /index.php/fm/article/view/3850/3075.

boyd, d., & Marwick, A. (2011, September 23). Bullying as true drama. *New York Times*. Retrieved from http://www.nytimes.com/2011/09/23/opinion/why-cyberbullying -rhetoric-misses-the-mark.html.

Bradshaw, C. (2013). Preventing bullying through positive behavioral interventions and supports (PBIS): A multitiered approach to prevention and integration. *Theory into Practice, 52*(4), 288–295. doi:10.1080/00405841.2013.829732.

Braithwaite, J. (1982). Enforced self-regulation: A new strategy for corporate crime control. *Michigan Law Review, 80*, 1466–1507.

Brown, A., Shifrin, D. L., & Hill, D. L. (2015, September, 28). Beyond turn it off: How to advise families on media use. *American Academy of Pediatrics News*. Retrieved from http://www.aappublications.org/content/36/10/54?sso=1&sso_redirect_count=1&nf status=401&nftoken=00000000-0000-0000-0000-000000000000&nfstatusdescription =ERROR%3a+No+local+token.

Brouwer, B. (2014, December 4). Study: Tweens choose YouTube as their favorite site. TubeFilter. Retrieved from http://www.tubefilter.com/2014/12/04/youtube-tweens -favorite-site.

Buckingham, D. (2011). *The Material Child*. Cambridge: Polity.

Buckingham, D., & Strandgaard Jensen, H. (2012). Beyond "Media Panics,". *Journal of Children and Media 6* (4): 413–429.

Bukowski, W. M. (2003). What does it mean to say aggressive children are competent or incompetent? *Merrill-Palmer Quarterly, 49*(3), 390–400.

Bulger, M., Burton, P., O'Neill, B., & Staksrud, E. (2017). Where policy and practice collide: Comparing US, South African and European Union approaches to protecting children online. *New Media & Society, 19*(5), 750–764.

Bullying Symposium 2013 Keynote Speaker Nancy Willard (2013, March 13). *YouTube*. Retrieved from https://www.youtube.com/watch?v=8ZlZwX4gqxU.

Bullying.uk. (n.d.). What to do if you are bullied on a social network. Retrieved from http://www.bullying.co.uk/cyberbullying/what-to-do-if-you-re-being-bullied-on-a -social-network.

Cain Miller, C. (2014, February 19). The loyal users of Google Plus say it is no ghost town. *New York Times*. Retrieved from http://bits.blogs.nytimes.com/2014/02/19 /the-loyal-users-of-google-plus-say-it-is-no-ghost-town/?_php=true&_type=blogs &_r=2.

Carr, J. (2013a). Facebook's Safety Advisory Board [Blog post]. Retrieved from https: //johnc1912.wordpress.com/2013/01/21/facebooks-safety-advisory-board.

Carr, J. (2013b). Non-disclosure agreements: enforced silence? [Blog post]. Retrieved from https://johnc1912.wordpress.com/2013/01/16/non-disclosure-agreements -enforced-silence.

Carr, J. (2016, March 31). John Carr on the GDPR: Poor process, bad outcomes. Retrieved from https://www.betterinternetforkids.eu/web/portal/news/detail?article Id=687465.

Carson, B. (2017, April 28). The Yik Yak App is Officially Dead. *Business Insider Nordic*. Retrieved from http://nordic.businessinsider.com/yik-yak-shuts-down-2017 -4?r=US&IR=T.

CBC News. (2013, August 7). N.S. Cyberbullying Legislation Allows Victims to Sue. Retrieved from http://www.cbc.ca/news/canada/nova-scotia/n-s-cyberbullying-legisla tion-allows-victims-to-sue-1.1307338.

Celizic, M. (2007, December 4). Attorney: Woman didn't know about online taunts. *Today News*. Retrieved from http://www.today.com/id/22096427/ns/today -today_news/t/attorney-woman-didnt-know-about-online-taunts/#.V6SwxpN94fE.

Centers for Disease Control and Prevention. (2014). Lesbian, Gay, Bisexual and Transgender Health. Retrieved from http://www.cdc.gov/lgbthealth/youth.htm.

Chang, C. (2010). Internet safety survey: Who will protect the children? *Berkeley Technology Law Journal, 25*(1), 501–527.

Chancellor, S., Pater, J., Clear, T., Gilbert, E., & Choudhury, M. D. (2016). #thygapp: Instagram content moderation and lexical variation in pro-eating disorder communities. Retrieved from http://www.munmund.net/pubs/cscw16_thyghgapp .pdf.

Charity Commission. (n.d.). Charity commission. Retrieved from https://www.gov .uk/government/organisations/charity-commission.

Charlotte Dawson's death puts cyberbulling back in spotlight. (2014, February 24). *ABC.* Retrieved from http://www.abc.net.au/news/2014-02-23/charlotte-dawson-death -puts-focus-on-cyber-bullying/5277904.

Chen, A. (2014, October 23). The laborers who keep dick pics and beheadings out of your Facebook feed. *Wired.* Retrieved from http://www.wired.com/2014/10/content -moderation.

ChiaVideos. (2012, October 11). Amanda Todd's story: Struggling, bullying, suicide, self harm [video file]. Retrieved from https://www.youtube.com/watch?v=ej7afkypUsc.

Christensen, L. M. (2009). Sticks, stones, and schoolyard bullies: Restorative justice, mediation and a new approach to conflict resolution in our schools. *Nevada Law Journal, 9*, 546–579.

Citron, D. K. (2014a). *Hate Crimes in Cyberspace.* Cambridge, MA: Harvard University Press.

Citron, D. K. (2014b, December 3). United States v. Elonis and the Rarity of Threat Prosecutions. *Forbes.* Retrieved from http://www.forbes.com/sites/daniellecitron/2014 /12/03/united-states-v-elonis-and-the-rarity-of-threat-prosecutions.

Civic Impulse. (2016). H.R. 2281–105th Congress: Digital Millennium Copyright Act. Retrieved from https://www.govtrack.us/congress/bills/105/hr2281.

Cohen, J. (2006). Social, emotional, ethical, and academic education: Creating a climate for learning, participation in democracy, and well-being. *Harvard Educational Review, 76*(2), 201–237. doi:10.17763/haer.76.2.j44854x1524644vn.

Cohen, J. E. (2012). *Configuring the Networked Self: Law, Code, and the Play of Everyday Practice.* New Haven, CT: Yale University Press.

Cohen, S. (1972). *Folk Devils and Moral Panics.* London: MacGibbon and Kee.

Coleman, J., & Hagell, A. (2007). *Adolescence, Risk and Resilience: Against the Odds.* Chichester, UK: John Wiley & Sons.

Collier, A. (2008, August 14). The latest technopanic. *Net Family News.* Retrieved from http://www.netfamilynews.org/the-latest-technopanic.

Collier, A. (2013, January 28). What we know and don't know about kids' online socializing: key study. *Net Family News*. Retrieved from http://www.netfamilynews .org/what-we-know-dont-know-about-kids-online-socializing-key-study.

Collier, A. (2014a, October 20). Of young people's (not just digital) citizenship. *Net Family News*. Retrieved from http://www.netfamilynews.org/young-peoples-just-digital -citizenship.

Collier, A. (2014b, July 18). Proposed "rightful" framework for internet safety. *Net-FamilyNews.org*. Retrieved from http://www.netfamilynews.org/proposed-rightful -framework-internet-safety.

Collier, A. (2016, January 10). Europe's big step backward for youth rights online, offline. NetFamilyNews.org. Retrieved from http://www.netfamilynews.org/europes -big-step-backward-for-youth-rights-online-offline.

Collier, A., & Nigam, H. (2010). *Youth safety on a living internet: Report of the Online Safety and Technology Working Group*. Retrieved from http://www.ntia.doc.gov/report /2010/youth-safety-living-internet.

Collins, L. (2008, January 21). Friend Game: Behind the online hoax that led to a girl's suicide. *The New Yorker*. Retrieved from http://www.newyorker.com/magazine /2008/01/21/friend-game.

Commission of the European Communities. (1996). *Illegal and Harmful Content on the Internet*. Brussels: European Communities.

Communications Decency Act, 47 U.S.C. 230. Retrieved from http://www.colum bia.edu/~mr2651/ecommerce3/2nd/statutes/CommunicationsDecencyAct.pdf.

Communicators with Doug Gansler. (2012, August 15). *C-SPAN*. Retrieved from http://www.c-span.org/video/?307537-1/communicators-doug-gansler.

Compassion Research Day. (2013). Retrieved from http://new.livestream.com/face booktalkslive/events/2564173.

Confederation of Family Organisations in the European Union. (2013). Cyberbul-lying: an overview. Retrieved from https://deletecyberbullying.files.wordpress. com/2013/02/euconference-cyberbullying-28-may-madrid-background-paper -coface.pdf.

ConnectSafely. (2012). A very brief history of US Internet safety. Retrieved from http://www.slideshare.net/ConnectSafely/legal-panel.

ConnectSafely.org. (2015). About ConnectSafely.org. Retrieved from http://www .connectsafely.org/about-connectsafely-org/.

ConnectSafely. (n.d.). About cyberbullying. http://www.connectsafely.org/wp-content /uploads/sc_cyberbullying.pdf.

Connolly, E. J., & Beaver, K. M. (2016). Considering the genetic and environmental overlap between bullying victimization, delinquency, and symptoms of depression/anxiety. *Journal of Interpersonal Violence, 31*(7), 1230–1256. doi:10.1177/0886260 514564158.

Constine, J. (2015, February 17). Yik Yak systematically downvotes mentions of competitors. *TechCrunch*. Retrieved from https://techcrunch.com/2015/02/17/yak gate/#abtw9P:b2w.

Constine, J. (2016, April 6). Yik Yak CTO drops out as hyped anonymous app stagnates. *TechCrunch*. Retrieved from https://techcrunch.com/2016/04/06/yik-yuck.

Corcoran, L., Guckin, C. M., & Prentice, G. (2015). Cyberbullying or cyber aggression? A review of existing definitions or cyber-based peer-to-peer aggression. *Societies (Basel, Switzerland), 5*(2), 245–255.

Corsaro, W. A. (2005). *The Sociology of Childhood*. 2nd ed. Thousand Oaks, CA: Pine Forge Press.

Craig, W. M., & Pepler, D. (2009). Introduction: Understanding and addressing bullying: An international perspective. In D. Pepler & W. Craig (Eds.), *Understanding and Addressing Bullying: An International Perspective* (pp. xix–xxvi). Bloomington, IN: Authorhouse.

Crawford, K., & Gillespie, T. (2016). What is a flag for? Social media reporting tools and the vocabulary of complaint. *New Media & Society, 18*(3), 410–428. doi:10.11 77/1461444814543163.

Critcher, S. (2008). Moral panic analysis: Past, present and future. *Sociology Compass, 2*(4), 1127–1144.

Cruz-Cunha, M. M., & Portela, I. M. (2014). *Handbook of Research on Digital Crime, Cyberspace Security, and Information Assurance*. Hershey, PA: IGI Global.

Curriculum: Understanding YouTube & Digital Citizenship: Lesson 4. (n.d.). Retrieved from https://docs.google.com/document/d/1SqtMEWNOkV8Zhr9QnAHNM4rs8m8s QJddTGrmV_XYans/edit?pli=1.

Cushing, T. (2013, August 12). UK Prime Minister calls ask.fm a 'vile site,' blames it for the behavior of some vile users. Retrieved from https://www.techdirt.com/arti cles/20130808/17522624116/uk-prime-minister-calls-askfm-vile-site-blames-it -behavior-some-vile-users.shtm.l

Cyberbullying law inspired by Rehtaeh Parsons' suicide takes effect. (2013, August 7). *The Star*. Retrieved from http://www.thestar.com/news/canada/2013/08/07/cyber bullying_law_inspiredly_by_rehtaeh_parsons_suicide_takes_effect.html.

Cyberbullying Research Center. (2013). *Cyberbullying: Neither an Epidemic nor a Rarity*. Retrieved from http://cyberbullying.org/cyberbullying-neither-an-epidemic-nor-a -rarity.

Cyberbullying Research Center. (n.d.). Cyberbullying facts. Retrieved from http://cyberbullying.org/facts.

Cybersmile Foundation. (2015). Cyberbulling & the law. Retrieved from http://www.cybersmile.org/advice-help/category/cyberbullying-and-the-law.

CyberWise. (2014). Digital citizenship. Retrieved from http://www.cyberwise.org/#!digital-citizenship/c1t53.

Dahl, J. (2014, January 17). "Rebecca's Law" aims to punish bullying in Fla. *CBS News*. Retrieved from http://www.cbsnews.com/news/rebeccas-law-aims-to-punish-bullying-in-florida.

Dale, B. (2015, August 12). Voice messaging beats phone calls and texts. Observer BusinessTech. Retrieved: http://observer.com/2015/12/voxer-zello-heytell-asynchronous-voice.

Damon, W. (2004). What is positive youth development? *Annals of the American Academy of Political and Social Science, 591*(1), 13–24.

Davidson, S. E. (2014). It is never too soon to start teaching digital citizenship. *International Society for Technology in Education, 41*(4), 32.

Davies, B. (2011). Bullies as guardians of the moral order or an ethic of truths? *Children and Society, 25*, 278–286.

Davies, C. (2014, May 6). Hannah Smith wrote vile posts to herself, say police. *The Guardian*. Retrieved from http://www.theguardian.com/uk-news/2014/may/06/hannah-smith-suicide-teenager-cyber-bullying-inquests.

DeAmicis, C. (2014, August 8). Meet the anonymous app police fighting bullies and porn on Whisper, Yik Yak, and potentially Secret. *Gigaom*. Retrieved from https://gigaom.com/2014/08/08/meet-the-anonymous-app-police-fighting-bullies-and-porn-on-whisper-yik-yak-and-potentially-secret.

DeAmicis, C. (2015, February 18). Yik Yak gives a better explanation of downvoting allegations. *Gigaom*. Retrieved from https://gigaom.com/2015/02/18/yik-yak-gives-a-better-explanation-of-down-voting-allegations.

Dearden, L. (2014, October 22). BeatBullying UK and MindFull charities suspend services as administrators called in. *Independent*. Retrieved from http://www.independent.co.uk/news/uk/home-news/beatbullying-uk-and-mindfull-charities-suspend-services-as-administrators-called-in-9810142.html.

de Haan, J., van der Hof, S., Bekkers, W., & Pijpers, R. (2013). Self-regulation. In: B. O'Neill, E. Staksrud & S. McLaughlin, *Towards a better internet for children? Policy pillars, players and paradoxes* (pp. 111–129). Göteborg, Nordicom.

d'Haenens, L., Vandoninck, S., & Donoso, V. (2013). How to cope and build online resilience? *EU Kids Online*. Retrieved from http://eprints.lse.ac.uk/48115/1/How%20to%20cope%20and%20build%20online%20resilience%20(lsero).pdf.

Delta, G. B., & Matsuura, J. H. (2013). Obscenity cases involving the internet. Chapter 12, Section 3. In: *Law of the Internet, third edition*. Retrieved via Westlaw database.

DeNardis, L. E. (2012). Hidden levers of internet control: An infrastructure-based theory of internet governance. *Journal of Information. Communicatio Socialis*, *15*(5), 720–738.

DeNardis, L. E. (2014). *The Global War for Internet Governance*. New Haven, CT: Yale University Press.

DeNardis, L., & Hackl, A. (2015). Internet Governance by Social Media Platforms. *Telecommunications Policy*. Advance online publication. Retrieved from http://www.sciencedirect.com/science/article/pii/S0308596115000592.

Dewey, C. (2014, December 1). A quick, jargon-free explainer to the Supreme Court case that will decide the limits of free speech online. *Washington Post*. Retrieved from http://www.washingtonpost.com/news/the-intersect/wp/2014/12/01/a-quick-jargon-free-explainer-to-the-supreme-court-case-that-will-decide-the-limits-of-free-speech-online.

Dewey, C. (2015, February 5). Twitter CEO Dick Costolo finally admits the obvious: Site has failed users on abuse. *The Washington Post*. Retrieved from http://www.washingtonpost.com/news/the-intersect/wp/2015/02/05/twitter-ceo-dick-costolo-finally-admits-the-obvious-we-suck-at-dealing-with-abuse.

Dickey, J. (2014, June 26). Meet the brothers behind the web's most controversial social network. *Time*. Retrieved from http://time.com/2923146/ask-fm-interview.

Dickey, M. R. (2013, May 31). These are the secrets people are actually sharing on the Whisper App. *Business Insider*. Retrieved from http://www.businessinsider.com/whisper-app-secrets-2013-5?op=1%3fr=US&IR=T&IR=T#depression-3.

Digital Media Law Project. (2008). United States vs. Drew. Retrieved from http://www.dmlp.org/threats/united-states-v-drew.

Digital Media Law Project. (2009a). Finkel vs. Facebook. Retrieved from http://www.dmlp.org/threats/finkel-v-facebook.

Digital Media Law Project. (2009b). Finkel Complaint. Retrieved from http://www.dmlp.org/sites/citmedialaw.org/files/2009-02-16-Finkel%20Complaint.pdf.

Digital media safety and literacy education and youth risk online prevention and intervention: Hearings before Subcommittee on Crime, Terrorism, and Homeland Security, 111th cong. (2009) (testimony of Nancy Willard). Retrieved from https://judiciary.house.gov/_files/hearings/pdf/Willard090930.pdf.

Digital Single Market. (2014). Better internet for Kids: CEO Coalition 1 year on. Retrieved from https://ec.europa.eu/digital-single-market/en/news/better-internet-kids-ceo-coalition-1-year.

Digital Single Market. (2015). Safer internet centers. Retrieved from https://ec.europa.eu/digital-single-market/en/safer-internet-centres.

Dinakar, K., Jones, B., Havasi, C., Lieberman, H., & Picard, R. (2012). Common sense reasoning for detection, prevention and mitigation of cyberbullying. *ACM Transactions on Interactive Intelligent Systems*, *2*(3), 1–30. doi:10.1145/2362394.2362400.

Donoso, V. (2011). Results of the Assessment of the Implementation of the Safer Social Networking Principles for the EU. Individual Reports of Testing of 14 Social Networking Sites. Retrieved from https://lirias.kuleuven.be/bitstream/123456789/458077/1/Individual+Reports+SNS+Phase+A.pdf.

Dormehl, L. (2015, January 28). 300 hours of footage per minute: Google explains why policing YouTube is so tough. *Fast Company*. Retrieved from http://www.fastcompany.com/3041622/fast-feed/300-hours-of-footage-per-minute-google-explains-why-policing-youtube-is-so-tough.

Dredge, S. (2014, October 23). Tumblr audience up to 420m as Yahoo predicts $100m revenues in 2015. *The Guardian*. Retrieved from https://www.theguardian.com/technology/2014/oct/23/tumblr-yahoo-revenues-2015-ads-nsfw.

Drezner, D. (2007). *All Politics is Global: Explaining International Regulatory Regimes*. Princeton, NJ: Princeton University Press.

Drotner, K. 1999. Dangerous media? Panic discourses and dilemmas of modernity. *Paedagogica Historica 35* (3): 593–619.

Drotner, K., & Livingstone, S. (2008). *International Handbook of Children, Media & Culture*. London: SAGE.

Dunn, R. (2013). Government to take a safeguarding position against websites like Ask.fm. Retrieved from http://epetitions.direct.gov.uk/petitions/48886.

Durkheim, E. (2002). *Moral Education*. New York: Dover Publications.

Durlak, J. A., Weissberg, R. P., Dymnicki, A. B., Taylor, R. D., & Schellinger, K. B. (2011). The impact of enhancing students' social and emotional learning: A meta-analysis of school-based universal interventions. *Child Development*, *82*, 405–432. doi:10.1111/j.1467-8624.2010.01564.

Dyer, E. (2014). Cyberbullying bill draws fire from diverse mix of critics. *CBC News*. Retrieved from http://www.cbc.ca/news/politics/cyberbullying-bill-draws-fire-from-diverse-mix-of-critics-1.2803637.

Earl, J., & Kimport, K. (2011). *Digitally Enabled Social Change: Activism in the Internet Age*. Cambridge, MA: MIT Press.

Elgan, M. (2015, July 29). Google+ is alive and well despite persistent media reports. Retrieved from http://www.eweek.com/cloud/google-is-alive-and-well-despite-persistent-media-reports.html.

Elgersma, C. (2016, February, 26). Snapchat, KIK and 6 more iffy messaging apps teens love. *Common Sense Media.* Retrieved from https://www.commonsensemedia.org/blog/snapchat-kik-and-6-more-iffy-messaging-apps-teens-love.

Englander, E. (2007). Is bullying a junior hate crime?: Implications for interventions. *American Behavioral Scientist, 51*(2), 205–212. doi:10.1177/0002764207306052.

Englander, E. (2015). What's bad behavior on the web? *Educational Leadership, 72*(8), 30–34.

Enhancing Online Safety for Children Act. 2015. No 24, 2015. Federal Register of Legislation. Retrieved from https://www.legislation.gov.au/Details/C2016C00781.

Esco, L., Richards, H., & Azuelos, L. (Producers). (2015). *FreeTheNipple* [Motion picture trailer]. U.S.A. Retrieved from http://www.freethenipple.com.

Espinoza, J. (2016, July 25). Girls gang up on boys in new cyberbullying craze called 'roasting,' expert warns. *The Telegraph.* Retrieved from http://www.telegraph.co.uk/education/2016/07/24/girls-gang-up-on-boys-in-new-cyberbullying-craze-called-roasting.

EU Kids Online. (2014). EU kids online: Findings methods recommendations (deliverable 1.6). Retrieved from http://eprints.lse.ac.uk/60512.

European Commission. (2009). Safer social networking principles for the EU. Retrieved from https://ec.europa.eu/digital-single-market/sites/digital-agenda/files/sn_principles.pdf.

European Commission. (2016). Corporate social responsibility. Retrieved from http://ec.europa.eu/growth/industry/corporate-social-responsibility_en.

Eighth European Forum on the Rights of the Child. (2013). *European Commission.* Retrieved from http://ec.europa.eu/justice/fundamental-rights/files/s3_forum_bullying_en.pdf.

Evans, N. (2013, August 7). Ask.fm run by Russian playboy brothers who make millions from troll site used to bully Hannah Smith. *Mirror.* Retrieved from http://www.mirror.co.uk/news/uk-news/askfm-run-russian-playboy-brothers-2134208.

Facebook. (2014). An update to news feed: What it means for businesses. Retrieved from https://www.facebook.com/business/news/update-to-facebook-news-feed.

Facebook. (2015a). Company Info. Retrieved from http://newsroom.fb.com/company-info/

Facebook. (2015b). Does Facebook allow photos of mothers breastfeeding? Retrieved from https://www.facebook.com/help/340974655932193.

Facebook. (2015c). Prevent Bullying. Retrieved from https://www.facebook.com/safety/bullying/?referer=safety_center.

Facebook. (2015d). Report a violation of Facebook terms. Retrieved from https://www.facebook.com/help/contact/274459462613911.

Facebook. (2015e) Safety is a conversation. Retrieved from https://www.facebook.com/safety/philosophy.

Facebook. (2015f). Statement of Rights and Responsibilities. Retrieved from https://www.facebook.com/legal/terms.

Facebook. (2016a). Help community: Facebook gives people around the world. Retrieved from https://www.facebook.com/help/community/question/?id=145104 2831788602.

Facebook. (2016b). Facebook Principles. Retrieved from https://www.facebook.com/principles.php.

Facebook. (2016d). What is social reporting? Retrieved from https://www.facebook.com/help/128548343894719.

Facebook. (2016e). What is the Support Inbox? Retrieved from https://www.facebook.com/help/545932948823931.

Facebook (2016f). Community standards. helping to keep you safe. Retrieved from https://www.facebook.com/communitystandards#.

Facebook (2017). What is the Facebook Safety Advisory Board and what work does it do? Retrieved from https://www.facebook.com/help/222332597793306/.

Facebook Help Center. (2016). How to report things? Retrieved from https://www.facebook.com/help/181495968648557?helpref=faq_content.

Facebook London Showcase. (2014, December 1). AntiBullyingPro. Retrieved from https://www.youtube.com/watch?v=MZrwGlLnHbg.

Facebook Newsroom. (2009, December 6). Facebook to enhance user safety through formation of Global Advisory Board. Retrieved from https://newsroom.fb.com/news/2009/12/facebook-to-enhance-user-safety-through-formation-of-global-advisory-board/.

Facebook refuses to add safety buttons saying they "confuse" and "intimidate" users. (2010, April 13). Telegraph. Retrieved from http://www.telegraph.co.uk/technology/facebook/7585688/Facebook-refuses-to-add-safety-buttons-saying-they-confuse-and-intimidate-users.html?mobile=basic.

Facebook Reporting Guide. (n.d.). Retrieved from https://fbcdn-dragon-a.aka-maihd.net/hphotos-ak-xpa1/t39.2178-6/851563_293317947467769_1320502878_n.png.

Facebook Safety. (2011, March 10). Details on social reporting. Retrieved from https://www.facebook.com/note.php?note_id=196124227075034.

Facebook Safety. (2012, February 13). Facebook awards $200,000 in digital citizenship research grants. Retrieved from https://www.facebook.com/notes/facebook-safety/facebook-awards-200000-in-digital-citizenship-research-grants/348583601829095.

Facebook Site Governance. (n.d.). Retrieved from https://www.facebook.com/fbsite governance.

Facer, K. (2012). After the moral panic? Reframing the debate about child safety online. *Discourse (Abingdon)*, *33*(3), 397–413. doi:10.1080/01596306.2012.681899.

Family Online Safety Institute. (2017). FOSI Mission and Values. Retrieved from https://www.fosi.org/about/mission/.

Family Online Safety Institute Annual Conference in Washington D.C. (2013, November 6–7).

Federal Communications Commission. (2016, October 25). Children's Internet Protection Act. Retrieved from https://www.fcc.gov/consumers/guides/childrens-internet-protection-act.

Federal Trade Commission. (n.d.). Children's Online Privacy Protection Rule ("COPPA"). Retrieved from https://www.ftc.gov/enforcement/rules/rulemaking-regulatory-reform-proceedings/childrens-online-privacy-protection-rule.

Federal Trade Commission. (2013, July 1). Revised Children's Online Privacy Protection Rule goes into effect today. Retrieved from https://www.ftc.gov/news-events/press-releases/2013/07/revised-childrens-online-privacy-protection-rule-goes-effect.

Federal Trade Commission. (2015, March 20). Complying with COPPA: FAQ. Retrieved from https://www.ftc.gov/tips-advice/business-center/guidance/complying-coppa-frequently-asked-questions#General Questions.

Fernback, J., & Papacharissi, Z. (2007). Online privacy as a legal safeguard: The relationship among consumer, online portal and privacy policies. *New Media & Society*, *9*(5), 715–734.

Fiegerman, S. (2015, August 2). Inside the failure of Google+. An expensive attempt to unseat Facebook. Mashable.com. Retrieved from http://mashable.com/2015/08/02/google-plus-history/#UQFRwn6XDPqZ

Finkelhor, D., Mitchell, K. J., & Wolak, J. (2000). *Online Victimization: A Report on the Nation's Youth*. Retrieved from http://www.unh.edu/ccrc/pdf/Victimization_Online_Survey.pdf

Fisk, N. (2017). *Framing Internet Safety: The Governance of Youth Online*. Cambridge, MA: MIT Press.

Foderaro, L. W. (2010, September 29). Private moment made public, then a fatal jump. *The New York Times*. Retrieved from http://www.nytimes.com/2010/09/30/nyregion/30suicide.html.

Franks, M. A. (2014, August 14). The many ways Twitter is bad at responding to abuse. *The Atlantic*. Retrieved from http://www.theatlantic.com/technology/archive/2014/08/the-many-ways-twitter-is-bad-at-responding-to-abuse/376100.

Fresco, A. (2009, November 18). Networking sites fail to protect children from abuse, says CEOP head. *Times*. Retrieved from http://technology.timesonline.co.uk/tol/news/tech_and_web/the_web/article6920945.

Frisen, A., Holmqvist, K., & Oscarsson, D. (2008). 13-year-olds' perception of bullying: Definitions, reasons for victimisation and experience of adults' response. *Educational Studies*, *34*, 105–117.

Frisen, A., Jonsson, A.-K., & Persson, C. (2007). Adolescents' perception of bullying: Who is the victim? Who is the bully? What can be done to stop bullying? *Adolescence*, *42*, 749–761.

Fukkink, R., & Hermanns, J. (2009). Counseling children at a helpline: Chatting or calling. *Journal of Community Psychology*, *37*(8), 939–948.

Fuller, R. W. (2003). *Somebodies and Nobodies: Overcoming the Abuse of Rank*. Gabriola Island, Canada: New Society.

Fuller, R. W. (2006). *All Rise: Somebodies, Nobodies and the Politics of Dignity*. San Francisco, CA: Berrett-Koehler.

Fuller, R. W., & Gerloff, P. (2008). *Dignity for All: How to Create a World without Rankism*. San Francisco, CA: Berrett-Koehler.

Gaggle (n.d.). Top social networks and apps kids use. Retrieved from https://www.gaggle.net/top-social-networking-sites-and-apps-kids-use.

Gallagher, F. (2015, May 6). How many users does Google+ really have? *TechTimes*. Retrieved from http://www.techtimes.com/articles/51205/20150506/many-users-google-really.htm.

Garcia-Martinez, A. (Summer, 2016). How Mark Zuckerberg led Facebook's war to crush Google Plus. *Vanity Fair*. Retrieved from http://www.vanityfair.com/news/2016/06/how-mark-zuckerberg-led-facebooks-war-to-crush-google-plus.

Gasser, U., & Schulz, W. (2015). Governance of Online Intermediaries: Observations from a Series of National Case Studies. Retrieved from https://publixphere.net/i/noc/page/NoC_Online_Intermediaries_Research_Project_Synthesis.

Gauthier, B. (2016, July 26). What Convention? For some on Twitter "the Bachelorette" is a lot more important. *The Salon*. Retrieved from http://www.salon.com/2016/07/26/what_convention_for_some_on_twitter_the_bachelorette_is_a_lot_more_important.

Geist, M. (2013, November 22). Lawful access returns under cover of cyber-bullying bill. *The Star*. Retrieved from http://www.thestar.com/business/2013/11/22/lawful_access_returns_under_cover_of_cyberbullying_bill.html.

Geoffroy, M.-C., Boivin, M., Arseneault, L., Turecki, G., Vitaro, F., Brendgen, M., et al. (2016). Associations between peer victimization and suicidal ideation and suicide attempt during adolescence: results from a prospective population-based birth cohort. *Journal of the American Academy of Child and Adolescent Psychiatry, 55*(2), 99–105. doi:10.1016/j.jaac.2015.11.010.

Giantasio, D. (2014, September 15). Anonymous apps like Whisper and Secret have a dark side. *Adweek.* Retrieved from: http://www.adweek.com/news/advertising-branding /anonymous-apps-whisper-and-secret-have-dark-side-160107.

Gibbs, S. (2016, March 4). Facebook to pay millions more in UK tax. *The Guardian.* Retrieved from: https://www.theguardian.com/technology/2016/mar/04/facebook -pay-millions-more-uk-tax-reports.

Gibson, C. (2016, September 6). They call it bunny hunting. *The Washington Post.* Retrieved from https://www.washingtonpost.com/lifestyle/style/they-call-it-bunny -hunting-how-authorities-warn-kids-about-online-predators/2016/09/06/2044ee40 -5980-11e6-9767-f6c947fd0cb8_story.html.

Gillespie, T. (2010). The politics of "platforms." *New Media & Society, 12*(3), 347–364.

Gillespie, T. (2015). Platforms intervene. *Social Media + Society, 1*(1), 1–2.

Gillham, B. (2000). *The Research Interview.* London: Continuum.

Gilden, A. (2013). Cyberbullying and the innocence narrative. *Harvard Civil Rights-Civil Liberties Law Review.* Retrieved from https://papers.ssrn.com/sol3/papers.cfm ?abstract_id=2208737.

Glaister, D. (2008, November 26). Neighbor found guilty on lesser charges in MySpace suicide case. *The Guardian.* Retrieved from https://www.theguardian.com/world /2008/nov/26/myspace-suicide-cyber-bully.

Global Kids Online. (2016). A framework for researching Global Kids Online. Forthcoming report from the GKO research network.

Goode, E., & Ben-Yehuda, N. (1994). Moral panics: Culture, politics, and social construction. *Annual Review of Sociology, 20*, 149–171.

Goodno, N. H. (2011). How public schools can constitutionally halt cyberbullying: A model cyberbullying policy that considers first amendment, due process, and fourth amendment challenges. *Wake Forest Law Review, 46*, 641–700.

Google. (2015a). Anti-bullying information for parents. Retrieved from https://support .google.com/plus/answer/2402979?hl=en.

Google. (2015b). Bring more to class with Google tools. Retrieved from https://www .google.com/edu/training/get-trained/?utm_referrer=.

Google. (n.d.). Terms and Policies. User Content and Conduct Policy. Retrieved from https://www.google.com/intl/en-US/+/policy/content.html.

Google. (2016a). Age Requirements on Google Accounts. Retrieved from https://support.google.com/accounts/answer/1350409?hl=en.

Google. (2016b). How to stop harassment & bullying on Google+. Retrieved from https://support.google.com/plus/answer/6006895?p=harassment&hl=en&rd=1.

Görzig, A. (2011). *Who bullies and who is bullied online?: A study of 9–16 year old internet users in 25 European countries*. London: EU Kids Online, London School of Economics and Political Science.

Görzig, A., & Macháčková, H. (2015). *Cyberbullying from a socio-ecological perspective: A contemporary synthesis of findings from EU Kids Online (Media@LSE Working Paper Series)*. London: London School of Economics and Political Science. Retrieved from http://www.lse.ac.uk/media@lse/research/mediaWorkingPapers/pdf/WP36-FINAL.pdf.

Görzig, A. (2016). Adolescents' experience of offline and online risks: Separate and joint propensities. *Computers in Human Behavior, 56*, 9–13.

Gov.uk. (2016, March 1). Child safety online: A practical guide for providers of social media and interactive services. Retrieved from https://www.gov.uk/government/publications/child-safety-online-a-practical-guide-for-providers-of-social-media-and-interactive-services/child-safety-online-a-practical-guide-for-providers-of-social-media-and-interactive-services.

Grandoni, D. (2014, April 25). Google+ isn't dead. It's just in a coma and on life support. *Huffington Post*. Retrieved from http://www.huffingtonpost.com/2014/04/25/google-plus-dead_n_5212819.html.

Great Speculations. (2016, March 23). How Yahoo is trying to drive revenues for Tumblr? *Forbes*. Retrieved from http://www.forbes.com/sites/greatspeculations/2016/03/23/how-yahoo-is-trying-to-drive-revenues-for-tumblr/#382dad5a18c4.

Greenberg, A. (2016, September 9). Inside Google's Internet Justice League and its AI-powered war on trolls. *Wired*. Retrieved from https://www.wired.com/2016/09/inside-googles-internet-justice-league-ai-powered-war-trolls/?mbid=social_twitter.

Grierson, J. (2017, May 22). "No grey areas." Experts urge Facebook to change moderation policies. *The Guardian*. Retrieved from https://www.theguardian.com/news/2017/may/22/no-grey-areas-experts-urge-facebook-to-change-moderation-policies.

Gunningham, N., & Rees, J. (1997). Industry self-regulation: An institutional perspective. *Law & Policy, 19*(4), 363–414.

Haigh, M. M., Brubaker, P., & Whiteside, E. (2013). Facebook: Examining the information presented and its impact on stakeholders. *Corporate Communications, 18*(1), 52–60.

Hamelink, C. J. (2003). Statement on Communication Rights. Paper presented at the World Forum on Communication Rights.

Hamilton, K. (2007, November 28). Broken lives on Waterford Crystal Drive. *Riverfront News*. Retrieved from http://www.riverfronttimes.com/2007-11-28/news/broken -lives-on-waterford-crystal-drive/full.

Hannah Smith: Ask.fm "happy to help police." (2013, August 6). *SkyNews*. Retrieved from http://news.sky.com/story/1124978/hannah-smith-ask-fm-happy-to-help-police.

Hannah Smith death: Father says daughter was victim of cyberbullies BBC News Leicester (2013, August 6). *BBC News*. Retrieved from http://www.bbc.com/news/uk -england-leicestershire-23584769.

Hannah Smith inquest: Teenager posted "online messages." (2014, May 6). *BBC News*. Retrieved from http://www.bbc.com/news/uk-england-leicestershire-27298627.

Hartling, L. M. (2010). Afterword in honor of Jean Baker Miller and Donald Klein. In E. Lindner (Ed.), *Gender, Humiliation, and Global Security: Dignifying Relationships from Love, Sex, and Parenthood to World Affairs* (pp. 175–176). Santa Barbara, CA: Praeger.

Hartling, L. M., & Luchetta, T. (1999). Humiliation: Assessing the impact of derision, degradation, and debasement. *Journal of Primary Prevention, 19*(4), 259–278.

Hasebrink, U., Göerzig, A., Haddon, L., Kalmus, V., & Livingstone, S. (2011). *Patterns of Risk and Safety Online: In-Depth Analyses from the EU Kids Online Survey of 9-to 16-Year-Olds and Their Parents in 25 European Countries.* London: EU Kids Online, London School of Economics and Political Science.

Hawley, P. H., Little, T. D., & Card, N. A. (2007). The allure of mean friend: Relationship quality and processes of aggressive adolescents with prosocial skills. *International Journal of Behavioral Development, 31*(2), 170–180.

Heath, A. (2016, March 8). Yik Yak becomes less anonymous as it struggles to remain relevant to students. *Tech Insider*. Retrieved: http://www.techinsider.io/yik-yak-becomes -less-anonymous-2016-3.

Held, T. (2007). Co-regulation in European Union Member States. *Communications, 32*(3), 355–362.

Hempel, J. (2016, January 14). Hey millenials, your mom is about to follow you on Snapchat. *Wired*. Retrieved from https://www.wired.com/2016/01/hey-millennials -your-mom-is-about-to-be-on-snapchat.

Henley, J. (2013, August 6). Ask.fm: Is there a way to make it safe? *The Guardian*. Retrieved from http://www.theguardian.com/society/2013/aug/06/askfm-way-to-make -it-safe.

Herba, C. M., Ferdinand, R. F., Stijnen, T., Veenstra, R., Oldehinkel, A. J., Ormel, J., et al. (2008). Victimisation and suicide ideation in the TRAILS study: Specific vulnerabilities of victims. *Journal of Child Psychology and Psychiatry, and Allied Disciplines, 49*(8), 867–876. doi:10.1111/j.1469-7610.2008.01900.x.

Hestres, L. E. (2013). App Neutrality: Apple's App Store and freedom of expression online. *International Journal of Communication, 7*(15), 1265–1280.

Hicks, D. (2011). *Dignity: Its Essential Role in Resolving Conflict.* New Haven, CT: Yale University Press.

Hill, M. (2014). By removing photos of childbirth, Facebook is censoring powerful female images. *The Guardian.* Retrieved from http://www.theguardian.com/com mentisfree/2014/oct/22/facebook-removing-childbirth-female-images.

Hillier, A. (2014, December 11). Former BeatBullying executives, including Ross Banford and Sarah Dyer, set up new company a week after liquidation. *Third Sector.* Retrieved from http://www.thirdsector.co.uk/former-beatbullying-executives-including -ross-banford-sarah-dyer-set-new-company-week-liquidation/management/article /1326181.

Hinduja, S. (2016, September 29). How social media helps teens cope with anxiety, depression and self-harm. Cyberbullying Research Center. Retrieved from http:// cyberbullying.org/how-social-media-helps-teens-cope-anxiety-depression-self-harm.

Hinduja, S., & Patchin, J. W. (2008). Cyberbullying: An exploratory analysis of factors related to offending and victimization. *Deviant Behavior, 29*(2), 129–156.

Hinduja, S., & Patchin, J. W. (2009). *Bullying beyond the Schoolyard: Preventing and Responding to Cyberbullying.* Thousand Oaks, CA: SAGE.

Hinduja, S., & Patchin, J. W. (2010). Bullying, cyberbullying, and suicide. *Archives of Suicide Research, 14*(3), 206–221. doi:10.1080/13811118.2010.494133.

Hinduja, S., & Patchin, J. (2016). *Bullying and cyberbullying laws.* Retrieved from http:// www.cyberbullying.us/Bullying-and-Cyberbullying-Laws.pdf.

Hopkins, N. (2017, May 22). How Facebook allows users to post footage of children being bullied. *The Guardian.* Retrieved from https://www.theguardian.com/news/2017 /may/22/how-facebook-allows-users-to-post-footage-of-children-being-bullied.

Hopkins, N., and J. Wong. (2017, May 21). Has Facebook become a forum for misogyny and racism? *The Guardian.* Retrieved from https://www.theguardian.com/news /2017/may/21/has-facebook-become-forum-misogyny-racism.

Hughes, T. (2016, February 5). Kik messaging app scrutinized in wake of Va teen's murder. *USA Today.* Retrieved from http://www.usatoday.com/story/news/nation /2016/02/04/kik-messaging-app-scrutinized-wake-va-teens-murder/79826224.

Humanium. (n.d.). The Convention on the Rights of the Child. Retrieved from http:// www.humanium.org/en/convention/signatory-states.

Hunt, E. (2016, July 20). Milo Yiannopoulos, rightwing writer, permanently banned from Twitter. *The Guardian.* Retrieved from https://www.theguardian.com/technol ogy/2016/jul/20/milo-yiannopoulos-nero-permanently-banned-twitter.

Hunter, S., Boyle, J., & Warden, D. (2004). Help seeking amongst child and adolescent victims of peer-aggression and bullying: The influence of school-stage, gender, victimisation, appraisal, and emotion. *British Journal of Educational Psychology, 74,* 375–390.

IAC. (n.d.). IAC. Retrieved from http://iac.com.

ICT Coalition. (n.d.). ICT coalition, Principles PDF. Retrieved from http://www.ict coalition.eu.

Ingram, M. (2016, June 2). Snapchat now has more daily users than Twitter does. *Fortune.* Retrieved from http://fortune.com/2016/06/02/snapchat-twitter.

Instagram. (2013). Terms of use. Retrieved from https://help.instagram.com/478745 558852511.

Isaac, M. (2016, August 2). Instagram takes a page from Snapchat and takes aim at it too. *New York Times.* Retrieved from http://www.nytimes.com/2016/08/03/technol ogy/instagram-stories-snapchat-facebook.html?module=WatchingPortal&region=c -column-middle-span-region&pgType=Homepage&action=click&mediaId=thumb_ square&state=standard&contentPlacement=6&version=internal&contentCollection =www.nytimes.com&contentId=http%3A%2F%2Fwww.nytimes.com%2F2016%2F08 %2F03%2Ftechnology%2Finstagram-stories-snapchat-facebook.html&event Name=Watching-article-click&_r=0.

Iowa Supreme Court holds that evidence of taunting is insufficient to constitute criminal harassment. *Harvard Law Review, 128*(7), 2058–2065. Retrieved from http:// harvardlawreview.org/2015/05/in-re-d-s.

Jenkins, P. (1992). *Intimate Enemies: Moral Panics in Contemporary Great Britain.* New York: Aldine de Gruyter.

Johnstone, B. (2002). *Discourse Analysis.* Oxford: Blackwell.

Jones, L. M., & Mitchell, K. J. (2015). Defining and measuring youth digital citizenship. *New Media & Society, 18*(9), 2063—2079. doi:10.1177/1461444815577797.

Jones, L. M., Mitchell, K. J., & Finkelhor, D. (2013). Online harassment in context: Trends from three youth Internet safety surveys (2000, 2005, 2010). *Psychology of Violence, 3,* 53–69. doi:10.1037/A0030309.

Jones, L. M., Mitchell, K. J., & Walsh, W. A. (2013). Evaluation of Internet child safety materials used by ICAC task forces in school and community settings: Final report. Retrieved from https://www.ncjrs.gov/pdffiles1/nij/grants/242016.pdf.

Jones, L. M., Mitchell, K. J., & Walsh, W. A. (2014). A content analysis of youth internet safety programs: Are effective prevention strategies being used? Retrieved from http://www.unh.edu/ccrc/pdf/ISE%20Bulletin%202_Contant%20Analysis%20 of%20Youth%20ISE%20FINAL-with%20appendix.pdf.

Judge orders end to Facebook cyberbullying under new law. (2014, February 11). *CBC News*. Retrieved from http://www.cbc.ca/news/canada/nova-scotia/judge-orders-end -to-facebook-cyberbullying-under-new-law-1.2531764.

June, L. (2016, March 18). Why did Facebook remove this photo of a woman and her newborn? *New York Magazine*. Retrieved from http://nymag.com/thecut/2016 /03/facebook-childbirth-censorship.html#.

Kaiser High School reports cyberbullying threats via social media app. (2015, November 22). *Hawaii News Now*. Retrieved from http://www.hawaiinewsnow.com /story/27449485/kaiser-high-school-reports-cyberbullying-threats-via-social-media -app.

Kapko, M. (2016, August 12). Cyberbullying continues to drag Twitter down. *The CIO*. Retrieved from http://www.cio.com/article/3107165/social-networking/cyber bullying-continues-to-drag-twitter-down.html.

Kaplan, A. M., & Haenlein, M. (2010). Users of the world, unite! The challenges and opportunities of social media. *Business Horizons, 53*(1), 59–68.

Katz, A. (2012). *Cyberbullying and E-safety: What Educators and Other Professionals Need to Know*. London: Jessica Kingsley.

Kelly, M. (2013, November 15). *The Sextortion of Amanda Todd. CBC*. [online documentary]. Retrieved from http://www.cbc.ca/fifth/episodes/2013-2014/the-sextortion -of-amanda-todd.

Kelly, M. (2014, December 5). *Amanda Todd: The Man in the Shadows. CBC*. [online documentary]. Retrieved from http://www.cbc.ca/fifth/episodes/2014-2015/stalking -amanda-todd-the-man-in-the-shadows.

Kiberd, R. (2016, August 5). YouTube's trolls are crying censorship over cyberbullying rules. Motherboard. Retrieved from http://motherboard.vice.com/read/youtubes -trolls-leafyishere-are-crying-censorship-over-cyberbullying-rules.

Kik. (2015, January, 29). 200 million users. Retrieved from https://blog.kik.com/2015 /01/29/200-million-users.

Kik Interactive. (2016a). I'm being harassed on Kik! What can I do? Retrieved from https://kikinteractive.zendesk.com/entries/23518788-I-m-being-harassed-on-Kik -What-can-I-do-.

Kik Interactive. (2016b). Is there a way to manage messages from new people? Retrieved from https://kikinteractive.zendesk.com/hc/en-us/articles/115006089428 -Manage-messages-from-new-people.

Kik Interactive. (2016c). Privacy policy. Retrieved from http://www.kik.com/privacy.

Kik Interactive. (2016d). Terms of service. Retrieved from https://www.kik.com/assets /Uploads/Kik-Terms-of-Service-Uploaded-May-9-2016.pdf.

Kik Interactive. (2016e). Home. http://kik.com.

Kik Interactive. (2016f). About. https://www.kik.com/about.

King, A. V. (2010). Constitutionality of cyberbullying laws: Keeping the online playground safe for both teens and free speech. *Vanderbilt Law Review, 63*(3), 845–884.

Kiss, J. (2010, April 7). Bebo: where did it all go wrong? *The Guardian.* Retrieved from http://www.theguardian.com/media/2010/apr/07/bebo-facebook.

Klein, J. (2012). *The Bully Society: School Shootings and the Crisis of Bullying in America's Schools.* New York: NYU Press.

Kling, R., Lee, Y., Teich, A., & Frankel, M. S. (1999). Assessing anonymous communication on the Internet: Policy deliberations. *The Information Society, 15*(2), 78–90. Retrieved from http://smg.media.mit.edu/library/Kling.AssessAnon.pdf.

Kobie, N. (2016, March 7). Linked to bullying and even murder, can anonymous apps like Kik ever be safe? Retrieved from https://www.theguardian.com/sustainable-business/2016/mar/07/anonymous-apps-cyber-bullying-security-safety-kik-yik-yak-secret.

Kofoed, J., & Ringrose, J. (2012). Travelling and sticky affects: Exploring teens and sexualized cyberbullying through a Butlerian-Deleuzian-Guattarian lens. *Discourse (Abingdon), 33*(1), 5–20.

Kosciw, J. G., E. A. Greytak, M. J. Bartkiewicz, M. J. Boesen, and N. A. Palmer. (2012). *The 2011 National School Climate Survey: The Experiences of Lesbian, Gay, Bisexual and Transgender Youth in Our Nation's Schools.* Gay, Lesbian and Straight Education Network (GLSEN). 121 West 27th Street Suite 804, New York, NY 10001. Retrieved from http://files.eric.ed.gov/fulltext/ED535177.pdf.

Kosciw, J. G., Greytak, E. A., & Diaz, E. M. (2009). Who, what, when, where, and why: Demographic and ecological factors contributing to hostile school climate for lesbian, gay, bisexual, and transgender youth. *Journal of Youth and Adolescence, 38*(7), 976–988.

Kosoff, M. (2015, December 11). 20 million people are sharing secrets on anonymous app Whisper every month. *Business Insider.* Retrieved from http://www.businessinsider.com/anonymous-app-whisper-has-20-million-monthly-users-2015-12.

Kosoff, M. (2016, April 7). Anonymous gossip app Yik Yak is in trouble. *Vanity Fair.* Retrieved: http://www.vanityfair.com/news/2016/04/anonymous-gossip-app-yik-yak-is-in-trouble.

Kowalski, R. M., Giumetti, G. W., Schroeder, A. N., & Lattanner, M. R. (2014). Bullying in the digital age: A critical review and meta-analysis of cyberbullying research among youth. *Psychological Bulletin, 140*(4), 1073–1137.

Kowalski, R. M., Limber, S. P., & Agatston, P. W. (2012). *Cyberbullying: Bullying in the DigitalAage.* Malden, MA: Wiley-Blackwell.

Kravets, D. (2009, September 30). Cyberbulling bill gets chilly reception. *Wired*. Retrieved from http://www.wired.com/2009/09/cyberbullyingbill.

Kunkel, D. 1990. The role of research in the regulation of US children's television advertising. *Science Communication 12* (1): 101–119.

Lampert, C., & Donoso, V. (2012). Bullying. In S. Livingstone, L. Haddon, & A. Görzig (Eds.), *Children, Risk and Safety on the Internet* (pp. 141–150). Bristol: Policy Press.

Lannin, S. (2014, December 3). Cyberbulling: Government crackdown to target social media sites. *ABC*. Retrieved from http://www.abc.net.au/news/2014-12-03/government -plans-cyber-bullying-crackdown/5935560.

Larson, R. W. (2000). Toward a psychology of positive youth development. *American Psychologist, 55*(1), 170–183.

Larson, J., Nagler, J., Ronen, J., & Tucker, J. (2016). Social networks and protest participation: evidence from 93 million Twitter users. Political Networks Workshops & Conference 2016. Retrieved from http://papers.ssrn.com/sol3/papers.cfm?abstract_id =2796391.

Latzer, M., Just, N., & Saurwein, F. (2013). Self- and co-regulation. Evidence, legitimacy and governance choice. In E. P. Monroe, S. G. Verhulst, & L. Morgan (Eds.), *Routledge Handbook of Media Law* (pp. 373–397). Oxon: Routledge.

Latzer, M., Price, M. E., Saurwein, F., & Verhulst, S. G. 2007. Comparative analysis of international co- and self-regulation in communications markets. Research report commissioned by Ofcom, September, Vienna: ITA at http://www.mediachange.ch /media/pdf/publications/latzer_et_al_2007_comparative_analysis.pdf.

Lawmaker modifies Audrie Pott sex-assault bill targeting teens. (2014, June 24). Retrieved from http://www.ksbw.com/news/central-california/hollister-gilroy/law maker-modifies-audrie-pott-sexassault-bill-targeting-teens/26644110.

LeafyIsHere. (2016, July 26). The YouTube rant: I'm getting banned off YouTube. Retrieved from https://www.youtube.com/watch?v=I5FLhS2YxmY&index=109 &list=WL.

Leiter, B. (2010). Cleaning cyber-cesspools: Google and free speech. In S. Levmore & M. Nussbaum (Eds.), *The Offensive Internet: Privacy, Speech, and Reputation*. Cambridge, MA: Harvard University Press.

Lenhart, A. (2015, April, 9). Teens Social Media & Technology Overview 2015. Retrieved from http://www.pewinternet.org/2015/04/09/teens-social-media-techno logy-2015.

Lereya, S. T., Winsper, C., Heron, J., Lewis, G., Gunnell, D., Fisher, H. L., et al. (2013). Being bullied during childhood and the prospective pathways to self-harm in late adolescence. *Journal of the American Academy of Child and Adolescent Psychiatry*, *52*(6), 608–618. doi:10.1016/j.jaac.2013.03.012.

Lerner, R. M., Fisher, C., & Weinberg, R. (2000). Toward a science for and of the people: Promoting civil society through the application of developmental science. *Child Development*, *71*(1), 11–20.

Levin, S., Wong, J. C., & Harding, L. (2016, September 9). Facebook backs down from napalm girl censorship and reinstates photo. *The Guardian*. Retrieved from https://www.theguardian.com/technology/2016/sep/09/facebook-reinstates-napalm-girl-photo.

Levmore, S. (2010). The Internet's anonymity problem. In S. Levmore & M. Nussbaum (Eds.), *The Offensive Internet: Privacy, Speech, and Reputation*. Cambridge, MA: Harvard University Press.

Lewis, P., & Rushe, D. (2014, October 17). Whisper app has published its new terms of service and privacy policy. *The Guardian*. Retrieved from http://www.theguardian.com/world/2014/oct/16/-sp-whisper-privacy-policy-terms-of-service.

Lievens, E. (2010). *Protecting Children in the Digital Era: The Use of Alternative Regulatory Instruments*. Leiden, Netherlands: Martinus Nijhoff.

Lievens, E. (2012). Risks for young users on social network sites and the legal framework: Match or mismatch? Paper presented at 23rd European Regional Conference of the International Telecommunication Society, Vienna, Austria. Retrieved from https://www.b-ccentre.be/download/b-ccentre_legal/B-CCENTRE%20Risks%20for%20young%20users%20on%20social%20network%20sites%20and%20the%20legal%20framework.pdf.

Lievens, E. (2016). Is self-regulation failing children and young people? Assessing the use of alternative regulatory instruments in the area of social networks. In S. Simpson, H. Van den Bulck, & M. Puppis (Eds.), *European Media Policy for the Twenty-First Century: Assessing the Past, Setting Agendas for the Future* (pp. 77–94). New York, NY: Routledge.

Lindner, E. G. (2006). *Making Enemies: Humiliation and International Conflict*. Westport, CT: Praeger.

Lindner, E. G. (2010). *Gender, Humiliation, and Global Security: Dignifying Relationships from Love, Sex, and Parenthood to World Affairs*. Santa Barbara, CA: Praeger.

Lipton, J. D. (2011). Combating cyber-victimization. *Berkeley Technology Law Journal*, *26*(2), 1103–1155.

Lipton, J. D. (2013). Cyberbullying and the First Amendment. *Florida Coastal Law Review*, *14*(99), 99–130.

Livingstone, S. (2009a). *Children and the Internet*. Cambridge: Polity Press.

Livingstone, S. (2009b). A rationale for positive online content for children. *Communication Research Trends*, *28*(3), 12–17.

Livingstone, S. (2016). Reframing media effects in terms of children's rights in the digital age. *Journal of Children and Media*, *10*(1), 4–12. doi:10.1080/17482798.2015.1 123164.

Livingstone, S., & Bulger, M. (2014). A global research agenda for children's rights in the digital age. *Journal of Children and Media*. doi:10.1080/17482798.2014.961496.

Livingstone, S., Carr, J., & Byrne, J. (2015). One in Three: Internet Governance and Children's Rights. Global Commission on Internet Governance. Retrieved from https://www.cigionline.org/publications/one-three-internet-governance-and-childrens-rights.

Livingstone, S., Haddon, L., Vincent, J., Mascheroni, G., & Ólafsson, K. (2014). *Net Children Go Mobile: The UK Report*. London: London School of Economics and Political Science.

Livingstone, S., Haddon, L., & Görzig, A. (Eds.). (2012). *Children, Risk and Safety on the Internet: Research and Policy Challenges in Comparative Perspective*. Bristol, UK: The Policy Press.

Livingstone, S., Haddon, L. G., Görzig, A., & Ólafsson, K. (2011). *Risks and safety on the internet: The perspective of European children—Full findings and policy implications from the EU Kids Online survey of 9–16 year olds and their parents in 25 countries*. LSE, London: EU Kids Online.

Livingstone, S., Mascheroni, G., Ólafsson , K., & Haddon, L. (2014). Children's online risks and opportunities: Comparative findings of EU Kids Online and Net Children Go mobile. Retrieved from http://netchildrengomobile.eu/reports.

Livingstone, S., G. Mascheroni, and E. Staksrud. (2017). European research on children's internet use: Assessing the past, anticipating the future. *New Media & Society* January 10:1–20.

Livingstone, S., Mascheroni, G., & Staksrud, E. (2015). Developing a framework for researching children's risks and opportunities in Europe. Retrieved from http://eprints.lse.ac.uk/64470/1/__lse.ac.uk_storage_LIBRARY_Secondary_libfile_shared_repository_Content_EU%20Kids%20Online_EU%20Kids%20Online_Developing%20framework%20for%20researching_2015.pdf.

Livingstone, S., Ólafsson , K., & Staksrud, E. (2011). *Social Networking, Age and Privacy*. London: EU Kids Online.

Livingstone, S., Ólafsson , K., O'Neill, B., & Donoso, V. (2012). Towards a better internet for children. EU Kids Online. Retrieved from http://www.lse.ac.uk/media@lse/research/EUKidsOnline/EU%20Kids%20III/Reports/EUKidsOnlinereportforthe CEOCoalition.pdf.

Long, J. D., & Pellegrini, A. D. (2003). Studying change in dominance and bullying with linear mixed models. *School Psychology Review, 32*(3), 401–418.

Lunt, P., & Livingstone, S. (2012). *Media Regulation: Governance and the Interests of Citizens and Consumers*. London: Sage.

Maag, C. (2007, November 28). A hoax turned fatal draws anger but no charges. *New York Times*. Retrieved from http://www.nytimes.com/2007/11/28/us/28hoax.html ?_r=0.

MacDonald, M. (2015, January 15). Year of probation for second man who pleaded guilty in Rehtaeh Parsons case. *The Globe and Mail*. Retrieved from http://www.theglobeandmail.com/news/national/rehtaeh-parsons-sentence/article22457916.

Macháčková, H., Dedkova, L., Ševčíková, A., & Cerna, A. (2013). Bystanders' support of cyberbullied schoolmates. *Journal of Community & Applied Social Psychology, 23*(1), 25–36. doi:10.1002/casp.2135.

MacKinnon, R. (2012). *Consent of the Networked: The World-Wide Struggle for Internet Freedom*. New York: Basic Books.

Magid, L. (2013, May 1). What is Snapchat and why do kids love it and parents fear it? (Updated). *Forbes*. Retrieved from http://www.forbes.com/sites/larrymagid/2013 /05/01/what-is-snapchat-and-why-do-kids-love-it-and-parents-fear-it.

Magid, L. (2014, August 14). IAC's Ask.com buys Ask.fm and hires a safety officer to stem bullying. Forbes. Retrieved from http://www.forbes.com/sites/larrymagid/2014 /08/14/iacs-ask-com-buys-ask-fm-and-hires-a-safety-officer-to-stem-bullying.

Marsden, C. T. (2011). *Internet Co-regulation. European Law, Regulatory Governance and Legitimacy in Cyberspace*. Cambridge: Cambridge University Press.

Marsden, C. T. (2012). Internet co-regulation and constitutionalism: Towards European judicial review. *International Review of Law Computers & Technology, 26*(2–3), 211–228. doi:10.1080/13600869.2012.698450.

Marwick, A. E. (2008). To catch a predator? The MySpace moral panic. *First Monday, 13*(6). Retrieved from http://journals.uic.edu/ojs/index.php/fm/article/view/2152 /1966.

Marwick, A., & boyd, d. (2014). "It's just drama": Teen perspectives on conflict and aggression in a networked era. *Journal of Youth Studies, 17*(9), 1187–1204.

Marwick, A. E., & Miller, R. W. (2014). Online Harassment, Defamation, and Hateful Speech: A Primer of the Legal Landscape. Fordham Center on Law and Information Policy Report No. 2. Retrieved from http://ssrn.com/abstract=2447904.

Maryland Attorney General. (2014). Attorney General Gansler secures settlement from Snapchat, Inc. Retrieved from http://www.oag.state.md.us/Press/2014/061214 .html.

Maryland Attorney General. (2013). AG Gansler launches pilot project with Facebook to address cyberbullying. Retrieved from http://www.marylandattorneygeneral .gov/press/2013/100313.pdf.

Masnick, M. (April 28, 2010). Anti-piracy group says: Child porn is great, since it gets politicians to block file sharing sites. *Techdirt*. Retrieved from https://www.tech dirt.com/articles/20100427/1437179198.shtml.

Matias, J. N., Johnson, A., Boesel, W. E., Keegan, B., Friedman, J., & DeTar, C. (2015). Reporting, reviewing, and responding to harassment on Twitter. *Women, Action, & the Media*. Retrieved from http://womenactionmedia.org/cms/assets/uploads/2015 /05/wam-twitter-abuse-report.pdf.

Mathews, K. J. (2007, October 17). New York Attorney General settlement with Facebook creates new model to protect children online. *Proskauer Privacy Law Blog*. Retrieved from http://privacylaw.proskauer.com/2007/10/articles/online-privacy/new -york-attorney-general-settlement-with-facebook-creates-new-model-to-protect -children-online/.

McCarthy, K. (2014 October 24). Whisper tracks its users. So we tracked down its LA office. This is what happened next. *The Register*. Retrieved from http://www.the register.co.uk/2014/10/20/whisper_doorstepping.

McGrath, P. (2015, February 7). Twitter CEO "ashamed" of how company handles cyber bullying, revenue growth threatened. *ABC*. Retrieved from http://www.abc .net.au/news/2015-02-06/twitter-ceo-ashamed-of-cyber-bullying-attacks/6076108.

McGraw, P. (2015, May 6). It's time to stop the cyberbullying epidemic. *Huffington Post*. Retrieved from http://www.huffingtonpost.com/entry/stop-cyberbullying_b_6647990.

McLaughlin, S. (2013). Regulation and legislation. In: B. O'Neill, E. Staksrud & S. McLaughlin, *Towards a better internet for children? Policy pillars, players and paradoxes* (pp. 77–91). Göteborg: Nordicom.

McMillan, R. (2007, October 17). After New York investigation Facebook to beef up safety. Retrieved from http://www.networkworld.com/article/2287089/lan-wan/after -new-york-investigation--facebook-to-beef-up-safety.html.

Medina, D. A. (2014, November 12). This gossipy social network is getting huge on college campuses. *QUARTZ*. Retrieved from https://qz.com/291637/the-rise-of-this -anonymous-app-does-not-mean-that-more-are-on-the-way/.

Megan Meier Cyberbullying Prevention Act, H.R.1966, 111th cong. (2009).

Megan Meier Foundation. (n.d.a). Megan Meier Foundation. Retrieved from http:// www.meganmeierfoundation.org.

Megan Meier Foundation. (n.d.b). Megan's story. Retrieved from http://www.mega nmeierfoundation.org/megans-story.html.

Menesini, C., Codecasa, E., Beatrice, B., & Cowie, H. (2003). Enhancing children's responsibility to take action against bullying: Evaluation of a befriending intervention in Italian middle schools. *Aggressive Behavior, 29*(1), 10–14.

Mercury News. (2016, July 8). Magid: New Snapchat features provide a more lasting experience. Retrieved from http://www.mercurynews.com/2016/07/08/magid-new -snapchat-features-provide-more-lasting-experience.

Michels, S. (2008, November 26). Neighbor guilty in MySpace hoax case. *ABC News.* Retrieved from http://abcnews.go.com/TheLaw/Technology/story?id=6338498.

Milosevic, T. (2015a). Cyberbullying policies of social media companies: Towards digital dignity. Unpublished doctoral dissertation.

Milosevic, T. (2015b). Framing cyberbullying in US mainstream media. *Journal of Children and Media, 9*(4), 492–509.

Mishna, F. (2012). *Bullying: A Guide to Research, Intervention and Prevention.* Oxford: Oxford University Press.

Mishna, F., Saini, M., & Solomon, S. (2009). Ongoing and online: Children and youth's perceptions of cyber bullying. *Children and Youth Services Review, 31*(12), 1222–1228.

Mitchell, R. (1998). Sources of transparency: Information systems in international relations. *International Studies Quarterly, 42*, 109–130.

Mitchell, K. J., Finkelhor, D., & Wolak, J. (2012). Risk factors and impact of online sexual solicitation of youth. *Journal of the American Medical Association, 285*(23), 1–4.

Mitchell, K. J., Ybarra, M., & Finkelhor, D. (2007). The relative impor- tance of online victimization in understanding depression, delinquency, and substance abuse. *Child Maltreatment, 12*, 314–324. doi:10.1177/ 1077559507305996.

Mitchell, K. J., Ybarra, M. L., Jones, L. M., & Espelage, D. (2016). What features make online harassment incidents upsetting to youth? *Journal of School Violence, 15*(3), 279–301. doi:10.1080/15388220.2014.990462.

Monaghan, J. (2011). Social networking websites' liability for user illegality. *Seton Hall Journal of Sports and Entertainment Law, 21*(2), 6.

Montgomery, K. C. (2007). *Generation Digital: Politics, Commerce and Childhood in the Age of the Internet.* Cambridge, MA: MIT Press.

Montgomery, K. C. (2015). Youth and surveillance in the Facebook era: Policy interventions and social implications. *Telecommunications Policy.* doi:10.1016/j.telpol .2014.12.006.

Montgomery, K. C., Gottlieb-Robles, B., & Larson, G. O. (2004). Youth as e-citizens: Engaging the digital generation. Retrieved from http://www.civicyouth.org/PopUps /YouthasECitizens.pdf.

Morgan, B., & Yeung, K. (2007). *An Introduction to Law and Regulation: Text and Materials*. Cambridge: Cambridge University Press.

Morris, K. (2012, October 19). Inside the sick pedophile ring that blackmailed girls like Amanda Todd. *Daily Dot*. Retrieved from http://www.dailydot.com/society/sick -pedophile-ring-blackmail-amanda-todd.

Morris, I. (2015, July 31). Google+ is officially an endangered species thanks to You-Tube. Retrieved from http://www.forbes.com/sites/ianmorris/2015/07/31/google -plus-is-dying-thanks-to-youtube/#20286284b670.

Morrison, B. (2002). Bullying and victimization in schools: A restorative justice approach. *Trends and Issues in Crime and Criminal Justice, 219*, 1–6.

Moscaritolo, A. (2014, January 22). Study: Facebook to lose 80 percent of users, become the next MySpace. *PC News*. Retrieved from http://www.pcmag.com/article2 /0,2817,2429794,00.asp.

Murphy, L. (2012, October 17). Did Anonymous unmask the wrong guy in its hunt for the man who allegedly drove a teen to suicide? *Slate*. Retrieved from http://www .slate.com/blogs/future_tense/2012/10/17/amanda_todd_suicide_did_anonymous _dox_the_wrong_guy.html.

National Association of Attorneys General. (2008). Attorneys General announce agreement with MySpace regarding social networking safety. Retrieved from http://www .naag.org/publications/naagazette/volume_2_number_1/attorneys_general _announce_agreement_with_myspace_regarding social_networking_safety.php.

Navarro, J. N., Marcum, C. D., Higgins, G. E., & Ricketts, M. L. (2016). Addicted to the thrill of the virtual hunt: Examining the effects of Internet addiction on the cyberstalking behaviors of juveniles. *Deviant Behavior, 37*(8), 893–903. doi:10.1080/ 01639625.2016.1153366.

NetAware. (2017). Sites, apps and games we've reviewed so far. *NSPCC*. Retrieved from https://www.net-aware.org.uk/networks/?order=-popularity.

Net Children Go Mobile. (n.d.). Home. Retrieved from http://netchildrengomobile.eu.

Net Family News. (2015). About us. Retrieved from http://www.netfamilynews.org /aboutus.htm.

Newman, A. L., & Bach, D. (2004). Self-regulatory trajectories in the shadow of public power: Resolving digital dilemmas in Europe and the United States. *Governance: An International Journal of Policy, Administration and Institutions, 7*(3), 387–413.

News O2. (2016, April 6). Children reveal riskiest social media sites. Retrieved from http://news.o2.co.uk/?press-release=children-reveal-riskiest-social-media-sites-new -net-aware-guide.

Newsroom.fb.com. (2016). Stats. Retrieved from http://newsroom.fb.com/company -info.

New York State Attorney General. (2014). A.G. Schneiderman and IAC announce new safety agreement to protect children and teens on newly acquired Ask.fm site. Retrieved from http://www.ag.ny.gov/press-release/ag-schneiderman-and-iac-announce-new -safety-agreement-protect-children-and-teens-newly.

Nguyen, C. (2015, November 6). An attempted suicide forced Tumblr community to open its eyes about bullying. The Motherboard. Retrieved from: http://motherboard .vice.com/read/an-attempted-suicide-forced-a-tumblr-community-to-open-its-eyes -about-bullying.

Nocentini, A., Calmaestra, J., Shultze-Krumbholz, A., Scheithauer, H., Ortega, R., & Menesini, E. (2010). Cyberbullying: Labels, behaviors and definition in three European countries. *Australian Journal of Guidance & Counselling, 20*(2), 129–142.

Nova Scotia Cyberbullying Law goes too far. (2014, February 17). *The Globe and Mail*. Retrieved from http://www.theglobeandmail.com/globe-debate/editorials/nova-scotias -cyber-bullying-law-goes-too-far/article16907312.

NSPCC. (2016, April 6). 50% of children admit to seeing sexual or violent content online. Retrieved from https://nspcc.org.uk/fighting-for-childhood/news-opinion /net-aware-reveals-risky-social-media-sites.

Office of the Children's eSafety Commissioner (n.d.). The Enhancing Online Safety for Children Act 2015. Retrieved from https://esafety.gov.au/about-the-office/legislation.

Ohler, J. (2011). Digital Citizenship Means Character Education for Digital Age. *Kappa Delta Pi Record, 48*(1), 25–27.

Olson, P. (2013, November 10). Teenagers say goodbye to Facebook and hello to messenger apps. *The Guardian*. Retrieved from https://www.theguardian.com/tech nology/2013/nov/10/teenagers-messenger-apps-facebook-exodus.

Olweus, D. (2012). Cyberbullying, an overrated phenomenon? *European Journal of Developmental Psychology, 9*(5), 520–538.

Omand, G. (2015, August 5). Rehtaeh Parson's father credits Anonymous for reopening investigation. *CBC*. Retrieved from http://www.cbc.ca/news/canada/nova-scotia /rehtaeh-parsons-s-father-credits-anonymous-for-reopening-investigation-1.3177605.

O'Neil, L. (2014, November 25). "Yik Yak" is the latest anonymous messaging app to cause trouble among teens. *CBC News*. Retrieved from http://www.cbc.ca/newsblogs /yourcommunity/2014/11/yik-yak-is-the-latest-anonymous-messaging-app-to-cause -trouble-among-teens.html.

O'Neill, B. (2013). Who cares? Practical ethics and the problem of underage users on social networking sites. *Ethics and Information Technology, 15*(4), 253–262.

O'Neill, B. (2014a). *Policy Influences and country clusters: A Comparative analysis of Internet safety implementation. LSE*. London: EU Kids Online.

O'Neill, B. (2014b). First report on the implementation of the ICT Principles, Retrieved from http://www.ictcoalition.eu/gallery/75/ICT_REPORT.pdf.

O'Neill, B., & Staksrud, E. (2012). Policy implications and recommendations: Now what? In S. Livingstone, L. Haddon, & A. Görzig (Eds.), *Children, Risk and Safety on the Internet: Research and Policy Challenges in Comparative Perspective* (pp. 339–354). Bristol: The Policy Press.

Ortutay, B. (2014, March 24). Anonymous apps like Secret and Whisper find a niche in Silicon Valley. *San Jose Mercury News*. Retrieved from http://www.mercurynews.com/business/ci_25409802/anonymous-apps-like-secret-and-whisper-find-niche.

Parents: Cyber Bullying Led to a Teen's Suicide. (2007, November 19). *ABC News*. Retrieved from http://abcnews.go.com/GMA/story?id=3882520.

Parliament of Australia. (n.d.). Enhancing Online safety act for children. Retrieved from http://parlinfo.aph.gov.au/parlInfo/download/legislation/bills/r5387_aspassed/toc_pdf/14260b01.pdf;fileType=application%2Fpdf.

Patchin, J. W. (2013). Cyberbullying: Neither an epidemic nor a rarity. Retrieved from http://cyberbullying.us/cyberbullying-neither-an-epidemic-nor-a-rarity.

Patchin, J. W. (2014, November 26). The case for including intent in a definition of bullying. Cyberbullying Research Center. Retrieved from http://cyberbullying.org/intent-define-bullying.

Patchin, J. W. (2014). Summary of our research (2004–2014). Retrieved from http://cyberbullying.us/summary-of-our-research.

Patchin, J. W., & Hinduja, S. (2012). *Cyberbullying Prevention and Response: Expert Perspectives*. New York: Routledge.

Payton, J., Weissberg, R. P., Durlak, J. A., Dymnicki, A. B., Taylor, R. D., Schellinger, K. B., & Pachan, M. (2008). The positive impact of social and emotional learning for kindergarten to eighth-grade students: Findings from three scientific reviews. Technical report. Collaborative for Academic, Social, and Emotional Learning (NJ1).

Pearce, N., Cross, D., Monks, H., Waters, S., & Falconer, S. (2011). Current evidence of best practice in whole-school bullying intervention and its potential to inform cyberbullying interventions. *Journal of Psychologists and Counsellors in Schools*, *21*(01), 1–21. doi:10.1375/ajgc.21.1.1.

Perez, S. (2014, August 14). IAC agrees to work with regulators on cyberbulling protections following Ask.fm deal. *TechCrunch*. Retrieved from http://techcrunch.com/2014/08/14/ask-com-agrees-to-work-with-regulators-on-cyberbullying-protections-following-ask-fm-acquisition.

Pesta, A. (2014, April 8). Who are you calling a bully? *Cosmopolitan*. Retrieved from http://www.cosmopolitan.com/lifestyle/advice/a6303/twelve-year-old-bully.

Pew Research Center. (2012). Teens fact sheet. Retrieved from http://www.pewinter net.org/fact-sheets/teens-fact-sheet.

Phaneuf, W. (2012, July 26). Source: Voxer approaches 70M users, encouraged by global smartphone adoption. *PandoDaily*. Retrieved from https://pando.com /2012/07/26/voicetext-app-voxer-expands-encouraged-by-global-smartphone -adoption.

Phillips, W. (2015). *This Is Why We Can't Have Nice Things: Mapping the Relationship between Online Trolling and Mainstream Culture*. Cambridge, MA: MIT Press.

Poole, E. (2013). Hey girls, did you know? Slut-shaming on the Internet needs to stop. *University of San Francisco Law Review*, *48*(221), 221–260.

Popkin, S. (2009, May 15). Cyberbullying laws won't save your children. *MSNBC*. Retrieved from http://www.msnbc.msn.com/id/30751310/ns/technology_and_sci-ence-tech_and_gadgets/t/cyberbullying-laws-wont-save-your-children/#. ULRAYIdfATa.

Powles, J., & Chaparro, E. How Google determined our right to be forgotten. *The Guardian*. Retrieved from https://www.theguardian.com/technology/2015/feb/18/the -right-be-forgotten-google-search.

Prensky, M. (2001). Digital natives, digital immigrants. *On the Horizon*, *9*(5). Retrieved from http://www.marcprensky.com/writing/Prensky%20-%20Digital%20 Natives,%20Digital%20Immigrants%20-%20Part1.pdf.

Preston, P. (2016, September 11). Face it, Mr. Mark Zuckerberg, you're a news editor too. *The Guardian*. Retrieved from https://www.theguardian.com/technology/2016 /sep/11/facebook-news-censorship-stick-to-social-media.

Pritchard, E. D. (2013). For colored kids who commit suicide, our outrage isn't enough: Queer youth of color, bullying and the discursive limits of identity and safety. *Harvard Educational Review*, *82*(2), 320–345.

Proskauer. (2008, January 15). State Attorneys General announce agreement with MySpace to protect children online [Blog post]. Retrieved from http://privacylaw .proskauer.com/2008/01/articles/online-privacy/state-attorneys-general-announce -agreement-with-myspace-to-protect-children-online/

Protalinski, E. (2014, October 28). Facebook passes 1.38B monthly active users and 864M daily active users, with a third now mobile only. *Venturebeat*. Retrieved from http://venturebeat.com/2014/10/28/facebook-passes-1-35b-monthly-active-users -and-864m-daily-active-users-with-a-third-now-mobile-only/

Prout, A. (2005). *The Future of Childhood*. Abingdon, UK: RoutledgeFalmer.

Puppis, M. (2010). Media governance: A new concept for the analysis of media policy and regulation. *Communication, Culture & Critique*, *3*(2), 134–149.

Raiche, R., & Williams, C. (2013, September 12). Polk County Sheriff Grady Judd: Girl was bullied before jumping to her death. *AbcActionNews*. Retrieved from http://www.abcactionnews.com/news/region-polk/lakeland/polk-county-sheriff-grady-judd-to-brief-media-on-death-of-12-year-old-rebecca-sedwick-of-lakeland.

Rawlinson, K. (2014, January 23). Mother of girl, 15, who killed herself, condemns suicide blogs. *The Guardian*. Retrieved from http://www.theguardian.com/uk-news/2014/jan/23/tallulah-internet-suicide-blogs.

Raymond, M., & DeNardis, L. (2016). Multi-stakeholderism: Anatomy of an inchoate global institution. CIGI paper series, Retrieved from https://www.ourinternet.org/sites/default/files/publications/Multi_Stakeholderism%20-%20Denardis%20et%20al.pdf.

REACH of Macon County. (2013). Change how you handle under-age usage and cyber bullying on the Whisper App [online petition]. Retrieved from https://www.change.org/p/whispertext-llc-change-how-you-handle-under-age-usage-and-cyber-bullying-on-the-whisper-app.

Read, A. (2016, July 27). Why Snapchat Memories will be pivotal (and why marketers are so excited). Retrieved from https://blog.bufferapp.com/snapchat-memories.

Rebecca Ann Sedwick, 12-year-old Florida girl, commits suicide after online bullying. (2013, December 9). *Huffington Post*. Retrieved from http://www.huffingtonpost.com/2013/09/12/rebecca-ann-sedwick-bulli_n_3915883.html.

Rebecca Ann Sedwick suicide: Two arrests made in death of bullied Florida girl. (2013, October 15). *CBS*. Retrieved from http://www.cbsnews.com/news/rebecca-ann-sedwick-suicide-2-arrests-made-in-death-of-bullied-florida-girl.

Regulation (EU) 2016/679 of the European Parliament and of the Council of 27 April 2016 on the protection of natural persons with regard to the processing of personal data and on the free movement of such data, and repealing Directive 95/46/EC (General Data Protection Regulation) (Text with EEA relevance). Retrieved from http://eur-lex.europa.eu/legal-content/en/TXT/?uri=CELEX%3A32016R0679.

Rehtaeh Parsons, Canadian girl, dies after suicide attempt; Parents allege she was raped by 4 boys. (2013, April 9). *Huffington Post*. Retrieved from http://www.huffingtonpost.com/2013/04/09/rehtaeh-parsons-girl-dies-suicide-rape-canada_n_3045033.html.

Rehtaeh Parsons case to be reopened by police. (2013, April 12). *CBC News*. Retrieved from http://www.cbc.ca/news/canada/nova-scotia/rehtaeh-parsons-case-to-be-reopened-by-police-1.1309465

Rehtaeh Parsons suicide: Web calls on Anonymous to act after Nova Scotia teen's death. (2013, April 10). *The Huffington Post Canada*. Retrieved from http://www.huffingtonpost.ca/2013/04/10/rehtaeh-parsons-suicide-anonymous_n_3052495.html.

Report of the Round Table on Advertising. (2006). Retrieved from http://ec.europa .eu/consumers/archive/overview/report_advertising_en.pdf.

Rey, P. J. (2012, February 1). There is no "Cyberspace." *Cyborgology*. Retrieved from https://thesocietypages.org/cyborgology/2012/02/01/there-is-no-cyberspace/

Riley Huntley. (2012, October 15). Amanda Todd—Transcript of video. Retrieved from http://pastebin.com/rMX6fWKU.

Robertson, A. (2016, August 11). Twitter secretly filtered tweets during Obama Q&A, says report. *The Verge*. Retrieved from: http://www.theverge.com/2016/8/11/1243 0552/twitter-barack-obama-askpotus-abusive-tweet-filtering-harassment

Robinson, J. P., & Espelage, D. L. (2012). Bullying explains only part of LGBTQ-hetero-sexual risk disparities: Implications for policy and practice. *Educational Researcher*, *41*(8), 309–319.

Robson, S. (2013, August 16). A purple coffin and mourners wearing onesies: Heartbro-ken family and friends gather at funeral for teenage troll victim Hannah Smith. *Mail Online*. Retrieved from http://www.dailymail.co.uk/news/article-2395484/Hannah-Smith -funeral-Family-friends-gather-cyberbully-victim-Lutterworth.html.

Rudd, A. (2013a, August 19). Hannah Smith suicide: Teenager used Ask.fm in secret after being banned from going on it by worried father. *Mirror*. Retrieved from http:// www.mirror.co.uk/news/uk-news/hannah-smith-suicide-teenager-used-2184385.

Rudd, A. (2013b, August 9). Hannah Smith suicide: Ask.fm hire law firm to carry out independent audit. *The Mirror*. Retrieved from http://www.mirror.co.uk/news/uk -news/hannah-smith-suicide-askfm-hire-2145631.

Ruedy, M. C. (2008). Repercussions of a MySpace teen suicide: Should anti-cyberbul-lying laws be created? *North Carolina Journal of Law & Technology*, *9*(2): 323–346.

Rushe, D., & Lewis, P. (2014, October 19). Whisper chief executive answers privacy revelations: "We're not infallible." *The Guardian*. Retrieved from http://www.the guardian.com/world/2014/oct/19/-sp-whisper-chief-executive-on-privacy -revelations-were-not-infallible.

Ruskin, B. (2015, December 11). Court strikes down anti-cyberbullying law created after Rehtaeh Parson's death. *CBC News*. Retrieved from http://www.cbc.ca/news /canada/nova-scotia/cyberbullying-law-struck-down-1.3360612.

Rusli, E. M. (2014, November 24). Yik Yak, big in schools, is a hit with investors too. *The Wall Street Journal*. Retrieved from http://www.wsj.com/articles/year-old -messaging-app-yik-yak-draws-big-valuation-1416791097?mod=WSJ_hpp_sections _smallbusiness.

Rusli, E. M., & Elder, F. (2014, November 25). Yik Yak incidents highlight new social-media risks. *Wall Street Journal*. Retrieved from http://www.wsj.com/articles/yik-yak -incidents-highlight-new-social-media-risks-1416965963.

Russel, J. (2014, August 22). Apple removes Secret from the App Store in Brazil because it breaches local free speech law. *The Next Web*. Retrieved from http://thenextweb.com/apps/2014/08/22/apple-removes-secret-app-store-brazil-breaches-local-free-speech-law.

Russo, A., Watkins, J., Kelly, L., & Chan, S. (2008). Participatory communication with social media. *Curator, 51*(1), 21–31.

Sacco, D., Silbaugh, K., Corredor, F., Casey, J., & Doherty, D. (2012). *An Overview of State Anti-bullying Legislation and Other Related Laws*. Retrieved from http://cyber.law.harvard.edu/sites/cyber.law.harvard.edu/files/State_Anti_bullying_Legislation_Overview_0.pdf.

Sandle, P., & Humphries, C. (2013, October 30). Tech start-ups bring jobs to low-tax Ireland. *Chicago Tribune*. Retrieved from http://articles.chicagotribune.com/2013-10-30/business/sns-rt-us-ireland-tech-20131030_1_tax-rate-tax-rules-tax-bill.

Saul, H. (2013, August 19). Ask.fm "will be safer from online bullying" as owners introduce new features. *Independent*. Retrieved from http://www.independent.co.uk/news/uk/home-news/askfm-will-be-safer-from-online-bullying-as-owners-introduce-new-features-8774234.html.

Schneider, S. K., Smith, E., & O'Donnell, L. (2013a). Bystander intervention behaviors related to cyberbullying in a regional census of high school students. Paper presented at 141st APHA Annual Meeting and Exposition, Boston, MA.

Schneider, S. K., Smith, E., & O'Donnell, L. (2013b). Social media and cyberbullying: Implementation of school-based prevention efforts and implications for social media approaches. Retrieved from http://www.promoteprevent.org/sites/www.promoteprevent.org/files/resources/Social_Media_and_Cyberbullying_FinalReport-EDC_0.pdf.

Schulz, W., & Held, T. (2004). *Regulated Self-Regulation as a Form of Modern Government*. Luton, UK: University of Luton Press.

Scott, S., & Isaac, M. (2016, September 9). Facebook restores iconic Vietnam War photo it censored for nudity. *New York Times*. Retrieved from http://www.nytimes.com/2016/09/10/technology/facebook-vietnam-war-photo-nudity.html?_r=1.

Senden, L. (2005). Soft law, self-regulation and co-regulation in European law: where do they meet? *Electronic Journal of Comparative Law, 9*(1).

Ševčíková, A., & Šmahel, D. (2009). Cyberbullying among Czech Internet users: Comparison across age groups. [Journal of Psychology]. *Zeitschrift fur Psychologie mit Zeitschrift fur Angewandte Psychologie, 4*, 227–229.

Shamberg, S. (2013, June 1). Tweens and Instagram: How to do it right? Retrieved: http://www.huffingtonpost.com/scott-shamberg/tweens-instagram-how-to-d_b_2992049.html

Sharwood, S. (2014, January 22). Australia floats plan for national social media regulator. *The Register*. http://www.theregister.co.uk/2014/01/22/australia_floats_plan _for_national_social_media_regulator.

Sharwood, S. (2015, March 4). Australia's social media law for children all but passes. *The Register*. Retrieved from https://www.theregister.co.uk/2015/03/04/australias _social_media_censorship_law_for_the_children_passes/.

Shift, & the Institute for Human Rights and Business (2013). ICT Sector Guide on implementing the UN guiding principles on business and human rights (for the European Commission), Retrieved from https://www.ihrb.org/pdf/eu-sector-guidance /EC-Guides/ICT/EC-Guide_ICT.pdf.

Shontell, A. (2014, Jun 27). 13-year-old describes how kids are bullied on Snapchat. *Business Insider*. Retrieved from http://www.businessinsider.com/how-kids-are -bullied-on-snapchat-2014-6

Shontell, A. (2015, January 3). Snapchat is a lot bigger than people realize. *Business Insider*. Retrieved from http://www.businessinsider.com/snapchats-monthly-active -users-may-be-nearing-200-million-2014-12.

Silver, C. (2016, July 5). Snapchat use rises among adults. *Forbes*. Retrieved from http://www.forbes.com/sites/curtissilver/2016/07/05/snapchat-use-rises-among -adults-to-the-chagrin-of-teens/#51eddd464e47.

Simmons, R. (2014, November 10). The secret language of girls on Instagram. *Time*. Retrieved: http://time.com/3559340/instagram-tween-girls.

Slonje, R., & Smith, P. (2008). Cyberbullying: Another main type of bullying? *Scandinavian Journal of Psychology*, *49*(2), 147–154.

Smith, C. (2016a, July 14). By the numbers: 50+ amazing Google+ statistics. Expanded-Ramblings, DMR. Retrieved from http://expandedramblings.com/index.php/google -plus-statistics.

Smith, C. (2016b, October 1). By the numbers: 180+ Instagram statistics. Expanded-Ramblings, DMR. Retrieved from http://expandedramblings.com/index.php/impor tant-instagram-stats.

Smith, C. (2016c October 26). 145 amazing YouTube statistics. Retrieved from http:// expandedramblings.com/index.php/youtube-statistics.

Smith, J. D., Schneider, B. H., Smith, P. K., & Ananiadou, K. (2004). The effectiveness of whole-school antibullying programs: A synthesis of evaluation research. *School Psychology Review*, *33*(4), 547–560.

Smithers, R. (2011). Terms and Conditions: Not reading the small print can cause big problems. Retrieved from https://www.theguardian.com/money/2011/may/11 /terms-conditions-small-print-big-problems.

Smith-Spark, L. (2013, August 9). Hannah Smith suicide fuels calls for action on Ask .fm cyberbullying. *CNN*. Retrieved from http://edition.cnn.com/2013/08/07/world /europe/uk-social-media-bullying.

Snapchat not covered by cyberbullying laws. (2014). *ZDNet*. Retrieved from http:// www.zdnet.com/article/snapchat-not-covered-by-cyberbullying-laws.

Snapchat. (n.d.a). Community Guidelines. Retrieved from https://support.snapchat .com/a/guidelines.

Snapchat. (n.d.b). Safety Center. Retrieved from https://www.snapchat.com/safety.

Snapchat. (n.d.c). Snapchat Support: I Need Help. Retrieved from https://support .snapchat.com/en-US/i-need-help.

Snapchat (n.d.d) Snapchat Support: Live Stories. Retrieved from https://support .snapchat.com/en-US/about/live-stories.

Snapchat (n.d.e). Snapchat Support: Stories. Retrieved from https://support.snap chat.com/en-US/about/stories.

Snapchat. (2016). Terms of Service. Retrieved from https://www.snapchat.com /terms.

Solon, O. (2017, May 25). Underpaid and overburdened: The life of a Facebook moderator. *The Guardian*. Retrieved from https://www.theguardian.com/news/2017 /may/25/facebook-moderator-underpaid-overburdened-extreme-content.

Solove, D. J. (2007). *The Future of Reputation: Gossip, Rumor, and Privacy on the Internet*. New Haven, CT: Yale University Press.

Solove, D. (2013). *Nothing to Hide: The False Tradeoff between Privacy and Security*. New Haven, CT: Yale University Press.

Stalla-Bourdillon, S. S. (2009). Making intermediary internet service providers participate in the regulatory process through tort law: A comparative analysis. *International Review of Law Computers & Technology, 23*(1), 153–165.

Staksrud, E. (2013a). *Children in the Online World: Risk, Regulation and Rights*. London: Ashgate.

Staksrud, E. (2013b). Online grooming legislation: Knee-jerk legislation? *European Journal of Communication, 28*(2), 152–167.

Staksrud, E. (2015). Counting children. On research methodology, ethics and policy development. In H. Ingierd & H. Fossheim (Eds.), *Internet Research Ethics* (pp. 98– 121). Oslo, Norway: Cappelen Damm Akademisk.

Staksrud, E., and J. Kirksæther. (2013). He who buries the little girl wins! Moral panics as double jeopardy. In *Moral Panics in the Contemporary World*, (pp. 145–167), ed. C. Critcher, J. Hughes, J. Petley and A. Rohloff. New York: Bloomsbury.

Staksrud, E., & Livingstone, S. (2009). Children and online risk: powerless victims or resourceful participants? *Information, Communication & Society 12*(3), 364–387. Retrieved from http://eprints.lse.ac.uk/30122/1/Children_and_online_risk_%28LSERO_version%29.pdf.

Staksrud, E., & Lobe, B. (2010). Evaluation of the implementation of the Safer Social Networking Principles for the EU, Part 1: General report (Study commissioned by the European Commission), Retrieved from http://ec.europa.eu/information_society/activities/social_networking/docs/final_report/first_part.pdf.

Statista. (n.d.a). Number of monthly active WhatsApp users worldwide from April 2013 to January 2015 (in millions). Retrieved from http://www.statista.com/statistics/260819/number-of-monthly-active-whatsapp-users.

Statista. (n.d.b). Cumulative total of Tumblr blogs between May 2011 and July 2016 (in millions). Retrieved from https://www.statista.com/statistics/256235/total-cumulative-number-of-tumblr-blogs.

Statista (n.d.c). Number of monthly Instagram users from January 2013 to June 2016 (in millions). Retrieved from https://www.statista.com/statistics/253577/number-of-monthly-active-instagram-users.

Statista (n.d.d). Number of monthly active Twitter users worldwide from 1st quarter 2010 to 2nd quarter 2016 (in millions). Retrieved from https://www.statista.com/statistics/282087/number-of-monthly-active-twitter-users.

Statista. (n.d.e). Number of registered Kik Messenger users worldwide from November 2012 to February 2016. Retrieved from https://www.statista.com/statistics/327312/number-of-registered-kik-messenger-users.

Steinhauer, J. (2008, November 26). Verdict in MySpace suicide case. *New York Times*. Retrieved from http://www.nytimes.com/2008/11/27/us/27myspace.html?_r=1&hp.

Stopbullying.gov. (2012). What is cyberbullying? Retrieved from http://www.stopbullying.gov/cyberbullying/what-is-it/index.html.

Stopbullying.gov. (March 31, 2014). Key components in state anti-bullying laws. Retrieved from http://www.stopbullying.gov/laws/key-components/index.html.

Strohmeier, D., Yanagida, T., & Toda, Y. (2016). Individualism/collectivism as predictors of relational and physical victimization in Japan and Austria. In P. K. Smith, K. Kwak, & Y. Toda (Eds.), *School Bullying in Different Cultures: Eastern and Western Perspectives* (pp. 259–279). Cambridge: Cambridge University Press.

Stump, S. (2013, November 22). Fla. teen cleared of cyberbullying: I didn't do "anything wrong." *Today News*. Retrieved from http://www.today.com/news/fla-teen-cleared-cyberbullying-case-i-didnt-do-anything-wrong-2D11632710.

Subrahmanyam, K., & Šmahel, D. (2011). *Digital Youth: Advancing Responsible Adolescent Development*. New York: Springer.

Surbramniam, V., and J. Whalen. (2014, December 14). Amanda Todd stood up to stalker in Facebook conversation. *CBC News*. Retrieved from http://www.cbc.ca/news /canada/amanda-todd-stood-up-to-stalker-in-facebook-conversation-1.2860471.

Suski, E. (2016, April 13). You can't stop bullying just by passing a law. *The Guardian*. Retrieved from https://www.theguardian.com/commentisfree/2016/apr/13/anti -bullying-law-punishment-nevada.

Svantesson, D. J. B. (2005). The characteristics making internet communication challenge traditional models of regulation. What every international jurist should know about the internet. *International Journal of Law and Information Technology*, *13*(1), 39–69.

Swart, E., & Bredekamp, J. (2009). Non-physical bullying: Exploring the perspectives of grade 5 girls. *South African Journal of Education*, *29*, 405–425.

Swearer, S. M., & Espelage, D. L. (2011). Expanding the social-ecological framework of bullying among youth: Lessons learned from the past and directions for the future. *Educational Psychology Papers and Publications*. Paper 140. Retrieved from http://digital commons.unl.edu/edpsychpapers/140.

Tambini, D., Leonardi, D., & Marsden, C. (2008). The privatization of censorship: Self-regulation and freedom of expression. In D. Tambini, D. Leonardi, & C. Marsden (Eds.), *Codifying Cyberspace: Communications Self-Regulation in the Age of Internet Convergence* (pp. 269–289). Abingdon, UK: Routledge/ UCL Press.

Tang, X. (2013). Shame: A different criminal law proposal for bullies, 61CLEV. ST. *L. REV.*, *649*, 651.

Taraszow, T. (2013). The influence of NGOs on safer internet policy making. In B. O'Neill, E. Staksrud, & S. McLaughlin (Eds.), *Towards a Better Internet for Children? Policy Pillars, Players and Paradoxes*. Goteborg: Nordicom.

Taylor, C. (2013, March 15). Formspring, the pioneering "ask me anything," anonymous Q&A platform, is shutting down. *TeachCrunch*. Retrieved from https://tech crunch.com/2013/03/15/formspring-the-pioneering-anonymous-qa-platform-is -shutting-down.

TheInternetOffendsMe. (2013, April 9). The real story behind Facebook moderation and your petty reports. [Blog post]. Retrieved from https://theinternetoffendsme. wordpress.com/2013/04/09/the-real-story-behind-facebook-moderation-and-your -petty-reports.

Thornberg, R. (2015). Distressed bullies, social positioning and odd victims: Young people's explanations of bullying. *Children & Society*, *29*, 15–25.

The Stream. (2014, March 10). Florida advances bill to make bullying a crime. *Al Jazeera*. Retrieved from http://america.aljazeera.com/watch/shows/the-stream/the -stream-officialblog/2014/3/10/florida-advancesbilltomakebullyingacrime.html.

ThirdParent, T. (2015, February, 19). We still think Yik Yak is manipulating posts naming competitors. Retrieved from http://thirdparent.com/we-still-think-yik-yak -is-manipulating-posts-naming-competitors.

Thomson, I. (2014, October 17). Careless Whisper? Anonymous messaging app accused of stalking users, blabbing to Feds. *The Register*. Retrieved from http://www.theregister .co.uk/2014/10/17/careless_whisper_company_denies_its_tracking_anonymized_users.

Three U.S. teens arrested for sexual battery after girl's suicide. (2013, April 12). *CBC News*. Retrieved from http://www.cbc.ca/news/world/3-u-s-teens-arrested-for-sexual -battery-after-girl-s-suicide-1.1312171.

Tokunaga, R. S. (2010). Following you home from school: A critical review and synthesis of research on cyberbullying victimization. *Computers in Human Behavior*, *26*(3), 277–287.

Troianovski, A., and S. Raice. (2012, June 4). Facebook explores giving kids access. *The Wall Street Journal*. Retrieved from https://www.wsj.com/articles/SB1000142405 2702303506404577444711741019238.

Tsaliki, L. (2007). The construction of European identity and citizenship through cultural policy. In K. Sarikakis (ed.), *Media and Cultural Policy in the European Union*, pp. 157–182. Amsterdam: Rodopi.

Tsui, B. (2014, March 19). Friends With Benefits: Inside Facebook's Compassion Research Day. *Pacific Standard*. Retrieved from http://www.psmag.com/nature-and -technology/friends-benefits-facebook-sociologists-social-media-74781.

Ttofi, M. M., & Farrington, D. P. (2011). Effectiveness of school-based programs to reduce bullying: A systematic and meta-analytic review. *Journal of Experimental Criminology*, *7*(1), 27–56.

Tuchman, G. (1978). *Making news: A study in the construction of reality*. New York: Free Press.

Tumblr. (2015, June 2). Tumblr staff. Retrieved from: https://staff.tumblr.com/post /120551226975/hey-tumblr-welcome-to-your-better-blocking.

Tumblr. (2016). Community guidelines. Retrieved from https://www.tumblr.com /policy/en/community.

Tumblr. (n.d.a). Counseling and prevention resources. Retrieved from https://www .tumblr.com/docs/en/counseling_prevention_resources.

Tumblr. (n.d.b). How can we help? Retrieved from https://www.tumblr.com/help.

Tumblr. (n.d.c). Harassment. Retrieved from https://www.tumblr.com/abuse/harassment.

Tumblr. (n.d.d). Harm to minors. Retrieved from https://www.tumblr.com/abuse /minors.

Twitter. (2016a). Safety center. We're Committed to building a safer Twitter. Retrieved from https://about.twitter.com/safety.

Twitter. (2016b). Trust and safety council. Retrieved from https://about.twitter.com /safety/council.

Twitter. (2016c). Trusted resources. Retrieved from https://support.twitter.com/groups /57-safety-security/topics/274-handling-issues-online/articles/20171366-trusted -resources.

Twitter. (2016d). The Twitter rules. Retrieved from https://support.twitter.com/arti- cles/18311-the-twitter-rules.

Twitter. (2016e). The Twitter for good blog. Retrieved from https://blog.twitter.com /twitter-for-good.

Twitter. (2016f). Twitter privacy policy (effective January 27, 2016). Retrieved from https://twitter.com/privacy?lang=en.

Twitter. (2016g). About: Company. Retrieved from https://about.twitter.com/company.

Twitter (2017). Twitter for Good. Retrieved from https://about.twitter.com/company /twitter-for-good.

UK Council for Child Internet Safety. (n.d.). UK Council for Child Internet Safety. Retrieved from https://www.gov.uk/government/groups/uk-council-for-child-internet -safety-ukccis.

UK Council for Child Internet Safety. (2010). Good practice guidance for providers of social networking and other user-interactive services. Retrieved from https://www .gov.uk/government/uploads/system/uploads/attachment_data/file/251456/indus try_guidance_social_networking.pdf.

Underwood, M. M., Rish-Scott, M., & Springer, J. (2011). Bullying and suicide risk: Building resilience. *Social Work Today, 11*(5):10. Retrieved from http://www.social worktoday.com/archive/092011p10.shtml.

UNICEF. (2014). *25 Years of the Convention on the Rights of the Child. Is the World a Better Place for Children?* New York: UNICEF. Retrieved from www.unicef.org/publica tions/files/CRC_at_25_Anniversary_Publication_compilation_5Nov2014.pdf.

U.S. Department of Education. (2011). U.S. Education Department releases analysis of state bullying laws and policies. Retrieved from http://www.ed.gov/news/press-releases /us-education-department-releases-analysis-state-bullying-laws-and-policies.

U.S. House of Representatives Committee on the Judiciary, Subcommittee on Crime, Terrorism, and Homeland Security. Hearing on: Online Privacy, Social Networking, and Crime Victimization 112th cong. (2010) (testimony of Joe Sullivan). Retrieved from https://judiciary.house.gov/_files/hearings/pdf/Sullivan100728.pdf

U.S. teen's death eerily similar to Rehtaeh Parsons's story. (2013, April 12). *CBC News*. Retrieved from http://www.cbc.ca/news/canada/nova-scotia/u-s-teen-s-death-eerily-similar-to-rehtaeh-parsons-s-story-1.1371319.

Vaas, L. (2014, October 30). Snapchat escapes Australian cyberbullying crackdown, for now. *Naked Security*. Retrieved from https://nakedsecurity.sophos.com/2014/10/30/snapchat-escapes-australian-cyberbullying-crackdown-for-now.

Vaidhyanathan, S. (2011). *The Googlization of Everything: (and Why We Should Worry)*. Oakland: University of California Press.

van der Zwaan, J. M., Dignum, V., Jonker, C. M., & van der Hof, S. (2014). On technology against cyberbullying. In J. van den Hoven, N. Doorn, T. Swierstra, B. J. Koops, & H. Romijn (Eds.), *Responsible Innovation 1, Innovative Solutions for Global Issues no. 1* (pp. 369–392). Dordrecht: Springer.

van Dijck, J. (2013). *The Culture of Connectivity: A Critical History of Social Media*. Oxford: Oxford University Press.

van Geel, M., Vedder, P., & Tanilon, J. (2014). Relationship between peer victimization, cyberbullying, and suicide in children and adolescents: A meta-analysis. *JAMA Pediatrics, 168*(5), 435–442. doi:10.1001/jamapediatrics.2013.4143.

Van Royen, K., Poels, K., & Vandebosch, H. (2016). Help, I am losing control! Examining the reporting of sexual harassment by adolescents to social networking sites. *Cyberpsychology, Behavior, and Social Networking, 19*(1), 16–22.

Vandebosch, H., & Van Cleemput, K. (2009). Cyberbullying among youngsters: Profiles of bullies and victims. *New Media & Society, 11*(8), 1349–1371.

Vandoninck, S., d'Haenens, L., & Roe, K. (2013). Online risks. *Journal of Children and Media, 7*(1), 60–78. doi:10.1080/17482798.2012.739780.

Victor, D. (2016, August 3). Instagram posts may have escalated fatal standoff, police say. *The New York Times*. Retrieved from http://www.nytimes.com/2016/08/04/us/instagram-police-fatal-shooting-maryland.html?emc=edit_th_20160804&nl=todaysheadlines&nlid=61571261.

Voxer. (n.d.a). (Android) privacy mode. Retrieved from https://support.voxer.com/hc/en-us/articles/204332203--Android-Privacy-Mode.

Voxer. (n.d.b). Plans and pricing. Retrieved from http://voxer.com/plans-and-pricing.

Vreeman, R., & Carroll, A. E. (2007). A systematic review of school-based interventions to prevent bullying. *Archives of Pediatrics & Adolescent Medicine, 161*(1), 78–88.

Waldman, A. E., & Clementi, J. (2015, October 1). Ending the cyberbullying epidemic five years after Tyler Clementi's suicide. Retrieved from http://www.nydaily news.com/opinion/waldman-clementi-ending-cyberbullying-epidemic-article-1.2381804.

Wallace, K. (2014, April 21). Police file raises questions about bullying in Rebecca Sedgwick's suicide. *CNN*. Retrieved from http://edition.cnn.com/2014/04/18/living /rebecca-sedwick-bullying-suicide-follow-parents.

Wallace, K. (2015, January 9). Parents beware of bullying on sites you've never seen. *CNN*. Retrieved from http://edition.cnn.com/2013/10/10/living/parents-new-apps -bullying.

Wartella, E., & Jennings, N. (2000). Children and computers: New technology—old concerns. *Future of Children and Computer Technology, 10*(2), 31–43.

Warzel, C. (2016, August 11). A honeypot for assholes: Inside Twitter's ten year fail- ure to stop harassment. *BuzzFeedNews*. Retrieved from https://www.buzzfeed.com /charliewarzel/a-honeypot-for-assholes-inside-twitters-10-year-failure-to-s?utm _term=.el3b6Y7nv2#.mc6gPYvxmO.

Watertown teens arrested for Instagram bullying. (2014, July 8). *FoxCT*. Retrieved from http://foxct.com/2014/07/08/watertown-high-school-students-allegedly-caught -using-anonymous-instagram-account-to-harrass-others.

Wasko, J. (2008). The Commodification of youth culture. In K. Drotner & S. Living- stone (Eds.), *The International Handbook of Children, Media & Culture* (pp. 460–474). London: SAGE.

Wauters, E., Lievens, E., & Valcke, P. (2016). Empowering children through labeling in social networks: Illusion or solution? In M. Walrave, K. Ponnet, E. Vanderhoven, J. Haers, & B. Segært (Eds.), *Youth 2.0: Social Media and Adolescence: Connecting, Shar- ing & Empowering* (pp. 227–249). Springer.

Websites could be made to reveal names of cyber bullies. (2013, August 9). *London Evening Standard*. Retrieved from http://www.standard.co.uk/news/uk/websites-could -be-made-to-reveal-names-of-cyber-bullies-8753431.html.

WhatsApp. (2016a). Frequently asked questions. Retrieved from http://www.what sapp.com/faq/en/general/28030003.

WhatsApp. (2016b). Home. Retrieved from https://www.whatsapp.com.

WhatsApp. (2016c). Terms of service. Retrieved from https://www.whatsapp.com /legal/#key-updates.

What is a true threat on Facebook? (2014, December 1). *New York Times*. Retrieved from http://www.nytimes.com/2014/12/02/opinion/what-is-a-true-threat-on-facebook .html.

Whisper (2015a). Home. Retrieved from https://whisper.sh.

Whisper (2015b). Stories. Retrieved from https://whisper.sh/stories.

Whisper. (2016a). Terms of use. Retrieved from https://whisper.sh/terms.

Whisper. (2016b). Community guidelines. Retrieved from https://whisper.sh/guide lines.

White, P. (2014a, June 1). On the trail of Amanda Todd's alleged tormentor. *The Globe and Mail*. Retrieved from http://www.theglobeandmail.com/news/world/on -the-trail-of-amanda-todds-alleged-tormentor/article18935075/?page=all.

White, P. (2014b, June 25). Dutch police used controversial software in Amanda Todd case. *The Globe and Mail*. Retrieved from http://www.theglobeandmail.com /news/world/dutch-police-used-contentious-software-in-amanda-todd-case/article 19345909.

Whitworth, D. (2010, November 15). "New law needed" to stop bullying, says charity. *BBC*. Retrieved from http://www.bbc.co.uk/newsbeat/11746126.

Wilkinson, P. (2009, November 18). Social network sites criticized on bullying. *CNN*. Retrieved from http://edition.cnn.com/2009/TECH/11/18/cyber.bullying/index.html ?iref=allsearch.

Williams, R. (2016, March 25). Rise in teens shamed in cyberbullying videos. Sky-News. Retrieved from http://news.sky.com/story/rise-in-teens-shamed-in-cyberbullying -videos-10217480.

Wiseman, R. (2009). *Queen Bees and Wannabes: Helping Your Daughter Survive Cliques, Gossip, Boyfriends and the New Realities of Girl World* (3rd ed.). New York: Random House.

Wiseman, R. (2013, November). Masterminds and wingmen. Paper presented at the Family Online Safety Institute's Annual Conference, Washington D.C.

Wiseman, R. (2015). Speaking engagements. Retrieved from http://rosalindwiseman .com/programs/rosalinds-events.

Wolak, J., Mitchell, K. J., & Finkelhor, D. (2006). *Online Victimization of Youth: 5 Years Later*. Retrieved from http://www.unh.edu/ccrc/pdf/CV138.pdf.

Wolak, J., Mitchell, K. J., & Finkelhor, D. (2007). Does online harassment constitute bullying? An exploration of online harassment by known peers and online only contacts. *Journal of Adolescent Health, 41*(6), S51–S58. doi:10.1016/j.jadohealth.2007.08.019.

Wolf, J. (2012). The playground bully has gone digital: The dangers of cyberbullying, the first amendment implications and the necessary responses. *Cardozo Public Law, Policy and Ethics Journal* (note 575–610.)

Wong, J. C. (2016, February 17). What is Kik and should your child be using it? *The Guardian*. Retrieved from https://www.theguardian.com/technology/2016/feb/16 /what-is-kik-app-online-anonymous-tech-nicole-madison-lovell.

Woollaston, V. (2015, May 1). The secret's out: Anonymous app shuts down following legal battles and claims that it encouraged bullying. Retrieved September 6,

2016, from: http://www.dailymail.co.uk/sciencetech/article-3064077/The-secret-s
-Anonymous-app-shuts-following-legal-battles-claims-encouraged-bullying.html.

Xu, J. M., Jun, K.-S., Zhu, X., & Bellmore, A. (2012). Learning from bullying traces in
social media. In J. Chu-Carroll (Ed.), *The 2012 Conference of the North American Chapter
of the Association for Computational Linguistics: Human Language Technologies* (pp. 656–
666). Stroudsburg, PA: Association for Computational Linguistics.

Yale Center for Emotional Intelligence. (2013). Introducing the Facebook Bullying
Prevention Hub. Retrieved from http://ei.yale.edu/introducing-the-facebook-bullying
-prevention-hub.

Ybarra, M. L., & Mitchell, K. J. (2004). Youth engaging in online harassment: With
caregiver-child relationships, Internet use, and personal characteristics. *Journal of
Adolescence, 27*(3), 319–336.

Ybarra, M., & Mitchell, J. (2007). Prevalence and frequency of Internet harassment
instigation: Implications for adolescent health. *Journal of Adolescent Health, 41*(2),
189–195.

Ybarra, M., Mitchell, K., Kosciw, J., & Korchmaros, J. (2015). Understanding linkages
between bullying and suicidal ideation in a national sample of LGB and heterosexual youth in the United States. *Prevention Science, 16*(3), 451–462.

Yellin, S. (2013, February 27). Resetting one of the longest running cyberbullying
cases—DC v. RR. *Technology & Marketing Law Blog*, Retrieved from http://blog.eric-
goldman.org/archives/2013/02/resetting_one_o.htm.

Yiannopoulos, M. (2016, August 1). Milo on Sky News: Twitter ban made me a house-
hold name. *YouTube*. Retrieved from https://www.youtube.com/watch?v=FmctktE0xXI.

Yik Yak. (2014). Campus tour. Retrieved from http://www.yikyakapp.com/tour.

Yik Yak. (2016a). Terms. Retrieved from http://www.yikyakapp.com/terms.

Yik Yak. (2016b). Guidelines. Retrieved from http://safety.yikyak.com/community.

YouTube. (n.d.a). YouTube community guidelines. Retrieved from https://www.you
tube.com/yt/policyandsafety/communityguidelines.html.

YouTube. (n.d.b). Statistics. Retrieved from https://www.youtube.com/yt/press/en-GB
/statistics.html.

YouTube. (2016). YouTube help: Harassment and cyberbullying. Retrieved from
https://support.google.com/youtube/answer/2802268?hl=en&ref_topic=2803176.

YouTube.au. (2010, June 9). Terms of service. Retrieved from https://www.youtube
.com/static?gl=AU&template=terms.

YouTube.gb. (2010, June 9). Terms of service. Retrieved from https://www.youtube
.com/static?gl=GB&template=terms.

YouTubeCurriculum. (2012, July 6). YouTube digital citizenship curriculum [video file]. Retrieved from https://www.youtube.com/watch?v=vXw55E2JbPE.

Young, S. (2014, February 4). 9 facts parents need to know about Voxer app. Retrieved http://www.chicagonow.com/between-us-parents/2014/02/facts-parents-need-to-know-about-the-voxer-app.

Zetter, K. (2009, May 4). Probation and $5,000 fine recommended for Lori Drew. *Wired*. Retrieved from https://www.wired.com/2009/05/prosecutors-ask-for-fine-probation-for-lori-drew.

Zetter, K. (2010, March 18). Court: Cyberbullying threats are not protected speech. *Wired*. Retrieved from http://www.wired.com/threatlevel/2010/03/cyberbullying-not-protected.

Index